Homeschool Teacher

a practical guide to inspiring academic excellence

Grades K-8
Ages 4-14

Kate Laird

FOR PARENTS INSTRUCTING CHILDREN
LONG TERM * SHORT TERM * HELP AFTER SCHOOL

BAY BOOKS

ISBN:978-1532715716
ISBN-10: 1532715714

BAY BOOKS
CORDOVA, ALASKA

With Thanks

To Helen and Anna, for learning
To Hamish, for making it possible
To all my teachers, especially Sally and Dan

Anna and Helen should be considered co-authors of this book, for their willingness to have their elementary and middle school years discussed and dissected. Hamish took care of the bulk of boat maintenance and keeping us fed, as school became a bigger part of our lives with each passing year and this book took up any free time generated by the children's increasing independence.

A great many homeschooling parents, online and in real life, have contributed to my understanding of homeschool techniques and trials, pointed me to resources when I couldn't find the right ones, and listened to my comments, many of which became early drafts of the ideas in this book.

Education professors Tom Newkirk and Sarah Beck contributed their time and expertise to guide me in my research, providing sources and discussion, read early drafts, and helped transform this book from one family's story into a discussion of teaching and learning that I hope can help many families.

And finally, I must thank my loyal, bleary-eyed proofreaders Hamish, Helen, Sally, and Dan.

Table of Contents

Introduction

Helen woke at six and ate breakfast while reading about neanderthals in *Scientific American*, then started algebra.

Anna appeared at eight, read a couple of chapters of *Wild Swans* on her Kindle while dripping jam on the table, then disappeared to write a page or two on her novel. She wiped up the jam after being asked twice.

This book chronicles my experiments over twelve years of homeschooling, trying to find a balanced education for my children, demanding yet interesting, academic yet practical. In the end, I found it came down to *teaching,* whether in the form of hands-on, detailed instruction, or invisibly behind the scenes, writing a good syllabus and handing out deadlines. It came down to figuring out *how I had learned* – in grade school, at home, at Phillips Exeter and Harvard – and breaking down those techniques into teachable skills. It came down to answering the question, *why should we learn this?* in the clearest possible way, because teaching is only possible when students want to learn.

In our first year traveling with the children, ages 4 and 2, a mother of school-aged children warned, "You are so lucky not to have to deal with school." Like many parents we have met, she was giving up on her dreams because the demands of teaching her children were so great. "We must get them back to school for third grade / for sixth grade / for high school," is a common refrain.

We meet people who have been utterly failed by the local schools, whose children aren't taught, suffer bullying or racism, or parents who are working crazy hours and never see their children

1

in order to afford private schools. "I'm not as patient as you are," they say. "I could never teach my children. I can't even get them to clean up their rooms."

Or perhaps school seems to be going pretty well, but the parents aren't sure. "I don't really know what's going on. The teachers seem to be good enough." Their child has a bit of trouble with math or writing or reading, but they don't want to interfere. "I'm sure the teachers know what they're doing. I wouldn't know where to begin to help them."

The successful homeschool teachers I've met are not all patient. They shout sometimes. They need vacations. I certainly can't get the children to clean their room. Successful homeschool teachers do share a commitment to education and a dedication to whatever it was that made them choose to homeschool.

There are three general types of homeschoolers – long-term, short-term, and afterschoolers. Long-term homeschoolers plan to teach through many or all years of the child's education, whereas short-term homeschoolers do it for a year or two to avoid a difficult school situation or to enable the family to travel. Another common type of homeschooling is what I refer to as *afterschooling*, when the children attend a regular school, but receive extra help or the opportunity to advance after school or on weekends and vacations, or perhaps receive extra instruction in the home language, while attending school in a second language.

My husband Hamish and I run a high latitude charter sailboat, which means we are working for six-month seasons and could fit in, at most, six months of bricks and mortar school a year for the children. My own schooling was a paragon of security: the same rural-becoming-suburban school district from kindergarten to eighth grade, but I had heard enough from my father of what it was like to move in the middle of nearly every school year to know I didn't want it for my children.

Our work has taken us from the US to Greenland, Britain, Argentina, Chile, Antarctica, New Zealand, Japan and Alaska. Over twelve years of homeschooling, our daughters Helen and Anna have had school in remote regions where we spent weeks without seeing another person, in urban areas, and small towns where they can roam freely. They've studied in countries with busy, friendly libraries, and in places with no English-language books available at all.

Your children *can* learn at home, and with work on your part and theirs, they can learn just as much as they would if you put them into a great school. I hope this book helps you plan your own homeschool, gives you someone to argue with, and helps give your children a better education.

In ten years of homeschooling, I have made my share of mistakes, banged my head against the wall, but for the most part Helen and Anna were where I had hoped they would be at the end of middle school. They were voracious readers, with the stamina to read adult-level novels and histories as well as high-school level science texts. They had prodigious vocabularies, not from workbooks, but from reading. They wrote serviceably and fluently. They had strong backgrounds in science, and they began ninth grade math, while still in seventh and eighth grade. I wish they were further along in studying a second language, but any lack there is my fault entirely. They were interested in their studies, hard working, and self-motivated.

As I look back over what we have done, there are several crucial themes in the design of our homeschool. The most important has been my emphasis on creating assignments that are *always difficult, but never impossible*. This has helped the children develop an outlook that values challenges over easy successes, and emphasizes that hard work is the key to mastering any subject. In practice, this means that they do no fill-in-the-blank worksheets – all of their work pushes them, and the reward for doing well is more advanced work.

The second most important element is the *development of reading and writing stamina*. Stamina is more important than spending time on reading strategies and techniques. The best way to develop reading ability is through hours and hours and hours of reading. Likewise, doing hours and hours of writing (and developing skills like touch typing to make those hours more efficient) is a crucial element of a writing program. The longest chapters in this book are on reading and writing, because they drive the rest of education.

When Helen and Anna were four and three, I started thinking about school. It was obvious I'd have to teach them, but I wasn't having a lot of luck finding good examples of how to do it. A week after my college graduation in 1990, my first job was tutoring three children for a family sailing across the Pacific, so I had enjoyed a trial run of sorts, but I hadn't been satisfied with their fixed box curriculum, nor my rookie teaching. I began looking through the homeschooling books on the market, and found I could divide most of them into two piles: the conservative *classical education* families who believed school wasn't strict enough anymore, and the liberal *unschooling* families who believed children would learn what they needed to know at their own pace, at their own time.

Neither way fit with my understanding of how I'd learned, both in school and at home. The closest I could find was David and Micki Colfax, *Homeschooling for Excellence*[1] (and one of the boys described in the book had been my classmate at Harvard). But the world of homeschooling had changed dramatically in the quarter century since the Colfaxes wrote their book. Now there were program options – a bewildering variety of whole curricula, plus individual courses in math, writing, grammar, science, reading, and so on. I had the internet, replete with forums and reviews, guaranteed successes and solutions. (I count myself lucky that I usually only had about a quarter of the year with regular internet access at that time, because my mind might have imploded with all the possibilities.)

Around this time, my father sent me an article about the Robinson Curriculum. They offer one of the many curriculum choices out there, and sell a package of materials and a philosophy. A little examination of their website showed that all the materials were off copyright and available for free download, but I loved the image of the Robinson classroom: Mr. Robinson at his big desk, doing his paperwork, while dozens of little Robinsons beavered away teaching themselves at their desks of industry.

I imagined my children would be able to teach themselves in the same way. They weren't. I started thinking back to the fine teachers I had (both in the classroom and out), and how they structured learning and taught me how to teach myself. I stopped reading homeschooling books and started reading teaching books. Over the years, I absorbed the teaching philosophies – which are generally sharply divided on political lines – and created my own middle ground, borrowing ideas and techniques from all sides of the arguments.

This book is a summary of the things I wished I'd known when I started homeschooling twelve years ago, and a report on some things that went right, and some that went wrong. It's not the definitive answer to all the questions, but rather a starting point to the conversation. Homeschooling has been one long experiment, a pulling together of ideas and research and what actually worked with my children.

I've examined the theory of teaching from specialists and professionals. I'm neither. A homeschool teacher must be a jack of all trades, and above all, value education. I'm grateful for having had this chance to teach my children, to know them as well as I do, and also grateful for their patience with my "phases" as they call them, and my overly-enthusiastic trials of the next good idea.

A Word of Warning

I find both homeschooling and teaching books overemphasize the positive. Students are eager, happy, and brilliant, and teachers deliver perfectly executed lesson plans, targeted programs, and never waste any time. Let me make it clear right now: it is not always fun, it is not always easy, and it doesn't always work.

Thomas Newkirk, one of the few educational theorists to admit to inattentive students and bad classes, writes:

> There is an emotional turbulence and frequency of failure in my own teaching that I do not see reflected in many accounts . . . . In the classes I read about, everything seems to work; student writing is impressive, often deeply moving; the teacher seems to have achieved full participation of all members of the class. And what I find most hard to believe, the teacher never shows signs of despondency, frustration, anger, impatience or disappointment.[2]

If you are signing on for homeschooling, you will have your share of bad days, when you despair of your children learning anything. Those days are probably going to be worse than if you were teaching in a school, because there's no Staff Room to retreat to and you have a double role – that of a teacher unsatisfied with your performance and that of a parent who feels that his or her child is falling short.

Teaching is a job – a difficult, time-consuming, frustrating, thrilling, overwhelmingly satisfying job. I'd do it again.

Considering Homeschooling

Who Homeschools?

As a 2011 Department of Education survey[3] discovered,

- 1,700,000 American students are homeschooled (3.4% of school-aged children)
- Homeschoolers are split fairly evenly between urban, suburban, and rural (which means that rural homeschoolers are more common than their representation in the country as a whole)
- Homeschooled students are racially and ethnically diverse, with the percentages aligning within a few points of the nation's population as a whole (even closer if you consider the skew of rural homeschoolers)
- Parents' top four reasons for homeschooling were ranked:
    1. Concerns about the local school environment, such as safety, drugs, or negative peer pressure (25%)
    2. Other reasons, including family time, finances, travel, and distance from schools (21%)
    3. Dissatisfaction with academic instruction at other schools (19%)
    4. Desire to provide religious instruction (16%)

More recent articles have padded the total numbers – in August 2015, *Time Magazine* estimated 2 million; the same month, *Boston Magazine* 2.2 million, and so on; however the most recent national survey data I have is this 2011 study, which is undoubtedly low.[4]

These numbers do not include families who are homeschooling for part of the year because of illness or travel, nor does it include the many afterschoolers. Of the children who attend regular bricks and mortar schools (public and private), 64% have parents who engage in some form of afterschooling, ranging from simply checking that homework is done to active tutoring. There are a lot of homeschool teachers out there.

When I read blogs and forums from homeschooling families, they back up the trends described by this survey, and in addition, a great many families have decided to homeschool because the local public schools were not meeting the needs of learning disabled, gifted, or twice-exceptional (gifted *and* learning disabled, often called 2E) children. Even in places with strong public schools, over-worked teachers may not be able to devote enough time to the outliers.

Another reason, which surprised me, was many families had withdrawn their children from public schools because there was *too much* religion embedded in the school's outlook and instruction. In the early days of American homeschooling, a majority were doing so for religious and geographic reasons, but today, homeschooling for academic and social reasons is rapidly becoming the norm.

Is Homeschooling Right for Your Family?

Do You Have the Time to Teach?

The Robinson vision of the parent working at his desk on his own projects while the children study is not the norm. Homeschooling elementary school requires a large investment of time on behalf of the teacher. I often tried to sneak in other projects during school hours, but school went better when I did not. We seemed to get away with our schedule of six months of intensive school, followed by six months of relaxed schooling, where my work demands ate into school time (and the children exploited my lack of focus and only studied the things that interested them). In elementary school, my time commitment was four or five hours a day, seven days a week, six months a year. In middle school, Helen and Anna did more schoolwork, but much more of it was independent, so while I still needed to be at home for five or six hours a day, seven days a week for six months of the year, I had more time to work on other projects at the same time. During my work season, I spent two or three hours a day on school on my infrequent days off.

For those of you adding up – and I only did it for the first time while writing this paragraph – having school seven days a week for six months is roughly the same as nine months of US public school with weekends and vacations: 180 days. (British state schools have 195 class days a year). Helen and Anna do get a few days off in that time period, of course, but we ignore the calender week.

Another option is to find an outside tutor to teach some or all of the schooling. I often use the word "parent" in this book, and I expect most of its readers will be parents teaching their children, but it is equally appropriate for unrelated tutors structuring a homeschool. Recent college graduates often make good tutors, and they are sometimes willing to trade their teaching for an adventure – I was very happy to work for room and board and a sailing voyage across the Pacific when I was twenty-two.

How Long Will You Homeschool?

Homeschooling for a year or two for extraordinary circumstances means you can be more minimalistic in your schooling –if the trip / job / sabbatical will take you into another culture for a relatively short period of time, your children will probably get as much out of the new environment as they would out of an extra couple of hours of schooling every day.

If you are homeschooling in order to give your children a break from school, but plan to put them back in with their peers at the end of a year, however, you may feel far more pressure than the long-term homeschoolers, because you need to keep up. Laurie Brodie, writing in *Brain, Child* magazine, describes this as the most difficult type of homeschooling, because there is little support in homeschooling groups or books.[5]

For these short-term homeschoolers, beginning with more structure can help – it is easy to relax rules as the year progresses but much harder to transition to a stricter regime. However, whether on the road, around the kitchen table, or in a hospital room, short-term homeschoolers can take comfort in the idea that they don't need to do it all; as long as they match the local school's goals for math, the children will probably re-integrate well. With only a few students, you will likely be able to do a better job than local schools on instilling reading and writing stamina, and you can then pick and choose between other subjects based on either student-led interests or parent-led focus on weaker areas.

What are Your Goals?

It can be helpful to think explicitly about your goals for homeschooling, especially if you are considering teaching your children at home for many years, or conversely, if you are afterschooling, because you will be adding on hours to an already packed day. Short-term homeschoolers can afford to be more relaxed in their overall goals, although they may have immediate goals defined for them by local school authorities.

Goals for my children:

- Knowing how to research and to value the process
- A thorough, facts-grounded background in history, math, science, and literature
- The ability to express ideas, arguments, and analysis in writing and speaking
- An appreciation for the world of arts, music, and sports
- Reasonable proficiency in at least one other language
- Understanding and appreciation of other cultures and nations
- Preparation for college/university

Your list may not look exactly the same. I used to have "knowing how to learn" on the list and changed it to "knowing how to research." Research is something I do every day; the learning is unconscious. You may have more goals than I do, you may have fewer. I do think that it is important for children to be doing college preparatory work regardless of their (and your) aspirations. I know many people who decided not to go to college and then went in their late twenties, and it was enormously valuable for them – maybe even more so than for all those who started at eighteen.

A well-educated person has read[*] and remembered a lot of books. That's the most important point. From there comes understanding of literature, history, science, applied mathematics, and the two things most directly measurable: a huge vocabulary and clutter of background knowledge that, as E.D. Hirsch points out in *Cultural Literacy*, makes understanding everything easier.[6] (I agree completely on that point; I disagree about the best way to get there.)

A well-educated person can write clearly and concisely, whether in revised material or a quick email. Grammar, spelling, and punctuation have to be standard.

A well-educated person can do algebra and uses it in day-to-day life.

A well-educated person can speak a second language.

That's it: reading, writing, arithmetic, and language. For me, those are the important things, in order. Your list might shuffle things around, and of course there's art, music (which may really make you smarter), public speaking, health, sports, and so on. But the heart of an education is found in these four things.

But how do you get there? How do you take the child who is sitting on the floor trying to eat a Cheerio through his nose and turn him into this mythical well-educated person?

---

[*] For most people, reading text directly will be the most memorable; for others, listening to audio books is a valid and useful substitute.

How We Learn

Automatic or Thoughtful?

I divide learning into two types, based on the differences in the kind of retention we want students to have: *automatic* and *thoughtful*. Politicized educational theorists (both academic and homeschooling) often push us towards one or the other, regardless of the topic under study, but I see a critical role for both in the classroom.

I think of *automatic learning* as the subjects that require mastery and automaticity – as in the joke about "How do you get to Carnegie Hall?" there is only one answer: practice, practice, practice. When I took the PADI Scuba Diving course in college, the drill drove me crazy. We did the same moves, over and over. And then over and over again. I dove occasionally for the next 25 years, without much deliberate practice of the skills, when one afternoon my regulator failed eighty feet below the surface. I did not have a single conscious thought about it – my left hand swept out without being told, scooped up my spare regulator, shoved it in my mouth, and pushed the button to clear the water out. The emergency – and it could have killed me – was over before I had the chance to think about it, before my diving partners even noticed I was in trouble. All that drill came back to me, and my hands moved automatically, without conscious direction.

Automatic learning applies to anything you need to know that has to be perfect. Times tables, addition facts, musical instruments – any subject where repetition will help you master it. Teachers deride "drill and kill" exercises for being boring, but practice is the only way to succeed at something like math facts or music and the only way to stay alive in scuba diving.

The problem starts when teachers use the same method of drilling facts for the *thoughtful learning* subjects. When history is dates, science is memorized diagrams, literature is descriptive terms, and writing is diagramming sentences, the students never have a chance to really understand.

I ask myself, do my children need to know this particular fact or skill in ten or twenty years? If the answer is yes (and they don't already know it), then it needs to go in the automatic learning category and needs to be practiced, which usually involves nagging.

In contrast, we can never master the *thoughtful learning* subjects of history, literature, science, advanced mathematics, or writing. What we can do is revisit those subjects over and over in different forms, until we have knowledge approaching that of an expert, until we have truly mastered the vocabulary and the ideas. You don't get those vocabulary words from flashcards, but rather from reading them, listening to them, speaking them, writing them. There is no set list of things you need to know for these subjects, despite what the purveyors of AP exam preparation courses would want you to believe.

Automatic learning subjects include early reading, math facts, musical instruments, handwriting, typing and keyboarding, and spelling. Thoughtful learning subjects include history, science, literature, writing, and advanced math. There is a slight bias towards automatic subjects in the first six years of school, and towards thoughtful subjects in the last six, but there is a place for both types of learning throughout elementary, middle, and high school. (And of course some topics have elements of both – think of the automaticity needed to operate a clutch, gas pedal and gear shift simultaneously on a manual transmission car, and the experience-driven, evaluative, thoughtful learning needed to make driving decisions.)

The automatic subjects are those where you learn the best and the fastest by doing the *same* thing over and over again; the thoughtful subjects are those where you learn the best by doing *similar* things over and over again, by reading different versions of a history, for example, or writing another paper. These are the subjects where you learn best by over-reading and retaining the gist of the idea. In science or history, for example, it is far easier to learn ten textbook pages' worth of material by reading an entire book on the topic, rather than the ten dense pages in a textbook. The textbook may be helpful, but it will work better *after* students have some familiarity with the subject. All the "chapter previewing" in the world won't help you understand a chapter on World War II as well as developing a basic understanding (and interest) through family stories, novels, and films, followed by a general-audience history book, and then (and only then) an analytical account such as you might find in a history textbook.

Intelligence is Not Fixed

Success in academics comes from hard work. American and European children are often cursed by a label that stays with them throughout their educations. Whether that label is "smart" or "stupid," it is a terrible liability. Children labeled "stupid" give up and never try to learn; what's the point? We understand that pretty well, and try not to use the "stupid" label, but "smart" can be equally destructive. Why should a "smart" child study? He shouldn't need to. "Smart" children fear that if they do have to work at a class, maybe they're not really smart, and they don't want to lose that lovely epithet by admitting that maybe they need a bit of extra help, or maybe they do need to work, or maybe they do need to study in order to pass.[7] When I was growing up, my father told me his secret to being a great student in college: he studied on the weekends when everyone else was away, so that he could waltz through the week without any apparent effort.

Most of the time, what we refer to as talent is actually practice. Daniel Willingham in *Why Don't Students Like School?* cites an article in *Psychological Review* where researchers surveyed professional musicians, music academy students labeled "best" and "good," and those students studying to become music teachers. The difference? Both the professionals and the students labeled "best" had put in 11,000 hours of self-reported practice before the age of twenty. The "goods" came in at just under 9000 hours, and the future music teachers at slightly over 6000.[8]

Do you remember that child with a phenomenal talent at drawing? What did she do all day? What did her notebooks look like? She drew. Every recess, she sketched, every lecture, she doodled. She practiced.

What about the best musician? He played for hours after school, performed in concerts at the weekend, and tapped his fingers idly on the desk when he was supposed to be doing his math exercises.

The soccer player, the swimmer, the writer, the math whiz. Almost without exception, the children at the top of the game at the end of middle school are the ones who put in the hours. A friend's son is known as a math whiz. People think he's gifted, but he's not. He loves it. He loves it so much that he asked his mother to find him a tutor over the summer. He's possibly the only person ever to carry a calculus textbook on a backpacking trip. He loves the puzzle, and I suspect he also loves impressing people with his precociousness. But he's not precocious; he works hard.

According to Daniel Willingham, research backs up the idea that intelligence can be developed. He writes:

> Americans, like other Westerners, view intelligence as a fixed attribute, like eye color. If you win the genetic lottery, you're smart; but if you lose, you're not. . . . The destructive cycle is obvious: students want to get good grades so that they look smart, but they can't study to do so because that marks them as dumb. In China, Japan, and other Eastern countries, intelligence is more often viewed as malleable. If students fail a test or don't understand a concept, it's not that they're stupid – they just haven't worked hard enough yet. This attribution is helpful to students because it tells them that intelligence is under their control.[9]

He goes on to note that "children do differ in intelligence, but intelligence can be changed through sustained hard work."[10] As a teacher and a parent, you can forget about the native intelligence – it's too late to engineer their DNA – and concentrate on the hard work side of it. An ethic of hard work will take your children further than "self-esteem," the popular buzz-word of 90s and 00s classrooms. Perhaps too, it can provide an alternate model to the "Tiger Mother" stereotype used to explain the widespread academic success of Asian American students. Families and communities who value education and hard work help their children on the road to intelligence.

Our job as homeschool teachers – and it's not always a comfortable fit with our job as parents – is to push the children to acquire knowledge when they don't necessarily see the point of it. Schools today complain about "helicopter" parents who hover over their children, trying to influence every decision the children make and controlling every aspect of their lives. I'd rather be an "outboard motor" parent: push, push, push, but ultimately give them freedom of their destination.

When you're teaching, try to take off the parent hat that sees the mere existence of your children as a praise-worthy miracle. Instead, save your praise for their efforts and their truly exceptional accomplishments (which doubtless will come after a lot of hard work on their part.) Save your praise for when it is deserved.[11] This can be tricky for the parent as teacher. We're used to applauding the slightest achievement of our children – everything they do seems quite amazing when we remember when they didn't have the dexterity to pick up a piece of food and stick it into their mouths. I catch myself saying "good" to Anna as she works through her spelling, when what I actually mean is, "correct." Spelling something correctly shouldn't be praised – it's not "good," it's the standard. What should be praised is the hard work she puts in to master the spelling words.

In his analysis of successful teaching techniques, *Teach Like a Champion*, Doug Lemov writes, "Champion teachers make a careful and intentional distinction between praise and acknowledgment, acknowledging when expectations have been met and praising when the exceptional has been achieved."[12]

Educational psychologist Carol Dweck's experiments with school children have shown that even one short episode of misguided praising can have a noticeable result on exam scores. Students who are praised for their effort try harder and do better on subsequent tests than those who are praised for their intelligence. In another study, the students who were given an extra fifty minutes of instruction in the idea that intelligence can be improved had a marked improvement on their math scores.[13]

Growth Mindset

Another phrase that you may hear is *growth mindset,* coined by Carol Dweck in her book *Mindset.* This is another way of saying what Daniel Willingham and others have stated – academic success comes from hard work, with the added idea that one's attitude sharply affects what one is able to learn. It's not the power of positive thinking, it's not saying that self-esteem is what matters in education; instead, Dweck writes: "A remarkable thing I've learned from my research is that in the growth mindset, you don't always *need* confidence .... [E]ven when you think you're not good at something, you can still plunge into it wholeheartedly and stick to it."[14]

Her research into even very young children has shown that if they have a *fixed mindset* they eschew challenges in favor of easy successes, whereas growth mindset children seek out challenges. Reading her book gave me a new way of looking at my academic successes – my parents had managed to instill in me the idea that I could do anything *if I worked hard at it.* (This was long before Dweck and Willingham.) In the first grade, I was desperate to catch up in math with the three girls whom I hero-worshiped. I did math during snack time, I did math during school bus rides, I did math at home. I caught up. All through school (both academics and sports), I had this attitude: if I wasn't successful it was because I hadn't worked hard enough at it yet.

I am far from being a complete growth mindset sort of person – I hate doing things badly, and there are times when I don't do things I would enjoy simply because I'll look bad doing them, but I do fundamentally believe that if I practice most things I can do it. Well, maybe not singing. People tell me I could, but I definitely don't have a growth mindset about singing.

Dweck makes it sound easy to turn children's mindsets around (and her examples about a few short comments before a task to change the nature of mindset do make it seem simple), but it isn't always so easy in practice. I have one daughter who is the poster child for growth mindset. She loves a challenge, she loves working hard, she doesn't mind being bad at things. I have another daughter who finds it harder going. We have certainly tried to instill a growth mindset in her (even before we knew the term), but it hasn't been the on/off switch that Dweck describes.

Dweck recounts interviewing college students, evaluating them for whether they were fixed mindset or growth mindset and then watching them through their college careers. The growth mindset students were far from immune to setbacks – depression, breakups, bad grades – but their reactions were completely different. When they failed or were miserable, they worked harder. When the fixed mindset students met the same obstacles, they switched off, preferring to make no effort so they could blame that lack of effort rather than themselves.[15]

I was introduced to Carol Dweck's work through an online course in teaching mathematics by Stanford professor Jo Boaler. Boaler finds particular relevance to mindset in mathematics, because so many people (students, teachers, and parents) have a fixed mindset about math, even if they don't have it in other subjects or parts of their lives. How many times have you heard someone say (or said yourself), "I'm just not good at math." Boaler's argument is that there is no such thing as "good at math," and she insists that anyone can master high school math.

It may take some students longer than others, but as Boaler points out, quick does not equal good. Fixed mindset, and by extension, stereotypes, are so pervasive in mathematics that in one of her studies, merely checking a box for male or female at the top of a math test makes female students do worse than when there is no such box.

Growth mindset is equally important for teachers as for students, especially homeschooling parents and elementary school teachers. Both must cover topics that they themselves didn't like or excel at in school and yet maintain enough enthusiasm to spark students' interest.

Salman Khan, the founder of the free online Khan Academy, which provides short insightful lectures on math and sciences to help tutor students, describes the learning process:

> People learn at different rates. Some people seem to catch on to things in quick bursts of intuition; others grunt and grind their way toward comprehension. Quicker isn't necessarily smarter, and slower definitely isn't dumber. Further, catching on quickly isn't the same as understanding thoroughly. So the pace of learning is a question of style, not relative intelligence. The tortoise may

very well end up with more knowledge – more useful, *lasting* knowledge – than the hare.[16]

Realizing this will help you stay in the growth mindset. In a school setting, the children who work more slowly are labeled as slow, often tracked into remedial classes, and never have the chance to catch up. Homeschoolers have a huge advantage in that the children can work at their correct level, without condemnation from their peers, and they can work at different "grade" levels in different subjects. This isn't a plug for "work at their pace" child-centered learning. I think most children do need to be pushed to acquire a solid education, but the pace can be matched to their needs in a homeschool program. Instead of never finishing the math book, year after year, which causes the student to fall further and further behind, we finish the math book when we finish the math book. It has nothing to do with the school calendar. One school year simply rolls into the next. We never finish a math curriculum before September, we often don't finish my goals for history (but since it's chronological history, it simply continues into the next year), and other subjects may have dividing points at different times of the year. I might drop several subjects if we're traveling, or slim down if we're having a hard push in one subject area, or the weather is unusually fine.

How Thinking Works

A chapter in *Why Don't Students Like School?* discusses how the brain thinks. As Daniel Willingham explains it, we have a working memory and a long-term memory: the working memory does all the processing of information, the actual thinking, whereas the long-term memory holds the facts. He contends that our working memory capacities are pretty fixed – there's no way to increase the RAM on this computer, but what we can change is the amount of information in the long-term memory. For example, if you have a math problem to solve – say 386 times 4 – if you have all the multiplication tables firmly in your long-term memory, it's an easy problem. If you don't know your multiplication tables absolutely, you'll have to pause and take up valuable space in your working brain to work out, say, what's four times six, well, three times six is eighteen, so eighteen plus six, is . . . um . . . twenty-four. That math problem is going to be a lot easier for a child who knows his times tables than one who doesn't. It's not innate math ability; it's the amount of facts in the long-term memory.

This isn't to say that some children don't start off a little better at math or a little better at reading. Helen seems to spell without effort, she struggled with elementary school math. Anna, nineteen months younger, has caught up to Helen in math, yet she is several years behind in spelling. There was probably an initial difference between them – and certainly Anna's particular learning difficulties are going to mean she has a tough time with spelling – but when I watched them at work in fifth and sixth grades, Anna flipped open the math page with enthusiasm and went straight to work, whereas Helen illustrated each word problem with great care, and every page without word problems was decorated with stylized dogs. If seventy-five percent of Helen's math time was spent gazing off into space or practicing her artwork, her artwork improved, and her math did not. That initial spark has turned into a real difference between them in math, but I believe very little of it is innate. Interestingly, in late middle school, Helen stopped illustrating her math book and began using that sketching ability to clarify the problems, and what had been an impediment to her learning transformed into an asset.

The relationship between facts in long-term memory and proficiency in working memory manipulations is fairly clear in mathematics – in fact, you can buy 250-flashcard sets just to drill those basic facts. But what about other subjects? Brain and education research appears to show that the amount of facts in the long-term memory is extremely important in other subjects. In order to read adult-level texts, you need to have a large body of cultural and historical knowledge that will be presumed by the author. This is going to have slight regional variations of course, but the core will be very similar for all writers in English.[17] But you can't order up a pack of 250,000-flash card facts for science, history, and literature, and drill them in to your memory. You learn this content slowly, with multiple repetitions, and you must think about it multiple times in order to shift that knowledge into your long-term memory, so that it is available when you need it. This is what makes higher level literacy and thinking possible, not simply the decoding of words that you learn in first and second grade.

Content in school is not a question of filler material to be manipulated as one develops skills. In order to be an educated adult, your children need to have this background knowledge, and an efficient school will focus on the acquisition of this knowledge, not by drilling the facts, but by reading, writing, and thinking about them. These are the *thoughtful learning* subjects I described earlier. A slow acquisition of this background knowledge, in context – not cramming for tests – will help your students retain this information forever.

It takes time and multiple repetitions to learn things properly. There's a reason why college students don't know as much as their professors – numerous scholars have pointed out that even students who have studied a subject thoroughly and done well on examinations, often fail to have an "expert" understanding of the subject matter when the subject is presented in a new context. Educational researchers often present this as a failure of education, but it seems to me to be more of a natural condition of learning abstract material. It might only take one repetition for a child to learn that the wood stove is hot, but truly understanding why the summer is hot will take diagrams, explanations, and multiple exposures over the years.

Howard Gardner blames this lack of understanding on pervasive child-contrived misconceptions,[18] but I think it is more likely simply that the students have not covered the topics enough times, and perhaps when children did ask the question in early childhood, they received the wrong answer, or no answer at all.

As George Nelson says in "Science Literacy for All in the 21st Century":

> In a classroom where science literacy is the goal, teaching should take its time.... [A]ny topic in science, mathematics, or technology that is taught in only a single lesson or unit is unlikely to leave a trace by the end of schooling.[19]

An experiment tested people fifty years after their last algebra exam, and the most important factor in their retention of math was how many years of math they'd done after algebra. It was better to get a C in algebra and keep studying math for four years than to get an A in algebra and stop there.[20]

The same can be said for history and literature. A perfect performance on a Friday date test or "prove you read it" questions do not translate into long-term retention or understanding that lets students (or the adults they become) transfer those ideas into other contexts.

Early Music?

There may be one way to enhance working memory – there is some evidence that early music instruction helps improve intelligence. A recent article in *Scientific American* reports: "Practicing a musical instrument appears to improve attention, working memory and self-control."[21]

The children have to actually play an instrument, rather than simply listening to it. The Oak Meadow homeschool program emphasizes the importance of music by including a recorder and recorder lessons in their packaged program (or of course, you could simply buy them separately). Since I have the musical knowledge of gravel, it was easier to wait until the children were older and could be more self-directed. We bought Helen an electronic piano keyboard for her twelfth birthday, and she taught herself from a downloadable digital program. She did a year on her own, before waylaying a woman playing at a small-town carnival and asking for lessons. Since then, she has continued to take lessons whenever we can find a teacher, and that has made a big difference.

Some homeschooling families are scornful of electronic keyboards because it is a digital instrument, rather than a real one, but digital instruments are generally much less expensive and don't need the maintenance of "real" instruments, plus students can practice with headphones. A boat or an apartment is a very small space, and it can feel even smaller on a rainy day with someone endlessly practicing scales. We met one boat where a child was learning to play the trumpet, which could be heard all across the anchorage – he has more tolerant parents than Helen and Anna do.

Hamish has taught himself how to play the guitar entirely by using the Justin Guitar program of videos and books, and that could work very well for a motivated older child. An electric guitar makes a surprisingly good instrument in a small space. Unamplified or with headphones, it's quite unobtrusive, quieter than an acoustic, and is less prone to changing shape with varying humidity levels. In addition, the same money will buy a better quality electric guitar than an acoustic, making it a good choice for beginners.

I don't discuss the study of music further in the subject area portion of this book, in part because I don't feel it is mandatory, in part because there are far better music teachers out there than I am, but it does seem to be able to improve intelligence, and of course it is a pleasure in its own right.

What About All These Intelligences?

Books on teaching, studying, and parenting often talk of students having multiple intelligences – Howard Gardner, for example, has a list of eight intelligences: linguistic, logical-mathematical, bodily-kinesthetic, interpersonal, intrapersonal, musical, naturalist, and spatial. These ideas have been extended into curricula thinking, and schools have tried to teach subjects through appealing to all the different intelligences, hoping to reach different students through different methods. However, both Daniel Willingham who discusses the question from a neuroscientist's perspective, and Gardner who articulated the initial concept, don't support the idea of trying to teach through all the intelligences (or "abilities" as Willingham prefers).

Willingham writes, "The different abilities . . . are not interchangeable. Mathematical concepts have to be learned mathematically, and skill in music won't help. Writing a poem about a golf club will not help your swing."[22]

Howard Gardner writes explicitly that Multiple Intelligence theory is not another way of describing "learning styles."[23] Instead, he describes the individual intelligences as a description of a type of "computational capacities." Different individuals have different blends of these intelligences, but rather than saying these intelligences represent how someone should be taught, he writes: "nearly every cultural role of any degree of sophistication requires a combination of intelligences."[24]

In the prototype MI classroom, Project Spectrum, Gardner notes that each child's year-end report:

> describes the child's personal profile of strengths and weaknesses and offers specific recommendations about what might be done at home, in school, or in the wider community to build on strengths as well as bolster areas of relative weakness.[25]

In other words, the differing intelligences are not seen as ways to teach children, but raw material to work with, and it is as important to *shore up weaknesses as to teach to strengths*. In this book, I emphasize strengthening of the two classical areas of academics, what Gardner would call logical-mathematical and linguistic intelligences. In a homeschooling situation, with its individualized classroom that Gardner calls for in *The Unschooled Mind* and elsewhere, other intelligences can easily be emphasized, brought into the classroom, and unschooled outside it.

Both Gardner and Alfred Binet (who developed the first IQ test in Paris in 1900) posit their work with an ideal of helping children learn. Binet's idea was to identify children who needed extra help to reach academic success – with the assumption that they *could* reach academic success – but instead it has been turned into an absolute, inescapable benchmark, a brand on the forehead of competence or incompetence in cultures that do not believe in malleable intelligence. In cultures without that belief, the diagnosis becomes destiny: students are tracked by their IQ test results, and those with poor scores are written off.[26]

In practice, Gardner's theory also suffers from an effective pigeon-holing of students. It may not be as definitive as Binet's IQ numbers, but it seems that in many classrooms the idea of "multiple intelligences" is used to excuse not trying to improve weaknesses, instead of as a way to maximize student engagement and understanding.

Learning Styles

Learning styles is another concept that is often discussed by homeschoolers and classroom teachers. While most parents would have an easy time categorizing their children as visual, auditory, or kinesthetic learners, it's not something I've let dictate my homeschool curriculum decisions. As with the concepts of intelligences, I think it is as important to shore up weaknesses as teach to strengths.

Helen and Anna's preferred styles are evident in what they do outside of school time, but I'm not one to spend hours planning out projects to cater to those styles – they'll take care of that. One sculpts and whittles and climbs mountains at a run. The other writes stories, and paces back and forth while chewing over plot lines and math problems. They both take in information by reading, by listening, and by hands-on experiments. This may not have been their "preferred" natural style, but both have learned to work in all domains.

Despite the enthusiasm for categorizing children's learning styles, there is some disagreement as to whether it's a true division. For example, Gary Stix, writing in *Scientific American,* regards it as a myth:

> The notion that a pupil tends to learn better by favoring a particular form of sensory input — a "visual learner" as opposed to one who listens better — has not received much validation in actual studies. For this and other myths, public perceptions appear to have outstripped the science.[27]

A teacher who can present information in different ways can reach many students. It may not be because she is successfully teaching to different intelligences or learning styles, but rather because the third or fourth time around the rest of the students get it.

I find when trying to learn something myself, three is a magic number – the first time I hear a term (like "asthenosphere" when studying Earth Sciences), it is shocking and foreign, and makes me miss out on the next five minutes of the lecture, because my brain is trying to come to grips with asthenosphere. The next time I hear it, I still don't know what it means, even though I looked it up after the last lecture, but it troubles me less: oh, yes, asthenosphere, better look that up again after the lecture. The third time I hear it, provided I did actually go look it up again in the meantime, I know it, and my mind processes it effortlessly. In my own case, I think the style I worked with last would be the one that seemed to help me learn, even though it was simply third time lucky. In addition, most learning styles discussions refer to the three types *visual, auditory, kinesthetic,* but in my case and many others', this triumvirate leaves out the most important part of learning, which is writing down ideas, thinking about them, and discussing them.

Despite study after study[28] noting that teachers can't consistently place children in one learning style or another, and that trying to teach to differing learning styles doesn't change outcomes, schools, homeschooling curricula, teachers and parents embrace the idea. It has recently migrated to the U.K., where a *Guardian* article describes:

> In one school in Cheshire, children wear lapel badges to indicate their preferred style; in a Kent primary school, children have labels on their desks to show whether they are auditory, kinaesthetic or visual.[29]

I have good guesses as to how Helen and Anna would be labeled if they were in a "learning styles" classroom, but they both respond extremely well to straight-forward, academic instruction, as long as they have enough breaks. Time out to move and think is usually missing from bricks and mortar schools, but can be enormously helpful in processing ideas. Anna usually goes for a brisk walk around every twenty minutes. Yes, Anna has a harder time sitting still, but that doesn't mean that she would learn better by acting in a play about Ancient Egypt, than she would by reading and writing about it.

The fastest way to learn about history is to study history. The fastest way to learn about math is to do math. The fastest way to learn about reading literature is to read literature and write about it, not make a diorama out of pasta in a shoe box. When I was given this particular assignment at age eleven, I remember thinking I could have read an entire novel in the time it took me to make the diorama.

If your goal for homeschooling is to combine efficiency, hard work, and academic focus, there will be plenty of time for your children to make dioramas in their own time. And often, the school-thinking will persist into this play time. A couple of years ago, Anna spent an afternoon with a seven-year-old boy and about 100 small plastic animals. Anna explained the plot to us at great length later that evening, including the feudal structure of the animals' society. They were taking what they'd learned in history and applied it to the society they'd created. I am sure that helped cement their historical knowledge, but I suspect it worked even better for being student-instigated, rather than an assigned project.

This is an area where I think unschoolers are absolutely right. While I'm not comfortable with an entirely child-led curriculum, I firmly believe that students teach themselves an enormous amount when they're left alone. One of my main aims for our school is to craft a schedule that will push my children to study all subject areas, but in the minimum time possible to allow them space and time for discovery.

Principles of Teaching

Always Difficult, Never Impossible

Always difficult, never impossible has turned into the background philosophy for our school. If school isn't difficult, your students should be doing something else with their time, and if it is impossible, they will only become frustrated. Impossible was Anna in her early spelling days, Helen in her early math days. I hung on too long in both cases, hoping that they would suddenly have a breakthrough, but the level was simply too high. The spelling workbooks were too simple for Helen and assigning them to her was a waste of her day.

If you're writing your own curriculum, it is perhaps easier for you to tweak the levels of the assignments to suit the children; you can assign a review sheet if it's hard or just the odd-numbered problems if it seems easy. But if you are teaching from a boxed or online program, it is important to keep tabs on what your children are learning, even if they do most of their work independently. Helen and Anna have no problem in declaring, "this is too easy!" and asking to be let off the work, but they are slower to admit that something is impossible. (Of course, there are children with the reverse tendency – carefully guarding the easy work, and too quick to declare the problems impossible.)

Having this philosophy for the school also helps a bit when the children declare that something is difficult; the answer is simply, "of course it is!"

In the past, boxed curricula were fixed, and it was impossible to accelerate or decelerate individual subjects, but now several of the programs offer the opportunity to do an accelerated math program, or in the case of Calvert, there is also an add-on program aimed at children with reading, writing, and spelling difficulties. I have no direct experience of this program, nor have we met any families using it, but it looks worth investigating.

We met a family who homeschooled for a year in town before leaving on their sailboat, and while this may not be practical for most families, it could be a good idea to have a warm up for homeschooling if you know you are planning to leave civilization behind, rather than starting the big move and the homeschooling at the same time. It will give you the chance to make sure your programs and materials are pitched at the right level for your students while there is still a chance to raise or lower the grade level. On the other hand, for some children, leaving their friends behind will be so tough that to start early would just be discouraging.

Most whole curriculum and individual subject programs offer placement tests, but it is still worth having at least a month to make sure the fit is right. We didn't have this opportunity because we had already been out sailing for two years before Helen started school in earnest, but it would have saved us some false starts, particularly in math.

Unschool When You Can; Teach When You Must

There is a homeschooling philosophy called *unschooling*, where the children pursue their own interests at their own pace; some call this *child-directed learning* or *eclectic homeschooling*, although eclectic homeschoolers generally have considerably more structure than true unschoolers. The "eclectic" label covers a wide swath of homeschooling styles, ranging from nearly unschooling to a rigorously academic program like the one described in this book.

To my mind, true unschooling is very unlikely to achieve the sort of well-rounded, academic background that I want for my children. Unschooling can also diminish a student's chances of attending college. My Harvard roommate now does interviews for Harvard, and she described an amazing interview with a bright, articulate high school student, but she reluctantly recommended against his admission because he had never written a single paper in the high school years, and she could find no evidence that he was prepared for college level academic work. Homeschoolers often do very well in the college admissions process, but you must be prepared to show proof of academic work over the years.

However, if there are topics that your children are particularly interested in, you can take those subjects off the school syllabus. In our case, that was reading. My children will read in preference to almost every other activity, and several times I have even had to ban "reading before school" because I was unable to pry them away from their novels to do their math. There's no need or benefit to turning that hobby into "school."

Much of our science work, current events, and art are also unschooled. Your children will have different interests, but if there is some subject that they pursue without much guidance, let them do it; just make sure that they keep up the work in the other subjects during school time.

Homework?

Homework is now assigned at a younger age; in many states it is mandatory from the first grade on. I don't think it's reasonable to expect most children to work independently at that age. If they do complete their homework, it's because their parents are supervising it, and that just means that the children whose parents are invested in their educations do their homework, and those whose parents are too busy do not, and the separation between educationally-advantaged and educationally-disadvantaged kids is merely exacerbated by school, not narrowed. Certainly when you are homeschooling, there is no benefit to the children doing "homework" in the early grades. Even in middle school, my children rarely did work outside of school hours.

Independent work, however, is important. In early elementary school, I found nearly every subject needed relatively close supervision and instruction; by middle school the ratios are more nearly reversed, and I could assign a long-term writing project, and expect the completed drafts printed up and on my desk on the due date. However, I was still very much present when we tackled difficult science, history, and literature assignments.

Their Questions

As Marina Koestler Ruben reminds us in *How to Tutor Your Own Child:* "No question is stupid. No matter how ridiculous a question may sound – or how obvious the answer may seem – if a student is asking you in earnest, you should not chastise, judge, or mock in response. Take any request for information seriously."[30]

It can be particularly hard to hold your temper and answer reasonably when the question is about a topic that you went over in great detail six months earlier. I try to remember that it usually takes many repetitions, in-depth discussions, and manipulation of ideas for information to be learned permanently. I will, however, admit to numerous days when I run out of patience and answer, "the same as it was last week."

Sometimes, you need to answer a question with the answer. Sometimes you need to answer it with a question. The trick is knowing which to use, and when to stop pushing and start explaining. It is something I've improved at over the years, so I was interested to read in Doug Lemov's *Teach Like a Champion*: "Ten minutes of teacher-driven background and then getting right to reading is usually worth an hour of, 'Who can tell me what Nazis were?' Efficiency matters."[31] This has inspired me to add in a few minutes of background at the beginning of discussions or readings. One of the advantages of being a homeschool teacher is I know how much my students actually know, far better than a classroom teacher could. I talk to them at mealtimes and after watching movies and reading books; I know exactly what the history teacher taught, because I'm the history teacher, too.

I used to go through a guided reading with Helen and Anna, and break off in the middle of the reading to ask, "What does that mean?" or "Do you remember that event?" Now, I have become better at starting off before the reading and saying "Here's some background" and giving them a mini lecture on the topic, to clear up anything that I think will confuse them. If it is a topic we've already studied, then I ask questions to gauge their memory. If they start faltering on the memory, I switch to background mode.

This is not the time to criticize them for not remembering; it's a sign to you that your techniques of teaching them how to learn are not working as well as they might. You don't want to turn this pre-reading time into an exam; you want to get on with the reading at hand.

What if you don't know the answer, to either your questions or their own? First of all, admit it. Then see how you can go about finding it out. If you're in a home, boat or R.V., carry as many science and history textbooks as you can, an encyclopedia (the Encyclopedia Britannica is available on DVD), and subject specific books such as the Dorling Kindersley Eyewitness books, particularly about subjects that interest your children. If you're living in remote regions, you can't rely on the internet to answer these questions, and even if you have internet access, you probably shouldn't rely on Wikipedia as you never know how accurate the answer may be. If you don't have regular internet access, but can send email or texts, it can be useful to have a collection of friends with good research skills. Once, I sent an emergency email to my best friend: do frogs have tracheae? We had spent about half an hour going through frog dissection sketches, but couldn't find a trachea. Back came a detailed email: they do. We also keep a list in the back of the school assignment book of things to look up when we do have internet access. For students, watching you help them find an answer, even if you can't find it, is far more valuable than shrugging off the question and dismissing it.

Your Questions

One of the skills you'll develop in homeschooling is asking a series of questions, to push your students to make connections and make them think about the material.

So, where do you come up with these questions? The first and easiest strategy is to avoid asking them – instead, ask your children to do a reading, and then to summarize the reading in their own words. When they're finished, read their summaries, and ask questions about what they've written. Do you think they've missed a crucial point? Ask them about it. You can also ask them to make value judgments on the material, especially in history and literature. Make them back up what they think – the question,

"Why do you think that?" is one of the best ones, applicable to almost every topic. Make sure they point to specific references in the reading (or lecture, or whatever media you are discussing). Ask "What is the evidence for that?"

Make sure you give students enough time to come up with good answers. Writing short answers or notes on an answer in a notebook can help them prepare for responding to questions out loud. Fill-in-the blank workbooks train students to answer the question with a minimum of sentence structure and complexity. Your questions should be the opposite: slightly open-ended, perhaps without a specific right answer (unless it's "what's six times seven" of course). Written answers should be in complete sentences (usually restating the question so that the answer can stand alone without the question). You may find that students' spelling and punctuation in these short answers will lag behind their best work. That shows they are thinking hard and doesn't need to be corrected.

- Can you summarize what happened in your own words? (I usually do this through writing assignments.)
- Write down three reasons that [whatever the event] might have happened.
- What is your evidence for that?
- Why do you think [whatever you're studying] might have happened as it did?
- When discussing living plants and animals, ask "What could be an evolutionary reason for that? How would it help the animal survive?"

Because these are open-ended questions, you can keep recycling them over and over again. The goal is to make your student think about the material, not to formulate a quiz, so your knowledge does not need to be as precise as theirs. After Helen and Anna read all eighteen volumes of the Roman Mysteries by Caroline Lawrence, their knowledge of life in Ancient Rome was far, far greater than mine, but when it came time to study the subject in school, I could still use these same questions.

When you're asking questions, don't stop at one. Even if a student gives a good response to your question, you can "stretch it" (to use one of Doug Lemov's phrases from *Teach Like a*

Champion) and ask another question that will stretch his knowledge of the subject.

Schools, homeschooling programs, and articles about education often talk about teaching "critical thinking." They may use the phrase "teach children to think like experts" or "apply [scientific] thinking" or something similar. As Daniel Willingham discusses in *Why Don't Students Like School?*, however, it is impossible to think critically about something unless you understand it. Teach content first. As your students understand more, they will naturally think about it in greater depth. Susan Wise Bauer and Jessie Wise's *The Well-Trained Mind: A Guide to Classical Education at Home* promotes the idea that students study chronological world history three times – once in elementary school, once in middle school, and again in high school. The basic story is unchanged, but the complexity with which students approach the material changes dramatically.

The first time around in elementary school, history is simply stories about people and places, without much analysis or questioning. However, by the time the cycle comes around in middle school, and your students reach the same material again, the story is slightly familiar and students are ready to ask questions about sources and make comparisons –

- How do we know that?
- Can you detect any biases in the author's approach?
- How is this like [another event in history]?
- How is it different?

The US Department of Education Practice Guide also stresses the importance of asking good questions, and instructs teachers to:

> Ask questions that elicit explanations, such as those with the following question stems: why, what caused X, how did X occur, what if, what-if-not, how does X compare to Y, what is the evidence for X, and why is X important? . . .

... Ask questions that challenge students' prior beliefs and assumptions, thereby promoting more intensive and deeper reasoning.[32]

Ultimately, in late middle school and high school, students will begin to self-generate these questions, and use them as the basis for essays and experiments. However, it will be much easier for students to transition into self-questioning if they have had years of answering your questions, making summaries and evaluating material, and organizing their thoughts. Good questions can give them the basis for the analytical "critical thinking" they will be expected to do later, but I found it much more straightforward to teach a habit of inquiry rather than an isolated skill of critical thinking.

Budget Teacher Time

Although I insist that teaching is "my job" for much of the year, and I say that I think of myself as a teacher, I seldom do as much day-to-day preparation as a classroom teacher would. I'm lazy that way. I prefer to spend time planning the syllabus, choosing the books, and so on, but day to day, it helps to have the minimum preparation time possible, which leaves me more time to check the day's work.

I have met homeschooling families who do far more day-to-day preparation than I do; in one family we met, the teaching parent (they did six weeks each in rotation) spent twenty minutes or so a day preparing the next day's lessons. Especially with older students, spending some time organizing a list of specific questions with complex follow up questions before class may be worthwhile. I'm a bit more willing to wing it – ideally, I'd prepare more questions for them, but at this stage, I can still answer most of their questions off the cuff, and I am comfortable coming up with the next follow up question on my feet. Our best discussions come outside of class time, which is when I really see the academic progress Helen and Anna are making.

Even more important than the lesson preparation time, however, is the time spent checking your children's work immediately after they finish. First, this shows them the value you place on their studies. Second, the sooner you can make corrections or suggestions, the more they learn from it. Work left idle and ungraded is like a bag of cement left in a barn loft – it turns to solid concrete surprisingly quickly. The longer a student's paper lies unread or the math problems left unmarked, the personal connection between the student and work withers, and corrections have far less impact.

Back in the 90s, the children I taught on the Calvert system would send in papers to Calvert for grading, so they could receive the official accreditation. By the time the papers caught up to us *six months later,* the children were no longer the same person who wrote those papers and the comments and grades were meaningless. That is an extreme example, and hopefully one ameliorated by email, but students need your feedback, and they need it fast.

In school I used to be infuriated by teachers who gave us an assignment, and then took two weeks to grade the papers and get them back to us. Why should I work hard over it, if you don't even care? (Of course, as William Armstrong reminds us in *Study is Hard Work*, students need to remember they are not writing the paper *for* the teacher, but for themselves.)[33] The effect is even stronger when it's a parent doing the grading. When I taught English at the University of New Hampshire, many of my fellow teachers were forever returning papers a week or two after they'd been submitted. I assigned student papers due on a Friday and returned them on Monday, no matter what happened over the weekend, and I think my students responded extremely well to my interest in their work. (Or maybe they just liked having a free weekend.)

Towards the end of middle school, as I began to assign far more independent reading, much of my teacher time was taken up reading or skimming possible book choices a month or so ahead of the assignment. I'd spend several days when we had the internet using reviews and websites such as GoodReads to find suitable popular history and science books for example, and then read them myself just to make sure. If the book couldn't hold my attention, I took it off the syllabus. This is critical if you're making up your own syllabus, but even with a box curriculum, it can be worth pre-reading to make sure the books are worthwhile choices.

Making Schoolwork Relevant?

Many teaching programs emphasize making school and its content relevant to students, either through connecting areas of study to what's going on in the students' lives, or by having them create art projects that portray their understanding. The cult of the project is widespread in American schools in particular, and anecdotally, it seems that it is often the parents who have the most stake in these projects.

If you (and your children) enjoy arts and crafts projects, there is no harm in them, but if you are looking for ways to trim your school to the minimum time and the maximum efficiency, students will learn more information more quickly in the traditional ways of reading, discussing, and writing, although active children will need breaks and time to run around after sedentary sessions.

I have presented the idea of school to Helen and Anna as the assimilation of knowledge and skills: this is what they need to know to be educated, discerning adults, who can protect themselves from financial and emotional swindles, analyze the biases behind what they read, and be able to evaluate current events and policies on the basis of our rich human history.

An otherwise interesting article on homeschooling on boats makes the following assertion:

> Packaged programs often include irrelevant or impractical lessons, such as complicated science experiments unsuited to a rocking platform, or topics like the Industrial Revolution. Try getting your kids excited about that in, say, the Bahamas![34]

Most science projects can be adapted to life on a boat, and implying that you can't study the Industrial Revolution because you're in the Bahamas is appalling advice. Your students need well-rounded knowledge, and you are responsible for making sure they have the opportunity to learn it, especially if you're the only teacher they're going to have. Local history is of course interesting and a way in to learning the skills and techniques of history, but a succession of local history lessons piled on top of one another does not make a cohesive curriculum or give students the background information that is assumed of educated adult readers.

So much of modern curricula planning is about making school relevant, but I don't think we need to do that for our children. If it suits you to make elaborate lesson plans that incorporate your daily life into your school plans, great. But if you don't, you can also go through a slightly old fashioned curriculum, forget about making it relevant for your children, and let the connections come in non-school time. Knowledge makes things interesting.

A few years ago, we happened to be studying the feudal system in Europe in the Middle Ages, while visiting Kosrae in the Federated States of Micronesia. I made no attempt to make the studies relevant to our lives, yet they were. Just behind the local hardware store in Kosrae, there is an overgrown path to 500-year-old basalt ruins, which towered above us as we walked across coral courtyards. We had a slim brochure from the local museum to tell us about these ancient people. I would have struggled to make it into an academic history unit, but I wasn't trying to. We simply visited the site on a walk, yet school happened, because we talked about the ancients' feudal structure, and Anna commented that it was "convergent evolution." That comment wouldn't have happened without their thorough, academic study of European history and evolutionary science.

Some packaged curricula have classes in knitting and modeling in clay. It would never occur to Helen and Anna that knitting and modeling in clay were part of school, and in a homeschool situation, arts and crafts don't have to be. A cousin taught them to knit, and they model in clay and mud and build boats out of coconut husks. When I describe the curriculum we followed and make recommendations for grade level work, I have listed art as optional – it would be good for a child who has no interest in drawing or making things to have art classes, but in our experience, it's unnecessary for many homeschooled kids. Deprived of television, computer games, gangs of friends, and sometimes even the ability to run around and play, almost every boat kid we've met is an artist. We buy paper by the ream. The sheer volume of extremely "talented" boat kid artists is a testament to the power of practice. If artistic ability is merely a genetic talent, as it is often argued, there is no way there could be such a high percentage of good artists amongst the cruising community. It's practice.

I do use art as a way of learning, but not by making "crafts." Instead, I frequently ask Helen and Anna to copy maps and scientific drawings with pencil sketches – this is a fast way of learning. Being able to sketch out and label a human heart or the Mediterranean Sea is a very good way for students to learn the material, and I don't believe it matters what kind of "learner" they might be. Some children will be able to draw perfect replicas on the page, some won't, but regardless, the exercise is a useful one for building memory about the subject, and far more effective than labeling pre-drawn illustrations. It's easier to organize too – you just need some blank paper, pencil, and the source drawing; you don't have to buy (or search the internet for) blackline drawings.

In some families, music might be intrinsic to their lives and could be left off the curriculum with ease. In ours, however, Helen and Anna won't practice music without it being on the day's school schedule, although occasionally after school they carry on with their music and compose jingles together.

A Better Way to Drill

Much of the time, *thoughtful learning* will help your students retain facts and figures simply through the act of thinking about them in multiple contexts. Sometimes, however, the memory will elude them, and drill will become necessary. Math facts and second language vocabulary often aren't retained without focused study.

The key to this type of learning is spaced repetition and revision. Many different school programs incorporate this kind of drill – All About Spelling makes use of it, Gabriel Wyner in *Fluent Forever* stresses its importance in learning second language vocabulary, and the US Department of Education explains the research behind it in *Organizing Instruction and Study to Improve Student Learning*.[35]

When drilling math facts, for example, instead of sorting flashcards into "known" and "unknown," divide them into "instant recall," "hesitant," and "unknown." Revisit the unknown cards in the same session, the unknown and hesitant cards the next day, and the instantly recalled cards three or four days later. If the student still can instantly recall those answers, wait, don't discard them, but bring them out a week later for another round. This will be a more effective use of time than either drilling all the cards every day or discarding the instantly recalled cards forever. A formal way of doing this would be to use a box of flashcards with four dividers, known as a *Leitner Box*. (I learned the name from Gabriel Wyner; I'd been using the system for many years: a stack of index cards with dividers.) Every day, students go through Level 1, plus one of the higher level card stacks. The higher level cards are sorted anew to either drop back to Level 1 or rise to the next higher level.

For example:[36]

Table 1: Leitner Box Drill Schedule

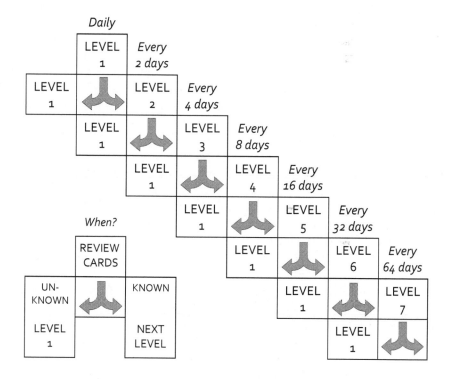

With math cards, there's a small number of cards that one needs to learn and four levels is sufficient; in second languages, the cards can number in the thousands. In *Fluent Forever*, Wyner recommends using a modified Leitner Box on a seven-level schedule. Each day, the user looks at ten to thirty new cards. If they are known, they go into Level 2. If not, they stay in Level 1, to be reviewed daily until they are known, and can shift to Level 2. Level 2 cards are reviewed every other day. If known, they go into Level 3, if not, revert to Level 1. A sixty-four day calendar may be found on Wyner's website [www.fluent-forever.com].

This kind of spaced drill or, as Wyner terms it, SRS (Spaced Repetition System) can be extended to many different subjects with a bit of imagination. For example, Helen learns a piano piece to perfection, but a few months later, she'll say, "I can't remember it!" Practicing every song one knows every day is impossible. Instead, I suggested she organize her sheet music box like a Leitner Box. Each day, she spends time practicing the current pieces, reviewing a different old piece each day, and at the end of the week, scheduling an extra practice session of the weakest. In the case of music, sixty-four days is probably too long a schedule, but a one month, four-level rotation can work well.

All About Spelling uses the same principle on a simplified schedule. In the program instructions, spelling word cards stay in "review" until "mastered," but the mastered cards don't disappear entirely. Every day, a handful of mastered cards are shuffled back into the daily review. When using this program with Anna, I found it worked best with an additional intermediate category of "well-known" cards, which I cycled through more frequently than the "mastered" cards, but didn't cover every day with the "review" cards. Essentially, I turned it into a four-level Leitner Box.

For older students working on a computer or tablet, Anki is a computer-based program that lets users make their own cards for this sort of review, and allows you to fine tune the review schedule with a bit of tweaking. I discovered it while we were studying Japanese; Wyner maintains that it is still the best tool available[37] for learning language vocabulary.

Quizzes often serve a similar function. Homeschoolers are sometimes reluctant to employ quizzes and tests, particularly in the elementary years, because of the evaluation aspect of testing. Too much testing can certainly contribute to a fixed mindset, but ungraded quizzing (or circling back to topics in discussion) can help students retain information. In *Organizing Instruction and Study to Improve Student Learning,* the Department of Education notes that students' retention is much higher for information that is revisited weeks or months after its original introduction, and goes on to assert:

> Laboratory experiments have repeatedly demonstrated that taking a test on studied material promotes remembering that material on the final test, a phenomenon called the "testing effect." ... [R]esearchers have found that having students take a test is almost always a more potent learning device than having students spend additional time studying the target material.[38]

The Department of Education pamphlet does not emphasize the point, but what they are discussing here is quizzing and testing information and techniques from *content-based* coursework, not the frequent standardized testing which is so common in US schools today.

Most students regard the instructions to "study" as instructions to read the material again, or, for more ambitious students, take notes on their notes. Most "studying" is done ineffectively, which is probably why the test effect is so profound – quizzes and intermediate tests are instances of forced recall under pressure, and the adrenaline of the test convinces the brain it is actually important material.

Homeschoolers who are adverse to "testing" can still make use of this effect, both through spaced drilling, and by circling around topics in their discussions and writing assignments. For example, if you're planning a year-long history syllabus, you can insert reminders to yourself to bring up old topics, either in the course of the school day or over dinner.

Imagination Time

In a homeschooling book, or at home making plans for the syllabus, it's easy to become so enthusiastic about the academic part of life that there isn't time for children to be children. Afterschooling parents in particular need to make sure that their children have time to play. Reading some of the hard core classical education books makes me wonder if the children ever go outside, play in the mud, howl at the moon.

When Helen and Anna had their brief six week stint of conventional schooling (in grades one and two) while visiting my parents, they set off for school in the dark, took the bus to school, were kept inside at recess because it was "too cold out," and climbed off the bus in the dusk. If they'd walked down the drive to my parents' house and had their much needed snack indoors, it would have been dark by the time they'd finished. Instead, my mother, at my request, met them every day at the bus with something to eat, which they wolfed down while still in their snow suits and mittens, earning a precious hour of play outdoors.

Children need time to be alone, as unsupervised as possible, working out their world. They need time to be bored and to figure out how to fill that time, without relying on adults, video games, or television to fill it for them. Po Bronson and Ashley Merryman describe a wildly successful program called "Tools of the Mind" in their book *NurtureShock*,[39] where preschoolers and kindergarteners learn imaginative and cooperative play.

One of the tasks Bronson and Merryman describe is children playing fire station. Each child is given a role, and they work out their play plan on paper beforehand. Essentially, the children are given roles in an improv theater. It reminded me of my kindergarten, where we played a long-running, class-wide game of *Emergency!*, a popular television show about firefighter-paramedics in LA. Perhaps we chose *Emergency!* because of the pole on the jungle gym. A few years later, it was the *Six Million Dollar Man* and the *Bionic Woman*, with everyone having set parts.

Imaginative games (even television-inspired ones) are important for children's developments, for empathy, and I suspect they are helpful in developing readers and writers, for what are readers and writers, but creators of another world in the medium of sedentary words, instead of the running, pole-sliding, three-dimensional world of kindergarten play?

Do modern children have enough play time to create this world of the mind? I don't have researched-based answers to this, but I do have a feeling that too many parent-directed (or coach-directed) activities, too many "quiet the children down with a screen" parenting decisions (whether it be television, a movie, or a game of Minecraft) get in the way of this part of intellectual development. Boredom is a precious childhood resource, not a scourge. It is from boredom that writers develop, readers emerge, artists draw, musicians play, creativity blooms.

My children were very lucky to spend most of their childhood in a predator-free wilderness, free from both possible human and animal threats. We were able to leave them alone, outdoors, without too much anxiety. I know I couldn't be that mother in New York who would let her child walk home alone from the park, but I sympathize with the concern that our children are now wrapped in protective bindings, never out of earshot of adult minders, never solving their own problems, never finding Mirkwood in a grubby tangle of trees.

Last year, we gave a slide show and talk about our travels, and at the end someone asked Helen and Anna if they were ever bored sailing across an ocean or living in the wilderness without the internet or television. Thirteen-year-old Anna took the microphone and announced, "Only boring people are bored." Of course we'd said that to them on occasion, but what we meant was: solve it yourself. The children knew that they couldn't come to us saying, "I'm bored" and expect us to provide a movie or a game. They now have an important life skill of being able to self-generate solutions, whether it is to read a book, draw a picture, write a story, create an imaginative world, or go for a hike. (Or even, perhaps, do their school work.)

What and When to Teach

Curriculum design is the hot topic in education. Every generation has a slightly different approach, every wave of education graduates has a mission and publishes its set of doctrines in books and articles. As a homeschooling parent without an education degree, how are you supposed to sift through that and find a way to teach your own school?

Early elementary school teachers have to occupy twenty to thirty young children for six hours a day. They can cover a lot of material, they can use early readers to coach late readers, and they are almost universally amazing people – I can't imagine facing thirty six-year-olds every day.

As a parent, doing one-on-one coaching with your child, there is only one thing you need to teach in the first year of school: reading.

If you live in a town, your local school district may require your children to start formal schooling at a certain age. This age varies widely around the world – six in most of the US, four or five in the UK, seven or eight in Finland.[40] When is the best time? It's going to depend on your children and your circumstances. Helen was ready to start to learn to read a few months before she turned five; Anna wasn't. She started at six.

Caroline Sharp, in a paper arguing against the practice of British children starting formal school at age four or five, concludes, "The best available evidence suggests that teaching more formal skills early (in school) gives children an initial academic advantage, but that this advantage is not sustained in the longer term." She further cautions, "there are some suggestions that an early introduction to a formal curriculum may

47

increase anxiety and have a negative impact on children's self esteem and motivation to learn."[41]

In September 2015, the UK government acknowledged that some students are not ready to begin at four, and is recommending that summer-born children be given the option of delaying a year.[42] This will help students whose families have the luxury of pre-school or staying at home; many children in families where all the adults work will continue to have to begin at four.

In each of their first years of schooling, Helen and Anna only studied reading, later handwriting, and played with math manipulatives (the teacherspeak word for objects used to help learn math such as beans, poker chips or color-coded rods). I considered the reading- and writing-only year "kindergarten." I started some more math with Helen about halfway through, and since we were living in the UK for a large part of that school year, I had to be inspected by the local school administrator, who was satisfied that we met the "Year One" requirements.

In most government-mandated curricula, one needs to do more in these early years, but three subjects were enough, and limiting our studies meant we could work harder on reading and writing. I am convinced that early reading is crucial to enjoying reading. If a child is nine years old and can only read the *Junie B. Jones* series, he won't enjoy reading, and chances are, he never will. Nine-year-olds who can read *Harry Potter* and *The Lord of the Rings* are going to be swept up in reading and the problem you'll have is getting them to do anything else. Reading is the most important skill you can teach early on, because a love of reading will guide much of the rest of their educations.

In a 2002 *Scientific American* article, "How Should Reading Be Taught?" the authors note that

> [C]hildren's facility with reading in the first grade usually provides a good indication of what their 11th-grade reading proficiency will turn out to be. Why? Because reading requires practice, and those who excel end up practicing the most. Hence, the gap between more and less able readers in the first few grades generally grows over the years.[43]

I'm not sure I buy the causality suggested here – that they excel, and therefore practice – I suspect rather that it's more that they practice and therefore excel. But I am sure that early competence and praise will make a child more likely to read for pleasure, and that reading well early means that a child can read the kind of books he likes listening to, not just simplistic tales (even though children's literature has progressed far beyond *Dick and Jane*).

By "early reading" I mean stressing reading in the first year or two of school, but I don't mean pushing your three- to six-year-olds to read before they are ready. It may be faster and easier to wait six months, as I certainly found with Anna. Different children are ready at different times, and as Dorothy Cohen pointed out back in 1972 in *The Learning Child*, "Nothing is really gained by an early start, and much can be lost of the experiences that support early reading."[44] The new Common Core guidelines suggest that a student be on the way to reading at the end of kindergarten, and reading by the end of first grade, and reading independently at grade level by the end of second grade.[45] (In most US states using the English / Language Arts Common Core standards, the kindergarten to second grade requirements have increased substantially, while the later grades often haven't changed much.)

British standards have children begin all day school a year earlier, and their expectations are roughly a year ahead of American students in reading levels. My suggestion is if your child doesn't read at a second grade level by age eight, and you've been consistently sharing books, reading aloud, and giving explicit instructions in phonics, it is worth seeking a second opinion in case there are learning difficulties that are interfering with learning to read. Age four to eight seems to be the usual range of reaching the ability to read short chapter books with numerous words on each page. I can't think of another child's milestone that has such a wide range.

Early elementary school (before age nine) is fairly fluid. Different students will reach academic readiness at different times. Helen and Anna are a case in point – I started teaching Helen to read just before she turned five, and she was a chapter book reader by six. However, in part because we started school in South America on a southern hemisphere schedule, she's officially a grade behind where she would be if she'd gone to school in the US, which I think is a boon for an August baby, and has made it possible for her to be "on grade level" in math. Anna wasn't reading chapter books until she was eight and a bit, but she has now caught up to roughly where Helen was at the same age (and she's actually caught up to Helen in math and they now do the same work).

This is the schedule we have followed. It may not meet the state or local requirements in your area; if you are reporting to a school district, you may need to add more subject areas, but if you aren't, here are nine years of school, pared to the essentials.

Elementary and Middle School Subjects

(For international equivalents of these US/Canadian grade levels, please see page 325.)

First Year of School

Kindergarten (age 5-6)

Table 2: Kindergarten Coursework

Teach	Reading	15 minutes / day
Teach	Introductory handwriting	15 minutes / day
Unschool if you can	Introductory math	15 minutes / day

Elementary School

Only include the elementary school items in the "school day" if they are not occurring independently. You may find that simply encouraging reading, art, or exercise is enough, and they will happen without your interference. Spelling isn't necessary for some children; it's critical for others. Teach your children, not a syllabus!

USA Grade 1-2 (age 6-8)

Table 3: Early Elementary School Coursework

Teach	Reading, handwriting, writing, math
Unschool if you can	Nature studies, art, physical exercise
Optional	History, music, second language

USA Grade 3-4 (age 8-10)

Table 4: Late Elementary School Coursework

Teach	Writing, math, history, science
Unschool if you can	Reading, nature studies, art, exercise
Skills Work	Handwriting, keyboarding (about age 9), spelling, math facts
Optional	Music, second language

Middle School

USA Grade 5-8 (age 10-14)

Table 5: Middle School Coursework

Teach/Assign	Writing, math, history, science, second language, music
Unschool if you can	Reading, nature studies, art, physical exercise, life skills, current events
Skills Work	Library research skills
As Necessary	Spelling, handwriting, keyboarding, math facts, vocabulary, grammar

Suggested Hours per Month

(italicized items can be unschooled / bracketed items are optional)

Table 6: Hours Per Month

	Kindergarten	Grades 1-2	Grades 3-4	Grades 5-8
Reading	10 hrs	*20 hrs*	*20-30 hrs*	*20-50 hrs*
Writing	1-5 hrs	15 hrs	30 hrs	20-50 hrs
Writing Skills	1-5 hrs	7 hrs	10-15 hrs	As necessary
Math	[1-10 hrs]	15 hrs	20 hrs	30-40 hrs
Science	*[1-10 hrs]*	*[10-15 hrs]*	*20 hrs*	30 hrs
History	[1-10 hrs]	[1-10 hrs]	20 hrs	30 hrs
Second Lang	[1-10 hrs]	[1-10 hrs]	[1-10 hrs]	20 hrs
Exercise	*30 hrs*	*30 hrs*	*30 hrs*	*30 hrs*
Art	*[1-10 hrs]*	*[1-10 hrs]*	*[1-10 hrs]*	*[1-20 hrs]*
Music	*[1-10 hrs]*	*[1-10 hrs]*	*[1-20 hrs]*	*[1-30 hrs]*

Excluding physical exercise, this rough time frame leads to less than an hour a day for kindergarten, approximately four hours of school per day for first and second grade students who go to school Monday to Friday, or just over three hours per day for those who have school seven days a week. Third and fourth graders will have six or seven hours of school a day Monday to Friday, or five and a half hours seven days a week. Fifth through eight graders will have eight or nine hours a day, or seven if they have school seven days a week.

This schedule counts both teaching time and independent work (homework), and in comparison with standard schools, saves a great deal of time in the younger grades, but is quite equivalent in the later grades. It would be fewer hours, but this schedule includes the added hours of a second language study, which is seldom taught in American middle schools.

In addition, the times below include independent reading, which I never had to include as part of school, so our actual hours of declared schoolwork were considerably fewer. Many home-schoolers do far fewer formal hours of schooling; many do far more.

Table 7: Sample Daily Time Commitment

	Typical School M-F	Homeschool M-F	Homeschool 7 Days
Kindergarten	3 hours + travel	< 1 hour	< 1 hour
Grades 1-2	6 hours + travel	3-4 hours	3-4 hours
Grades 3-4	6 hours + 1 hr homework + travel	6-7 hours	4-6 hours
Grades 5-8	6 hours + 2 hrs homework + travel	6-8 hours	5-7 hours

Of course, in order to achieve these time savings with homeschooling, the students have to be on task with the work, and that is not always the case. In the early years, we struggled to complete schoolwork in the three hours it should have taken: the school work took that much time, but the time devoted to sharpening pencils, sitting down, and passing notes (concealed in the inside of a ball point pen, it turns out) was almost certainly higher than in school with a sharp-eyed elementary school teacher. I discuss this further in Managing the Classroom, page 285.

One Year Minimalist School

I have homeschooled our children through every year, so my focus is on the long term, but if I were taking a single year to make a trip or a short-term life style change, I would strongly consider cutting down school to the bare minimum of reading, writing, and arithmetic. I'd require an hour a day of reading free-choice books, and roughly 20 hours per month each of writing and math (spread out through the year, or in a more conventional school-year format as suits your situation). I would try to cover a bit of history and science by including plenty of non-fiction in the books available for the free-choice reading. Local languages and skills such as keyboarding could be easily worked in as well.

Even with the continuity introduced by the Common Core in many states, different school districts have different goals and standards for different grades, and we expect children to move back and forth between schools without too much academic trouble. If your child studies a different path of history or science for a year or two, or even skips it altogether, it is not going to affect transitioning back into school. Keep up in math, exceed school requirements for reading and writing, and you will have done well by your children.

This is a simple amount of school to have while traveling: it requires a digital book reader loaded with as many books as you can possibly afford (don't forget the thousands of free books from Project Gutenberg), a stack of writing notebooks (you can buy them as you go), and the math book. If electrical access isn't a problem, a tablet with a separate keyboard can be both the book and the word processor for reading and writing, although I don't find reading backlit tablets as pleasurable as reading the non-backlit readers (and the tablets require far more frequent re-charging). Using a tablet with PDF-based math program such as Math Mammoth would even save the weight of a math book.

It's also a simple amount of school to have while staying at home. In her article, "One Good Year: A Look at Short-Term Homeschooling," Laura Brodie describes staying home with her daughter for fifth grade, where she tried to hit the fifth grade essentials for her school district, follow her daughter's interests in the Maya and dinosaurs, and most of all, do a lot of writing, a subject crowded out in many public schools overly concerned about test-prep.[46] Math is the one subject that short-term homeschoolers need to stay on top of if they want to put their children back into the same year in the same school district. (Parents willing to put their children back a grade after a year off have more freedom here, and I think a year of reading while exploring the world would benefit many children, but the social pressure of returning to the same school district will make this approach unappealing for most families.)

Many private schools (and a few large public schools) offer flexible math scheduling, where both semesters of each math course are offered each semester. This is usually done to benefit placement – a ninth grader might arrive ready to begin algebra, to begin second semester algebra, or skip it all together and begin geometry. However, this comprehensive scheduling can benefit families who want to take a semester off, because the student wouldn't have to keep up in math, but rather could slot back into the sequence where he left off. Almost all the traveling homeschooling parents we've met want to make sure they are back in town for high school, but in fact, this can be one of the easier times to short-term homeschool. Many high school schedules require five classes a term to graduate in four years, and a strong student could pick up a sixth class without too much difficulty, in order to skip a semester and still graduate on time. (However, be warned, it is generally not the easiest time socially.)

Deschooling

If you're starting from scratch teaching your children, you can ease into school very slowly, with a few reading exercises and some math games. If your children have come out of a public or private school, especially if they have had a difficult time there, they may benefit from some *deschooling* instead of rushing straight into a homeschooling routine.

This may happen naturally if you start homeschooling after a summer vacation, but at other times of the year, you may want to take more time off. It's an opportunity for you and your children to re-connect, to reintroduce yourselves, and to begin establishing your new relationship.

Do the things you couldn't do as a family while your child was in Monday to Friday school – go outside, sit around reading, visit a science museum, build something, paint, play music.

If you're planning on having a scheduled school program – I think of mine as unschool when you can / teach when you must – you may find it helpful to set a date when you'll begin. Some parents suggest a month of deschooling for every year the child has been in a bricks and mortar school. Honestly, I don't think I could handle eight months off for an eighth grader without panicking about it, but setting a specific date may keep you from rushing back to school too soon, and help your child make the transition from deschooling to a more formal type of homeschooling.

Unschoolers maintain this type of informal, child-led learning through the school years. That style of homeschooling has many strong proponents, but it is simply not in my comfort zone. One of my goals for homeschooling is to have richly educated children, ones who have mastered all subjects at the high school level, rather than specializing too soon. This means that sometimes I have to push them along to do work they aren't particularly interested in, although I have found that once they know a bit about a topic, it becomes interesting.

Afterschooling

Many children who are enrolled in full-time school could benefit enormously by some extra help or the opportunity to stretch themselves intellectually. Certainly much of my education was made up of *afterschooling*, and I know parents who have helped their children with mental math, pushed them further in mathematics, enrolled them in local schools in foreign countries, but kept up with mathematics, reading, and writing in their home language, and so on.

Afterschooling can be a short daily math drill, or it can be a full or half day of school on Saturdays and Sundays. The subject area chapters that follow can stand alone, so afterschoolers can focus on the area they are most concerned with.

When considering afterschooling programs, the two most valuable subjects are mental maths in the early years and free-choice reading in all years. Children in school often do not have sufficient time for either. If those areas seem satisfactory, then choose one of the other subject areas, perhaps for a Saturday – Sunday class.

Going ahead in mathematics requires some caution. A friend pushed ahead in math in the 70s, and her only option was to skip seventh grade so she could join the new algebra class on offer for eighth grade. She sometimes regrets the lack of preparation in other subject areas, and that missed seventh grade. Thirty years later, her son was allowed to push ahead in elementary school, so he was finished with seventh grade math when he began fifth grade at the middle school in the same school district. They did not have any program for math tracking, however, so he was put back into fifth grade math. This was a disaster, as he was bored out of his mind, distracted other students (surprise, surprise), and earned a reputation as a "bad math student," and judged ineligible for eighth grade algebra, not for his grades or test scores, but because he was inattentive in class. The story had a happy ending, however, as he studied algebra in his spare time (self-driven afterschooling), learned the whole course in six months, and changed schools to one with a placement test, where he passed out of algebra I. But had he not had the option to change schools, this might have been a problem that haunted him throughout his school years.

Few students are lucky enough to have teachers like the high school physics teacher, who knew just what to do when confronted with the future Nobel Prize winner Richard Feynman. Feynman recalls:

> One day [Mr. Bader] told me to stay after class. "Feynman," he said, "you talk too much and you make too much noise. I know why. You're bored. So I'm going to give you a book. You go up there in the back, in the corner, and study this book, and when you know everything that's in this book, you can talk again."[47]

The book was advanced calculus; when Feynman finished with that, Mr. Bader gave him the next volume.

For students hungry to push forward in math, the Art of Problem Solving series may be a good option, as it takes students deeper into each area of math. In some schools, it might be possible for accelerated math students to work problems at the back of the classroom at their own rate, although not all districts will allow this.

However, for most people, pursuing advanced work in reading, writing, science, or history is much less likely to cause problems meshing in with the local school than mathematics. In these subjects, primary schools typically do not have tracking, and there is no ceiling on how accomplished students can be. (In other countries, the same can be true in mathematics – Singapore, for example, usually has very difficult tests to allow exceptional students to differentiate themselves, without penalizing the merely above average. A grade of "A1" (equivalent to a US "A") is earned for a 75% score and above.)[48]

Remedial work in any subject is valuable. It is probably best for afterschoolers to choose the most difficult subject and concentrate on that, perhaps changing subjects as time goes by. An hour or two of focused attention a week can make a huge difference in academic performance, without shaming the student with remedial work during school time, or filling up too much of the week with schoolwork at the expense of physical exercise and play.

Another way is to afterschool like an unschooler. This is what my parents did with me: it never felt like *school*, but they surrounded me with books, discussion, and time to explore nature. They limited screen time, which was annoying, of course, even though in those days there were only three channels, and no internet. The reading, writing, history, and science sections will give you further ideas on ways to promote an education without it feeling like school.

Academic Goals

These are my goals for my children; you may have slightly different goals or priorities, but I've included this list as a starting point. It does not necessarily align with national or state standards – in some areas, I think it is important to exceed those standards; in math in particular, I think it is more important to be proficient than exactly on grade level.

End of Elementary School (age 10)

- Write a 3-5 page paper (double-spaced if typed), with sources, without quailing at the prospect
- Read long, complex chapter books, both fiction and non-fiction at a fifth or sixth grade level (search for "leveled book list" online)
- Spell at a fourth grade level (you can find lists online to check your student's level)
- Touch type / keyboard at 25 words per minute with accurate spelling
- Acceptable handwriting (printing, joined up writing, or a hybrid "italic" writing; joined up writing is the norm in the UK right from the start; many American states have now abandoned joined-up writing entirely, but I would recommend it, as it is considerably faster for writing essay exams and taking notes)
- Within 6 months of "grade level" in an appropriate math program
- General understanding of science and familiarity with the scientific method
- Several years' study of history and the ability to write several paragraphs about historical events, both summary of readings and simple analysis
- Able to follow written directions without adult supervision, for example follow science experiment directions or make a multi-step recipe

End of Middle School (age 14)

- Write a 5-8 page paper (double-spaced if typed), with sources, without quailing at the prospect
- Read long, complex books, both fiction and non-fiction at high school / adult level (search for "leveled book list" online)

- Write and speak with a high-school level academic vocabulary
- Spell at a sixth grade level (you can find lists online to check your student's level)
- Touch type / keyboard at 40 words per minute with accurate spelling
- Acceptable handwriting
- Within 6 months of "grade level" in an appropriate math program
- General understanding of science and familiarity with the scientific method; solid introduction to the following topics:
  - Evolutionary biology
  - Physics and chemistry
  - Earth sciences and astronomy
- The ability to read a high school level science textbook with some assistance
- Familiarity with the basics of experimentation, keeping lab notebooks, and dissection
- At least six years' study of history
  - Reading and understanding history from a variety of sources: high school level history textbooks, adult level popular history, middle school level textbooks
  - Able to write 2-4 page papers about historical events, both analysis and summary of readings
- Experience of at least one lecture-based course (online or on DVDs)
- The equivalent of one year of high school study in a second language, minimum
- Solid knowledge of world current events and a comfort with reading adult-level magazines such as *The Week*
- Basic computer skills (word processing, spreadsheet, layout and internet research)

Looking Ahead

In the American system, the testing for college is loaded towards the end of high school. Students may take the exams earlier, but they will generally score higher the longer they wait, except for some specific subject matter courses. Students will do best by following a general, broad range of studies throughout their school years, which will prepare them for the SAT or the ACT general exams, subject area exams, and occasionally AP (Advanced Placement) exams which are considered to be the equivalent of a year at an American university, and are similar to the British A-Level.

While most high schools require four years of English, three years of math, two years of science and history, and three years of a language for graduation, the extremely selective colleges expect four years of each plus a year of arts for admission. Competitive colleges typically look for four years of English, plus three years of everything else. Athletes should check NCAA requirements if they plan to compete at the college level.

In the British system, there are two cycles of exams, the GCSEs and the A-Levels, both of which are available to homeschooled students. Many schools offer the International Baccalaureate in place of A-Levels, but that exam is not currently available to homeschoolers. The GCSE preparation usually begins in Year 9 or 10, and the exams are usually taken at the end of Year 11 (about age sixteen). Most students take a broad range of classes and sit exams in five to eleven subjects. If a student is in school during these years, course work can count towards the grade, but homeschoolers will find it easiest to take the IGCSE, which is offered around the world and is exam-based only.

A-Levels are a two-year program (which may be followed by homeschoolers), taken in Years 12 and 13, or age 16-18. Throughout this book, I equate US grade level with the UK year level, and that is fairly accurate, although the British students are a year younger. English students are usually about a year ahead academically of American students by the end of secondary school (both countries finish up typically at eighteen), but most English universities are only three years (Scottish universities, however, are four years). The British system is much more focused after age sixteen – three or four subjects are usually studied at A-Level (I do know someone who took five), and at university students generally don't take the breadth of electives offered at most American universities.

Teaching and Learning Summary

- Encourage a growth mindset – most students can learn anything if they work at it
- Schoolwork should be always difficult, but never impossible
- If your students are studying a subject area on their own, let them run with it
- Focus your teaching time on the subjects your students find more difficult or uninteresting
- Emphasize reading and writing stamina
- Emphasize a blend of conceptual mathematics and basic facts to make the concepts easier
- Ask questions

Reading

Jump ahead if your child already knows how to read:

Early Elementary Reading (page 70)
Dyslexia and Other Difficulties (page 73)
Advanced Reading (page 82)

Beginning Reading

School begins when children are very small – by reading to them. All the time. Hamish and I can still quote any number of children's stories by heart; Helen and Anna remember none of them. But the important thing is that children learn that stories equate to entertainment (and cuddles and affection), and they watch you read for both pleasure and education.

Once, when Hamish was leaving for a month to work on a superyacht, he recorded himself reading a dozen of the girls' favorite stories. This was a great way to occupy them and gave them reading entertainment – but it has to come after hours and hours of sitting side by side with a parent – it's a supplement to reading together, not a substitute. Later, we let Stephen Fry do most of our reading aloud for us, as the Harry Potter stories repeated endlessly on long ocean passages.

The other reason to read children's picture books aloud is they often have far more complicated vocabulary than the typical adult conversation, television, or general elementary school books. In fact, the vocabulary in books read to pre-schoolers is often on par with that of the assigned literature in high school.[49] Of course, you'd have to read a lot more picture books to get a similar number of actual vocabulary words, but there are two important take aways from this – one, parents *must* read aloud to their children (and continue this throughout early reading instruction), and, two, children do need a different class of book for their early reading – the early reading books and chapter books are at a significantly lower vocabulary level than the read-aloud picture books, and that's a good thing. Children can polish their reading skills on phrases like, "Mat sat. Sam sat"[50] and at the same time learn vocabulary words like "soporific" from listening to Beatrix Potter.

For some children, reading aloud may be enough, or nearly enough. If your children do learn to read by your side without any apparent effort or phonics training, let them read! The only goal of reading instruction is proficient and enjoyable reading – not exposing children to drudgery. If your students read quite well, but you still have a nagging desire to work on their phonics, you can cover it as part of spelling lessons later on.

For many children, however, story time and book exposure is not enough. There are traditionally three main methods of teaching reading used in schools, although most teachers use a mix to teach their classes. The *phonics system* teaches children the sounds of letters and groups of letters, and allows them to "sound out" the words. The *sight-reading system* teaches them to recognize words that are used with high frequency in children's books and read rapidly from a collection of memorized words. The *whole language system*, which was in vogue when I taught Helen to read, emphasizes meaning-based experience, rather than sound-based, so there is no explicit instruction in how to sound out words. In some places, the debate still rages, but now many US educators are talking more about *balanced literacy*, which is melding explicit phonics instruction with whole language instruction.[51]

Most schools teach reading before or alongside writing, on the assumption that most children are physically capable of reading before they are capable of writing. Montessori schools teach writing first, and the children learn to read by reading their own writing. I didn't try this approach, but it's an interesting one. It does require a lot of organized work in the early years to develop the necessary dexterity.[52]

American teachers may dislike phonics because they were taught phonics the way I was: my memory of first grade includes several weeks on the schwa, a symbol found in dictionaries that looks like an upside-down e: ə. I remember making posters of the schwa, making up songs about it, and coloring it green. I did not learn to read that year.[53]

A 2002 article in *Scientific American* discussing the systems of teaching reading, research into the efficiency of those systems in the classroom, and the brain processes behind learning to read recommends taking a phonics-based approach:

> [R]eading must be grounded in a firm understanding of the connections between letters and sounds. Instructors should recognize the ample evidence that youngsters who are directly taught phonics become better at reading, spelling and comprehension than those who must pick up all the confusing rules of English on their own. Educators who deny this reality are neglecting decades of research. They are also neglecting the needs of their students. [54]

Furthermore, the authors recommend that most teachers follow a structured program as the most efficient way to teach children phonics.[55] I am not going to enter that debate, but I do know that a phonics-based system (and lots and lots of reading aloud beforehand) worked for us.

Good readers sight read. Fast readers sight read. The sight reading faction concluded children should be taught that way from the beginning because obviously it is the right way to read. It is. But, what happens when you get to a word you don't recognize? You have to slow down and sound it out. The basic skill of reading is breaking down words and sounding them out. Mechanics don't chant "righty tight-y, lefty loose-y" to themselves as they rebuild an engine, they just do it. But somewhere first, they had to learn the basic principles. Asking children to learn to read by simply exposing them to books is like plunking someone down in front of an eighty horsepower motor with a stack of seals and a jumble of tools saying, "rebuild this engine." It can work. Plenty of kids in my hometown learned mechanics in just this way – they'd buy an old wreck at fifteen and have it going by the time they were old enough for a driver's license. But it's not the most efficient way, and a lot of children are so put off by the intimidation of the whole engine that they just don't know where to start.

Many professional teachers become positively angry when discussing direct phonics instruction – Regie Routman describes it as "repetitive, military-like, whole class drills with scripted teacher materials . . . [that] focuses on sounds and words in isolation."[56] She argues that the call for phonics "is contrary to the wide body of research that puts meaningful encounters with print in social contexts as the most critical to emerging readers."[57]

A friend of mine worked extensively in reading education and trained as a Reading Recovery teacher. Many of her students had never handled a book before school – they didn't know how to hold it. That is what public school teachers are up against; it's easy to see the benefits of a whole-language approach, where all the children can come into contact with books and stories, to appreciate them before going through the hard work of learning to read. However, in a homeschooling situation, this immersion in books does not have to take place in "school time," but rather should be an intrinsic part of family life.

Another reason that the research about phonics instruction failed to inspire teachers was that in 2000, the National Reading Panel issued a report entitled, *Teaching Children to Read*, which emphasized the importance of phonics in teaching reading, and went on to note that (this wording is from 2003 summary pamphlet, *Put Reading First*):

> One of the major differences between good and poor readers is the amount of time they spend reading. Many studies have found a strong relationship between reading ability and how much a student reads. . . . Research, however, has not yet confirmed whether independent silent reading with minimal guidance or feedback improves reading achievement and fluency. Neither has it proven that more silent reading in the classroom cannot work; its effectiveness without guidance or feedback is as yet unproven. The research suggests that there are more beneficial ways to spend reading instructional time than to have students read independently in the classroom without reading instruction.[58]

I suspect many elementary school teachers had the same reaction I did, which is to shout, "Ridiculous!" Teachers are instructed to "encourage" students to read more at home, which is patently meaningless – six-year-olds whose parents push them are already reading at home, and the ones who don't have pushy parents won't read at home, even with teacher "encouragement."[59]

In several points in the document, *Put Reading First* discourages actual reading. Going through the pamphlet again (after a year-long cooling off period) I wonder if what perhaps they meant to say (or should have said) was children shouldn't be required to do silent independent reading until they can actually read at a first grade level. When I'd read the whole language method descriptions, I couldn't understand *how* the children were supposed to learn to read, and I knew if I'd been a first grader in a whole language classroom, given a book to read without knowing how, I would have talked, doodled, cried, or tipped over in my chair. I would not have tried to puzzle it out. However, once I could read, I never would have become a successful reader without thousands of hours of independent reading.

When I started the search for how to teach my children to read my only real starting point was that I hated every minute of my reading instruction, and it took me three years to read my first chapter book. No one (I hope) teaches first graders about the schwa anymore. Although whole language teachers talk about how they teach phonics "in conference,"[60] I didn't have the confidence in my own phonics knowledge to think I could teach reading through multiple readings of *Thomas the Tank Engine*. After all, I'd read most of the books in our library aloud – to the point of my knowing them by heart – yet neither daughter had shown any signs of learning to read.

I also wanted something fast. I remembered the screaming boredom of learning to read, and wondering why I should bother (probably because my parents read to me whenever I wanted). It seemed important to minimize the time of learning to read, so the children could get on with the important business of reading. In an article entitled "The Reading Wars," published in the *Atlantic*, Nicholas Lemann comments, "Even ... parents who consider themselves to be greatly concerned about their children's education, have tended to focus on high school and to assume that not much can go wrong in the world of angelic six-year-olds."[61] From the beginning, however, I had the opposite belief: that teaching reading was the most important job I had in all my homeschooling.

While researching, I came upon *Teach Your Child to Read in 100 Easy Lessons*. It is a "scripted program," which means your part in the play is clearly written out. The exact words you're expected to say are right there on the page. There is no need for preparation, no need to study up on the assignments the night before. I didn't in fact say exactly the words on the page, but I did go through the sequence of sounds in order and taught the stories as instructed. We did not do the writing practice, because that made the lessons too long.

There are several key factors in *Teach Your Child to Read*:

- The stories begin almost immediately, so the children have the satisfaction of reading
- Each lesson begins with some new material and practice, followed by a story
- The stories are all a bit odd, so it is impossible to guess the words; the children have to actually read it
- Parents are instructed to cover up the picture at the first reading so there is no chance of guessing[*]
- The first half of the book uses phonetic writing, for example the long e sound is written ē and the "th" sound is written with the two letters joined together. English pronunciation is extremely complicated, and so this is a great way to start students reading while they internalize the rules. (Students are gradually weaned off the crutch of phonetic writing in the second half of the book.)

Teach Your Child to Read is also a good resource for dyslexic children, who often need explicit phonics instruction.[62] Anna isn't dyslexic, but she does have some learning difficulties, although I

---

[*] Guessing is one of the biggest points of contention between the theories of teaching reading. Whole language teaching actively encourages guessing; *Teach Your Child to Read* actively discourages it. My unstudied opinion is that it is better to sound it out rather than guess because that way the student is not limited to the spoken vocabulary he already knows, but instead can learn to figure out words. They may not pronounce the new words perfectly, but that doesn't matter. Anna used to say "tarvern" instead of "tavern" after learning the word in *Lord of the Rings*, but that's better than guessing and reading it "tawdry" or "tarsier."

didn't figure this out until after she'd learned to read, and she had progressed to churning through the *Lord of the Rings*. It took her considerably longer to learn to read than it took Helen, but by the sixth grade she was reading at a high school level. It took patience and a couple of years to get her on track.

A lot of bitterness in the learn-to-read wars stems from using different terms to describe similar things. Sitting on the couch with Helen and Anna working through *Teach Your Child to Read* was a million miles away from Routman's description of "military-like whole class drills." For the first several weeks, Helen baulked at the size of the book, so I copied the reading onto index cards and put the book away. (By the time Anna started to read, she'd watched Helen work through the book, so it wasn't intimidating.) I think the key to avoiding the pitfalls often ascribed to direct phonics instruction is to teach it one on one, surrounded by books for the rest of the day. We had a bookcase at ground level; the children always had access to books, and every night had a bedtime story or three.

Halfway through kindergarten, Helen was reading at a second grade level; it took Anna until the end of first grade. I have to admit, however, not everyone was impressed. For a while I became a bit of a proselytizer for *Teach Your Child to Read,* telling everyone I knew with a pre-reading child how well it had worked, how quickly, how inexpensively, and I even gave away a few copies. No one I know gave it a try, neither those with children going into traditional schools, nor those homeschooling. I'm not entirely sure why – perhaps it was seen as too conservative, too strict, too much time, interfering with the school teacher's work.

If Anna had been the elder child, I might not have been so enthusiastic about *Teach Your Child to Read.* I might have blamed the book for her difficulties in learning to read, and then not tried it with Helen as a result. However, my research and my experience backs up the idea that systematic phonics combined with a family immersion in books is a great way for children, dyslexic and otherwise, to learn to read. If you don't like *Teach Your Child to Read,* you might find the *All About Reading* program more compelling (and potentially better for dyslexic children, although it is usually hard to tell if your children are dyslexic before you start reading instruction).

Independent Reading in Early Elementary (Grades 1-3)

Once a child knows how to read, she needs a lot of books. This is easy if you live near a library, but if you're out in the middle of nowhere, or in a country where you don't speak the language, you'll need to stock up. We bought a set of 500 children's books on eBay for fifty dollars; second-hand book shops can be a good source, and friends and relatives with older children may be ready to clear out a bookshelf. At this age, digital books aren't really a good option, and most children like books with lots of pictures, so you're better off with, well, if I have to pick a number, at least 100 children's books in the grade 1 to grade 3 range.

This is the trickiest time to do "on the road schooling." It's okay if you are on a boat or an R.V. with storage space for books, but if you're trying to go touring around by bus or plane, you might find it easier to wait until your children are out of the picture book stage and will be happy with a Kindle or other ebook reader. This difficulty is lessening, however, as more and more good children's books are available as ePub or Kindle format, and look great on a ten-inch tablet. I would still prefer to read paper books with young children when possible, given the concerns about backlit screens and melanin production. Researchers tell us that reading backlit screens at night or watching television before bedtime can interfere with sleep, whereas a non-backlit ebook reader appears to act more like a regular book.[63]

When I was in school, we used to have to write book reports on all the books we read. I loathed it. The important thing at this age is to read, read, read. It doesn't matter too much what it is (although I'm not that fond of Captain Underpants, and Junie B. Jones's grammar isn't exactly what you want your children to be learning).

If your students are not reading for an hour or so everyday at their reading level, then you should assign it as part of school, supervise it, and if you have to, ask them to keep book logs or other proof of what they've read. If they spend an hour a day or more reading on their own, stay out of it. That's an easy way to trim back on your "school day." Just make sure they read.

Elementary school children must be required to read, and read in great quantity, but children who choose their own books, and read for pleasure, entertainment and information, will become better readers. In *Holding on to Good Ideas in a Time of Bad Ones,* Thomas Newkirk points out: *"unless we can persuade students that reading is a form of deep sustained pleasure, they will not choose to read; and because they will not choose to read they will not develop the skills to make them good readers."*[64]

If your children are avid readers, they don't need to keep book logs, write book reports, or do any of the other "prove it" busy work of reading classrooms. A reading teacher needs some accountability with what happens when the students are outside of the classroom, but a homeschooling teacher knows how much reading is going on without the documentation.

When we had to provide homeschooling documentation for New Hampshire, our evaluating teacher had the excellent idea that I cut colored paper into strips, which the girls would use as bookmarks. When they finished a book, they would copy the title onto the strip, and staple it into a paper chain.

Once your students are hooked on reading, encourage them to vary the material a bit, but again, all that really matters is they are reading. Don't worry if they read the same book a dozen times. A friend's son was told by his third grade teacher that he "wasn't ready" to read *Harry Potter* books, so he was forbidden to read them at school reading time. Fortunately, he wasn't discouraged and read them at home – about ten times. Perhaps the teacher was right, he wasn't reading well enough to get everything out of the books on the first read, but it didn't matter. He was fascinated by the books, and so he read them again and again, and that improved his reading level far more than sitting in a classroom, eyes passing over words that he was "ready" to read, but held no interest.

Nancie Atwell in her excellent book, *The Reading Zone,* asks her students to categorize books as "just right," "challenge," or a "holiday." (She's adopted the terms from teacher Leslie Funkhouser.)[65] Ideally, your students' independent choice reading should fall into roughly a third of each type of book. Atwell's students keep reading logs, but simply keeping in touch with homeschool students over the dinner table can let you have an idea of how hard they are pushing themselves. If all their books are holidays, you can be a bit more proactive about your suggestions, if all are challenging, point them to some easier books to help them develop fluency.

Elementary school teachers frequently talk about Jeanette Veatch's "rule of thumb" where students open a book to a random page and read it. If they count up to five words on the page that they don't know, then it's too hard.[66] (This is probably the test that ruled out *Harry Potter* for my friend's son.) Can you imagine sitting down to a read a book where you didn't know five words on every page? It would be discouraging, heartbreaking and you'd probably give up on the book.

I take two lessons from imagining myself coping with five unknown words a page. First, interest in the subject matter is critical – it makes the student read, and read again. And maybe read again. Second, I think it points to the importance of having the skills of sounding out words on the page, even if that skill is employed for a relatively short period of time while sight reading develops.

Almost immediately after finishing their reading program, both Helen and Anna were able to sound out almost any word they came to. Of course, the more they read, the fewer times they had to stop and sound out words, because their sight-reading ability was increasing every day. Sounding out the new words rather than guessing meant that their sight-reading memories were accurate not haphazard. Books aimed at roughly second grade level didn't pose a challenge for them in terms of spoken vocabulary, so it was simply the new experience of seeing words written down that challenged them. When they did meet a word they didn't understand, they could make a good pitch at it, and come up with something very close to its actual sound. (Well, apart from "chaos." I too remember having trouble with that one.)

Anna had a lot more difficulty turning words into sight-reading words, and she was much more prone to just saying any old word that started with the same letter as the word on the page. It took her many more repetitions of sounding out a word before she knew it. But she could read: she could confront each word on the page and sound it out and read independently. She didn't have to employ strategies of guessing, looking at the picture, or any of the other methods that are frequently taught to early elementary school children. I am convinced that she would not have learned to read comfortably had she gone by the "Rule of Thumb" and tried to guess the unknown words. She cannot copy a list of words accurately when they are right in front of her unless she does it one letter at a time; she can't hold the image of the letters in her

72

mind long enough. But because she had the ability to sound out the words, she could read, and she read enough, over and over, that she did learn to sight read, and now she can read at an adult speed.

Dyslexia and Other Learning Difficulties

(Turn to page 82 for Advanced Reading if you want to skip this section.)

I missed this. I completely and utterly missed it. Anna is a more active child than Helen was – she was crawling at five months and has been on the move ever since. When she didn't want to learn to read at the same age, I put it down to this ceaseless energy. *She's not ready to sit still.* We went through the entire *Teach Your Child to Read* book, all one hundred lessons, but she still couldn't read, whereas Helen was ready to move straight into books and was reading at a second grade level after six months of reading instruction, just as it promised on the blurb on the back of the book.

With Anna, we had a few months off during charter season, and by the time we started reading lessons again, she'd forgotten everything. When Helen was that stage, I'd feared a big "summer vacation loss" but it didn't happen. She was able to take time off and come back nearly at the same level. Not so with Anna. I turned back to lesson 65 and restarted. This time we made better progress, but she was still not ready for books. For nearly a year afterward reading lessons had to be explicit and tutored. She read aloud, page after page, day after day from the *Spectrum* series of books, with me helping her read every word on the page. With Helen, I just left her alone with a stack of books.

When we finished with the *Spectrum Grade 2* books (and Anna was fed up with the content), I started her on some more interesting novels, but she still wasn't ready to fly solo. Every word she read for all of first grade was at my side, with me there to help her sound out each word she had difficulty with.

Finally, after months of this, it clicked. Anna read aloud her required selection in *Star in the Storm* by Joan Hiatt Harlow, a story about a Newfoundland dog who comes to the rescue in a small Canadian town. When we finished, she stayed in the corner of the settee and finished the book with no prompting. (On reading this paragraph, Anna noted, "The reason was, you were busy and you told me to read it on my own. I did, but Helen whined at me when I read out loud so I started to read silently. I still remember the wonderful feeling when I realized I could read anything.")

After that, she could read. In less than six months, she was dragging around *Harry Potter and the Deathly Hallows,* an impressively big book for an eight-year-old. (Anna does like big fat trophy books – the next book I remember her reading was the *Lord of the Rings*. She was particularly proud of this one as our 19 and 21-year-old charter guests were also reading it at the same time.)

Well, that's it then, she can read. Mission accomplished.

Then, I started to work with her on writing and her spelling.

Her handwriting was atrocious ("So was mine," said Hamish, and I took comfort from that, despite the fact that one of the reasons Hamish's writing had been bad was he'd broken his writing hand at age seven and from then on used his right hand for writing.)

Her numbers were often mirror imaged.

Her spelling was a jumble of letters. Often all the correct letters were there, but just in a completely mixed up order.

Sometimes her spelling was phonetically correct, but she was unable to go through a piece of her writing and circle the misspellings. Helen, by contrast, had been able to turn her reading ability directly into proofreading ability. When she didn't know how to spell a word, she at least could instantly look at it and recognize that it was wrong.

I simply could not understand how Anna's spelling could be so jumbled. I am afraid that my initial reaction was simply that she was lazy and she did not care about her schoolwork, and I drove myself crazy trying to figure out how to make her take more care with it. I set her to studying a highly recommended spelling program, but she even copied down the words wrong when working from the list.

I didn't actually figure it out until she was nine. Perhaps if she'd been in a regular school, a good teacher would have noticed it much earlier, but on the other hand, her constant restlessness and clowning around would have just caused her to be labeled as a disruptive child and in some parts of the world, teachers would have suggested Ritalin.

My big clue was one afternoon when Hamish's mother was in the hospital. The grandchildren wrote "Get Well" cards, and Anna burst into tears. It was a revelation to me: Anna was sobbing because her six-year-old cousin had tidier handwriting and better spelling. She *does* care.

It had been incredibly easy for me to dismiss her as lazy. I like to think I am a sensitive mother and am in touch with my children, but she'd never mentioned it was difficult for her – how could she; she had nothing to compare it with. I went online and searched for articles on dyslexia – at one point, I found a checklist of symptoms of dyslexic children. Nearly every item on the list described Anna. I'd been fooled because she could charge through the *Lord of the Rings* at eight, because she had her nose stuck in a book whenever she had the leisure time.

When she was evaluated for dyslexia, the professional educator described her not as dyslexic, but with various difficulties ranging from mild to severe, which explains why she could read so well, yet not be able to copy down a list of spelling words correctly side by side with the original.

Dyslexics Can Learn to Read

In 1995, Rosemary Fink studied successful adult dyslexics and noted that they had managed to reach a superior level of fluency and reading skill despite their earlier difficulties. The most important factor in their success was having *high interest* materials to read.[67]

Fink's study is a beacon of optimism for parents teaching dyslexic children. She chose a dozen highly successful dyslexics – successful in careers that required a lot of reading and writing, including a Nobel prizewinner. Fink writes:

> I expected to discover extraordinary bypass and compensation strategies. Presumably continual frustration with basic skills would lead dyslexics to avoid reading. To my surprise, I found that these dyslexics were avid readers. Although they had persistent troubles with basic, lower

level skills (letter and word recognition and phonics), they rarely circumvented reading. On the contrary, they sought out books; they did *not* bypass reading in order to learn.[68]

Although each of the individuals had a 3-4 year delay in reaching "fluency," due to their difficulties with basic decoding skills, she notes that the successful dyslexics in her study did not seem to need complete mastery in the lower level skills in order to reach reading mastery.[69]

According to Fink, it is important not to give up on children with reading difficulties, but to continue to work with them, both with reading and decoding instruction, but also with reading materials that target that student's particular interests. She concludes:

> These dyslexics' stories revealed a common theme: In childhood, each had a passionate personal interest, a burning desire to know more about a discipline that required reading. Spurred by this passionate interest, all read voraciously, seeking and reading everything they could get their hands on about a single intriguing topic.[70]

As with every child, the more children with reading difficulties read, the better they become. A reading program such as the one described by Nancie Atwell in *The Reading Zone,* based on high volume, high interest reading, is particularly important for students with reading difficulties.

If you have any inklings of reading or learning difficulties, don't be afraid to seek help from professionals. It is unlikely to cause problems with your plans to homeschool, as homeschoolers have a very strong track record of successfully teaching students with dyslexia and other difficulties. It's a perfect situation for many children, because they have one-on-one coaching, and the ability to work at different grade levels in different subjects. In fact, many homeschoolers have chosen that route *because* their children have difficulties.

The International Dyslexia Association [eida.org] is an excellent place to begin your research. They publish a series of Fact Sheets which are available for free download, which can help you evaluate your situation and decide whether or not you need to go to outside testing.

Understood [www.understood.org] is another good place to look for specific help and information.

Testing is often available at no cost through local schools, even for homeschooled students. Testing can be helpful because it will provide you with a formal diagnosis, which may be critical in receiving accommodations in future exams, such as the SATs or ACT. However, students who don't meet the criteria for official diagnosis may still benefit from some of the following techniques. In fact, many students who are formally diagnosed with dyslexia do learn to read and write well enough that they no longer qualify for special assistance or programs.

A Few Warning Signs

(Excerpted from the International Dyslexic Association Fact Sheet "Dyslexia Basics.")

What are the signs of dyslexia?

The problems displayed by individuals with dyslexia involve difficulties in acquiring and using written language. It is a myth that individuals with dyslexia "read backwards," although spelling can look quite jumbled at times because students have trouble remembering letter symbols for sounds and forming memories for words. Other problems experienced by people with dyslexia include the following:

• Learning to speak

• Learning letters and their sounds

• Organizing written and spoken language

• Memorizing number facts

• Reading quickly enough to comprehend

• Persisting with and comprehending longer reading assignments

• Spelling

• Learning a foreign language

• Correctly doing math operations

Not all students who have difficulties with these skills have dyslexia. Formal testing of reading, language, and writing skills is the only way to confirm a diagnosis of suspected dyslexia.[71]

In addition to these warning signs, I found the most significant one in Anna's case was an inconsistency in her abilities. In some subjects and techniques she was years ahead of expected "grade level," yet her reading was a year or so behind for several years, and her handwriting and spelling remained consistently behind. In mathematics, she was two years ahead of grade level, *as long as she didn't need to copy out the problems into a notebook.* Even when her fiction and non-fiction reading comprehension jumped ahead of grade level, her ability to solve word problems lagged several years behind the rest of her mathematics. These inconsistencies were an important clue (and should have been a red flag that she wasn't being lazy!). Looking at her academic performance as a whole made it evident that there were problems, even though she fit the range of "normal" in each individual area.

Basic Reading Instruction

The International Dyslexic Association points to the importance of using "Structured Literacy" (this means methodical, direct instructions in phonics) for dyslexic students, rather than using "whole language," "sight reading," or simply hoping they will pick up reading on their own.[72] The book we used, *Teach Your Child to Read in 100 Easy Lessons* can work for mildly dyslexic students, but may not be enough. *All About Reading* is highly recommended for any child, and may work when *Teach Your Child to Read in 100 Easy Lessons* does not. If I were starting over with a child like Anna, I would still begin with *Teach Your Child to Read* as it's only about $14 for a complete reading instruction package. However, if this isn't working, the next investment I'd make is *All About Reading* – the entire package of four levels plus "pre-reading," with accompanying books, readers, workbooks, and an interactive kit was just under $550 in 2016. (Most of it is re-usable if you are teaching a second or third child a few years later; if you are teaching two at the same time, you will need a second student kit.) It sounds like a very steep price, but it is considerably less expensive than professional assistance, where a simple evaluation can run over $1000.

It's important to remember that both these programs will work fine with non-dyslexic children -- you're not going to do any damage by using either of them, as long as you're sensitive to your students' understandings. If they seem to be getting everything effortlessly, you can speed up a bit. If they're struggling, slow down. Above all, keep reading instruction as brief and as lighthearted as you can, and continue reading aloud to your children every day, so they remember what a gift reading will be when they eventually understand it. As discussed in the last chapter, homeschooling with direct instruction is not as deadly to reading enjoyment as it can be in whole-class instruction, because students can work at their own pace.

If neither program is working for your child, and he has reached age eight or nine without making progress in independent reading, it is worth seeking some outside help, whether you choose to do it privately or through your local public schools.

Reading on Devices

Dyslexic students might want to try one of the two fonts especially developed to helped dyslexics, Dyslexie and OpenDyslexic. Dyslexie is free for home use and can be installed across a variety of platforms, and OpenDyslexic is free for all uses. If you suspect your child is dyslexic, it may be worth trying out these fonts on a computer or tablet; if they seem to help, it could be worth buying a Kobo ebook reader or one of the Amazon Kindles which allow users to select OpenDyslexic font. Amazon is slowly introducing the choice to their ebook readers, including some non-backlit ones. (Backlit screens may interfere with sleep patterns, but should present no problems when used during the daytime.)[73]

Links:

- Dyslexie font [www.dyslexiefont.com]

- OpenDyslexic [www.opendyslexic.org]

- Kobo Ebook Readers [www.kobobooks.com]

- Amazon Kindles [www.amazon.com]

Both the Dyslexie font and OpenDyslexic font may be downloaded free of charge to personal computers and used in writing programs such as Word or Open Office, which may help students with proofreading skills.

Many dyslexic students will find that they can learn to read standard books and fonts successfully. If at all possible, you should institute these aids as a help in learning to read, rather than a bypass for reading standard works. You may find older students can read accurately when they're alert, but need more assistance when they're tired, or they may be able to convert to reading standard books all the time after a few years of specialized fonts and read aloud programs.

Reading While Listening

For students who are formally diagnosed with dyslexia, Nancie Atwell in *The Reading Zone* particularly recommends the US National Library Service for the Blind and Physically Handicapped talking book program [www.loc.gov/nls/] for children who struggle with reading disabilities. These are not simply books on tape: the stories are read, but without special voices, background music or other props, so the students can learn to "connect auditory and visual input, enter the [reading] zone, and, over time, develop sight vocabularies that compensate for reading disabilities."[74]

I don't have any personal experience with this program, but it is free of charge for American children who qualify, and well worth a look if your children struggle to read. For students who do not meet the criteria, there are other options such as books on tape (often available from your local library) or Amazon Kindle's Whispersync, when used on a Amazon Fire tablet or an Android tablet. (In 2016, these are the only ebook reader devices that allow you to read and listen simultaneously. They call it "immersion reading." Although some Kindle models allowed readers to choose OpenDyslexic font on the readers, the ones which offered Whispersync were still unable to do so. I expect that will change soon, and it will make these devices a powerful tool for many readers with difficulties.)

Writing and Proofreading

Many dyslexic and dysgraphic students will have a difficult time with both printing and handwriting, and they may eventually find it far easier to type. (Dysgraphic students are those who don't have trouble with "decoding" words on the page, but have great difficult with "encoding" -- in particular, handwriting, spelling, and sometimes grammar.) With Anna, I did not let her type independently until she had reached a fourth grade spelling level, because I didn't want her to train her fingers to type misspellings. With help from *All About Spelling,* she reached this level in the sixth grade and began to write all her papers on the computer. I will discuss this further in the Writing-related Skills chapter on page 167.

Once students are ready to begin typing, it is possible to buy complete computer packages to help dyslexic students write accurately, but there are free work-arounds which can help all but the most severely affected students.

For example, I've paired the Dyslexie font with the OpenOffice word processing program to make proofreading easier. In OpenOffice, it is possible to convert document files into PDF documents, which then can be opened in Adobe Acrobat. The newest versions of the free Adobe Reader have a "read aloud" option, which is quite good, if slightly robotic. For older students proofreading their writing, it can be very helpful to have Adobe Acrobat reading the work aloud in a minimized file, while the student reads along in OpenOffice (or on a print out), making corrections. Each element is free for home use, in contrast to $800 or more for a complete dyslexic writing suite.

Homophones are words that sound the same but are spelled differently. These are often a real difficulty for dyslexic students who mistake *its* and *it's*, *their* and *there*, and so on. Because the alternatives are real words, the spell-check on a computer will not flag them. The easiest option is to do a final proofread online with Homophone Check [www.homophonecheck.com], which allows you to paste in a text. The program automatically highlights all the frequently mistaken homophones and give guidance on which to choose. (As a bonus, if you have selected Dyslexie or OpenDyslexic as your default browser font, the Homophone Check will show the text in that font.) Since we often do not have internet access, I wrote an OpenOffice macro for Anna to highlight her most often confused words.

Dragon Naturally Speaking can also be helpful for dyslexic or dysgraphic students. This will work better for older students who have substantial number of papers in computer files already, which helps the Dragon learn the student's writing style.

If these free or relatively inexpensive solutions are not working, you may find that there is funding available through your local public schools to try one of the comprehensive computer packages. In most of the US, this should be available to you even if you have opted to take your child out of the public school system.

Advanced Reading (Grades 3-8)

Advanced reading is a vital subject which will drive the rest of your children's educations. Yet, it can be easy to neglect because it requires quiet, sedentary time, and often seems like too much fun to be considered "school work." It is.

More than any other reading skills or strategies, students need stamina and perseverance, and the best way to instill this is with pleasure reading of both novels and non-fiction: no book reports, no posters, no literary analysis, no comprehension questions, just good, enthralling pages read.

If you're worried about justifying a reading program based on independent choice reading for late elementary and middle school, read Nancie Atwell's *The Reading Zone*. (Scuba divers, however, should skip the Nora Ephron quote in the first paragraph of the Forward, because the inaccuracies will put you in a bad temper for the first few chapters.)[75] Atwell was the 2015 winner of the Global Teacher Prize; by the time I discovered her marvelous book, Helen and Anna were eleven and ten. I wish I'd read it when they were seven and six, as it confirmed a lot of my own beliefs about the the the importance of reading for pleasure and not turning it into school, and it would have made me a lot less nervous about my "let them read" philosophy.

Helen and Anna grumble (somewhat forgivingly) about my "phases." I read about some way of teaching or learning and excitedly introduce it into school. They try it out for a few weeks or months and it either becomes a permanent fixture, or we abandon it. Sticky notes were one such phase, and probably the most dramatic failure.

I'd read that the best teachers taught elementary reading as a workshop, and the students were given pads of sticky notes to record their ideas and mark significant places in the book, so they could talk about them later. As a college student, I was a devotee of the sticky note, and my not so admirable technique of writing about literature would be to head to a coffee shop after dinner with the book, buy a large coffee, and read with my pen and sticky notes until I finished. I'd then retreat to my room, write the paper, zooming from one sticky note to the next, print it out, take it to breakfast, and re-write it over coffee and toast, return to my room to key in the changes, and print out a clean copy, and by dint of a mountain bike, have it under the professor's door by nine a.m. (It is sad but true that I actually achieved far higher marks while behaving in this way than I ever did during water polo season when all nighters were out of the question.)

I bought pads of sticky notes and told Helen and Anna that they should be marking up their books and attaching sticky notes to important paragraphs. Helen confessed to me this year: "It made me quit reading. I'd quite liked reading before that, but I hated the sticky notes." It turns out that she pretended not to read, and would steal away and read as a secret vice, rather than face my assignments.

Atwell describes her school:

> The K-6 teachers and I make time every day for our students to curl up with good books and engage in the single activity that consistently correlates with high levels of performance on standardized test of reading ability. And that is *frequent, voluminous reading*. A child sitting alone in a quiet room with a good book isn't a flashy, or more significantly, marketable teaching method. It just happens to be the only way anyone ever grew up to become a reader.[76]

Atwell doesn't assign "reading slips, book reports, [or] sticky notes . . . ." Instead, she talks to the students about the books they read, has them keep a list with ratings, give presentations to the class on books they recommend, and occasionally the students write letters to her or to each other about a book. I describe our school as having a "hands off" approach to reading, and I don't ask Helen and Anna to write letters or formally talk about the books, and they only rarely keep a list of books read, but I'm not completely ignoring them. I know what they're reading, and we do talk about the books, at a level similar to Atwell's letter. I buy books that I loved and recommend them, and Helen and Anna take out books from the library whenever we're near one (at last count I had a collection of nine library cards from four different countries). We have limited space on the boat, so we do all tend to read the same books, and we have all four of our digital readers on the same account, so when we purchase a book, we often all read it. It's a family version of a reading workshop, and, instead of being school work, the discussion simply happens at mealtimes or on a hike together.

We were also extremely fortunate in having a friend take a great interest in the girls' reading. Wal sent them packages of books a couple of times a year – dozens of novels, quite often the first volume of a multi-volume series, so they could take it up or not as they chose. It's one thing (and a very important one) for children to have parents and grandparents who encourage their reading, and demonstrate a love of reading, but Wal's generous gifts were more than simply books, they were proof that the outside world places a high value on reading. The brown packages of shiny new paperbacks did a tremendous amount to fuel Helen and Anna's obsession with reading.

Before I reached my frantic sticky notes and coffee-fueled paper writing stage, I had read nearly a thousand books, most of which I'd chosen. I read S.E. Hinton's *The Outsiders* in an evening, and read it again the following year. After I tutored three children sailing across the Pacific, I stayed in touch with the family. Six months after the thirteen-year-old had been reading adult novels quickly and with ease in our homeschool, I asked her what she was doing in school. She rolled her eyes. They were reading *The Outsiders*. Boring. How could that be? She showed me how: the whole class read the book, half a dozen pages a night, for *six weeks*. They had a 20-page handout of quiz-like fill-in-the-blanks and short answers to write as they dragged their way through the book. S.E. Hinton would be appalled. She wrote the book at her family's kitchen table when she was sixteen because she couldn't find a book she wanted to read. (To make matters worse, there's now a SparkNotes study guide for *The Outsiders*.)

On the other hand, homeschooled students usually don't have preconceived notions of what is hard and don't automatically groan about the classics, so don't be afraid to suggest them. I do try to focus on age appropriate material, however. Even in the sixth grade, Jane Austen would be easy reading for Helen and Anna, and friends have said their middle schoolers have enjoyed the comedy scenes but not the romance. But I want Helen and Anna to love Jane Austen, so I plan to save it for high school unless they choose to read it.

I have steered Helen and Anna away from retellings of the classics, written for children. I have flipped through a few of these condensed, simplified novels, and most are simply dreadful. The reason the originals are classics is because of the writing, not the plot. Jane Austen's plots are recapitulated in every Mills and Boon or Silhouette Romance ever written; it is Austen's use of language that makes her a master. Every classic was once modern, popular literature; it's endured for a reason. Your goal should be developing readers who can cope with the complex sentence structure and vocabulary in these books and poems, not simply giving them a quiz-show familiarity. Introduce classic literature when it is appropriate to your children's reading level and maturity, rather than teaching them that the classics are badly written summaries. If you do want to introduce the stories, it is less damaging to a love of literature to try a different medium – David Lean's *Oliver Twist* film or Odds Bodkin's oral retelling of *The Odyssey*.

Many homeschoolers follow a philosophy of Absolutely No TV. I love television and movies; we often watch them, but we have found it helpful to never offer TV as a solution to boredom. On long ocean passages, we never offered movies, just books on tape. (For the first day or so, we are all a bit too seasick to read.) The only time we ever say, "why don't you watch a movie?" is when Helen and Anna have fevers. They play outside pretty much every day, regardless of the weather. For the most part, sickbed movies excepted, we treat television and movies like books in that all watch together and talk about them afterwards.

Helen and Anna never watched much children's television, either. They never watched television cartoons, and they watched Disney movies at other people's houses. Because we are off the grid so much of the time, we tend to only watch television programs when they come highly recommended from various people, and we've bought the DVDs or the download. This means that we don't have to watch it to a schedule, and it also cuts down on the temptation for boredom TV. We're in it for the stories. Most of Helen and Anna's early television watching was natural history programming (and sometimes opera with my father); after age ten, we began to include more prime time drama, comedy, and many viewings of versions of Shakespeare's plays.

I used to tell the children that they couldn't watch a movie version of a book until they'd read the actual book, but I no longer do. In many cases, especially for strong readers, watching the movie first can be a valuable tool, particularly for historical novels. For example, Helen read *The Cruel Sea* by Nicholas Monsarrat the summer after eighth grade, every spare minute for several days. Earlier in the spring, as part of history, we'd watched the movie version, and though the book is far more complex and rich than the movie, she could better imagine the details with the movie in her mind. A 2015 teenager doesn't have the specific knowledge of corvettes, convoys, and submarines that any of Monsarrat's readers would have had when the book came out in 1951 and the memory of World War II was fresh indeed. Likewise, watching Ang Lee's *Sense and Sensibility* can help give a picture of 1811 privileged rural England, which Jane Austen's contemporary readers already had.

With fantasy, modern, futuristic or science fiction novels, however, I would hold off on the movie versions until after the children have read the books. Anna agrees with me – she's read *The Hobbit* and *The Lord of the Rings* many times over and disapproves heartily of all the liberties taken in the movie versions. I've spoken to many children and teenagers who feel no need to read *Harry Potter* because they've seen the movies, and they're missing out.

Building a library is our biggest homeschooling expense. I buy a lot of books at second hand shops and buy Kindle books when I can. When we are near a library, we use that. One of the best sources for book lists I've found is Nancie Atwell's students – they put lists of their favorite books online at the end of every year. There are lists for girls and boys, divided into school years from first grade to twelfth. The books change every year (and there is overlap between grades, of course). The lists can be found online at [www.c-t-l.org/kids_recommend.html].

You don't have to read every book your children read, but it can be helpful to know a bit about many of them, so you can evaluate whether or not a book is something you want your children to read. A friend gave Helen and Anna *The Boy in the Striped Pajamas* when we were studying World War II when they were ten and nine (and it is on Atwell's students' list for fifth and sixth grade, ages 10-12). I read it and thought it was a wonderful book, but I didn't think Helen and Anna were ready for it. They could have easily read the words, but they would have missed some of the horror of the story, and you can only ever read a book for the first time once. It will hit them a lot harder in high school.

When Hamish was eight, a new headmaster took over his boarding school. Every day after lunch, the boys were sent off to their beds to read for an hour. At the end of the books they particularly liked, they wrote a bit about the book on an index card and put it up on a enormous bulletin board. This was very similar to Nancie Atwell's book talks and book letters, and extremely progressive for a 1970s British boarding school, where the students were still beaten regularly. It turned those boys into readers. The books had to be from the school library (no comics, no magazines), but there was no other restriction on what the students could read. Nancie Atwell has a similar prescription:

"Books I don't – won't – stock anywhere in the classroom library include *The Guinness Book of World Records,* collections of sports statistics, comic books, repair manuals for dirt bikes, guides to computer gaming, Chicken Soup anthologies, and teen celebrity bios."[77] That doesn't mean, of course that your children can't read these things; these books and magazines simply don't count towards the goal of an hour a day immersed in pleasure reading.

In Atwell's experience, "the only gender difference that matters is girls tend to be able to find books on their own. Guys need adult help – teachers and parents who make it our business to keep an eye out for good stories for the boys in our lives."[78] Or simply go to Atwell's students for help: her lists for older students are divided into boys and girls (although there are many books that appear on both lists, and Helen and Anna in the seventh and sixth grade preferred the boys' list to the girls' list, which they found too heavy on the romance side).

Talking as a teacher under enormous pressure from testing and curricula, Atwell writes:

> First of all, I would give up any packaged or commercial program. When it comes to reading and writing, there are no substitutes for time engaged in the real thing. I'd give up vocabulary study and grammar study, and while I was at it, I'd give up book reports, public speaking, oral reports, projects, dialectical or double-entry journals, and graded class notes. As far as I can determine, there's no correlation between any of these activities and achievement in writing or reading except for negative effects – for example, the time that grammar study takes away from students in their English classes has actually been shown to have a detrimental impact on their abilities as writers and speakers.[79]

Atwell also doesn't stock series books in her classroom, but I disagree with this notion. Especially for reluctant readers, the warm bath of a series means that they are instantly engaged with the characters, and may do a lot towards turning them into readers. All the Rick Riordan books or all the Robert Muchamore books count as pages read, and a reluctant reader is far more likely to try something previously enjoyed than embark on something new.

If you are following a set curriculum, examine the way that it teaches literature. Are the books chopped up and discussed, chapter by chapter? Both Atwell and Kelly Gallagher in *Readicide* ask the teacher to imagine what it would be like if every time you went to the movies, someone turned the lights back on every fifteen minutes, gave you a quiz, and asked you to discuss the film so far. Gallagher describes the Los Angeles Unified School District's 2007 teacher's guide for Harper Lee's *To Kill a Mockingbird*. The guide, Gallagher reports, is "122 pages long – almost half the length of the actual novel." The details he describes of all the different activities and lessons piled onto the book are so mindbogglingly dull that I can't bring myself to type up the list, never mind assign it to children to do. Gallagher concludes: "If I were to follow this curricular guide step-by-step in my classroom, there is little doubt that my students would exit my class hating *To Kill a Mockingbird* forever. Worse, students who have been taught to hate *To Kill a Mockingbird* will find themselves much farther down the road toward hating all reading."[80]

Summer Vacation?

If you take a break from school during the year, whether in the summer or some other time of the year, make sure your students are still reading, ideally for the same hour a day minimum. As Kelly Gallagher writes in *Readicide*, it is vitally important that students continue to read year-round to avoid losing ground.

Looking Ahead to High School and College

Numerous studies report that as students age, they read less and less for pleasure. In addition, what they do read in school and for pleasure is less complex than it used to be. Donald Hayes and his colleagues analyzed the reading level in school textbooks over the twentieth century and charted a marked decline that paralleled the decline in top-scoring SAT scores over the century. (By looking only at top scoring students, Hayes has eliminated the argument that scores have decreased because of a larger pool of students.)[81]

Yet the required reading lists in high school haven't changed very much. The Common Core guidelines suggest *The Odyssey*, Ovid's *Metamorphoses*, Turgenev's *Fathers and Sons, The Grapes of Wrath,* and *Macbeth* for ninth and tenth graders; *Canterbury Tales, Don Quixote, Pride and Prejudice, Crime and Punishment, As I Lay Dying, A Farewell to Arms, Hamlet,* and de Tocqueville's *Democracy in America* for eleventh and twelfth graders.[82]

Carol Jago's suggestions for traditional classics include Anne Frank's *The Diary of a Young Girl, Romeo and Juliet, Lord of the Flies, Fathers and Sons, Brave New World, The Fall, Beowulf, Crime and Punishment,* and *The Odyssey.* Her textbook for Advanced Placement Literature includes *Hamlet, Heart of Darkness, Daisy Miller,* and *Antigone.*[83] Kelly Gallagher describes his inner city high school students reading *Hamlet, 1984, The Grapes of Wrath,* and *Dr. Jekyll and Mr. Hyde.*[84]

These books are challenging, even to strong readers who spend many hours a week curled up with a book. Yet, our eighth graders are reading less and less. Is it any wonder that high school students frequently turn to SparkNotes and Wikipedia entries to get the gist of the book and leave the actual words unread? Any wonder that they prefer *No Fear Shakespeare* to the real thing? The reading level expected of high schoolers has stayed relatively consistent through the years, while the expectations of elementary and middle schoolers has plummeted. Gallagher describes his students reading the first act of *Romeo and Juliet* as being in "survival mode, simply struggling to understand the text on a literal level."[85]

Penny Kittle in *Book Love,* says she was inspired to write the book after meeting a former student who had dropped out of the University of New Hampshire. He told her: "I didn't do that well. It was a lot of work, Mrs. Kittle. A lot of reading. . . . I never read that much in high school." Kittle then took informal polls of university professors and her former students, and notes that current US college students are consistently required to read 100-600 pages a week – far more than they had ever done in high school. She hypothesizes that lack of reading preparation could be a major factor in the oft-cited high college dropout rate.[86] Reading the SparkNotes guide for three or four classic novels a year is simply not adequate preparation for college.

It is not enough to score 90% on E.D. Hirsch's *Cultural Literacy: What Every American Needs to Know.* Mandating a reading list of too-difficult classic or contemporary literature simply means students are gaining a Bluffer's Guide knowledge of faint familiarity, and even if they do read these books, they rarely have a chance to leave "survival mode."

Nancie Atwell sends out a letter to the parents of her middle school students every year which notes:

> *There is no more important homework than reading.* Research shows that the highest achieving students are those who devote leisure time to reading. . . . Recently, the largest-ever international study of reading found that the single most important predictor of academic success is the amount of time children spend reading books, more important even than economic or social status. And one of the few predictors of high achievement in math and science is the amount of time children devote to pleasure reading.[87]

Stamina developed in books students love will prepare them for *The Odyssey* and *Hamlet* in high school. Reading hundreds of pages a week in middle school and high school is the only tool that will prepare them for reading hundreds of tough academic pages a week in college. Let them read.

Vocabulary

Vocabulary is best learned authentically, through speech and reading. William Armstrong in *Study is Hard Work* notes:

> The person who reads intelligently enjoys the very important added product of an improved vocabulary, for the proper pursuit of reading, sometimes without it even being consciously evident, is always increasing one's knowledge of words and the uses to which they may be put in order to gain a clearer understanding of what is read.[88]

The best way to improve vocabulary is to read. There are plenty of workbooks if this isn't working, but try reading first. The Kindle has a fabulous feature of a built-in dictionary; you merely highlight the word and the definition appears. All through school,

I knew I should get up off the couch and go find the dictionary, but I almost never did. Nevertheless, as Carol Jago points out in *With Rigor for All,* "Children who are readers add between 3,000 and 5,000 new words to their vocabulary every year through incidental exposure." She contrasts this with mere "300-400 words per year that can be taught through direct instruction."[89]

We tried the highly recommend *Vocabulary from Classical Roots* series, but it proved to be busy work, especially as Helen and Anna knew 80% of the vocabulary words already from encountering them in their free-choice reading. Fill-in-the-blank workbooks almost never work for us.

I'm not entirely sure I learned any words through studying vocabulary in the abstract. When I was in middle school, I had the good fortune to already know all the words in the vocabulary workbooks, and two teachers who administered placement tests. That was all good. They didn't quite figure out what to do with me afterwards, however, and in seventh grade, my teacher assigned me to read the dictionary (this taught me how to carry on long conversations with my friends without getting caught). In eighth grade, I was told to go off to the library and do the New York Times crossword puzzle (this taught me to hate crosswords). In neither year did I learn any new vocabulary during class time.

My teachers should have given me a book to read. They could have pushed me with an advanced reading list, or just let me alone to read books of my choice, which is how I'd developed the vocabulary in the first place.

We can help improve our children's vocabulary by not talking down to them. Even when children are quite little, they will soon learn the words at the limit of our vocabularies. In elementary school, one's spoken vocabulary will likely equal or exceed one's reading vocabulary.[90] (Later on, that may no longer be the case. There are hundreds of words that I struggle to pronounce and use in a sentence, but I have no trouble understanding them on the page.) In schools, there are large numbers of students who come from an educationally-impoverished background, without the advantages of a rich spoken language in the home, and teachers work hard to bring them up to the level of their more advantaged peers, but if you are planning to teach your children at home, you need to make sure that your talk at home is as advanced as it possibly can be.

At six, Helen was ill with a fever, and a friend brought her over a video of skateboarding penguins to watch. She lasted about five minutes and sighed, "I don't really hold with this anthropomorphic nonsense." It's a lot easier to say anthropomorphic than it is to read it or write it; and the early elementary years are a great time to learn language (she could be fluent in Chinese or Spanish or Finnish – or all three – if we'd studied it properly at that time).

In terms of second language ability, David Sousa in *How The Brain Learns* asserts that children between three and seven will learn to speak a second language like a native, eight to ten with eighty percent proficiency, and after seventeen with only fifteen percent efficiency.[91] Don't deprive your children of the full extent of your vocabulary because you think it's too hard for them.

Parenting guides suggest that children are unable to comprehend sarcasm. Really? Ours have been dishing it out for years. Sophisticated vocabulary and the advanced ways of thinking don't suddenly become easy at thirteen: it is far simpler to expose your children to these ways of speaking and thinking right from the start. They'll absorb it all easily. True immersion learning is by far the easiest way to learn a language – no studying, just repetition by fluent parents – and that's as true learning the first language as the second or third.

The US Department of Education's Best Practice Guide for *Improving Adolescent Literacy* notes that there is strong research support for the idea of explicitly teaching vocabulary, but then breaks down "explicit instruction" into two categories – learning words in isolation (outside of texts) with computer drill (or workbook drill) and learning practices to make students more effective learners of vocabulary on their own.[92]

In a homeschooling situation, the emphasis should be on learning vocabulary independently in the context of their reading. In schools, the teacher typically has far superior vocabulary to many of the students; in a homeschooling situation, provided you are speaking to your children with the richest vocabulary you can muster, the playing field is going to be more level.

The research appears to support vocabulary drill in workbooks, but then the guide goes on to admit that "Words are usually learned only after they appear several times. In fact, researchers estimate that it could take as many as 17 exposures for a student to learn a new word.... [T]he exposures are most effective if they appear over an extended period of time."[93] So you mustn't count on workbooks alone to achieve sufficient vocabulary for your students. That has to come through reading, and better yet, reading with the conscious desire to improve vocabulary by looking up mysterious words and learning in context.

Shakespeare

Many homeschooling books will tell you to start teaching Shakespeare in middle school. Many bricks and mortar schools have students read Shakespeare – often *Romeo and Juliet* – in the eighth grade; it has come to be the mark of a "good school." (And the new US Common Core guidelines suggest *Macbeth* for ninth graders.) But most of these children have never watched Shakespeare, and many "rigorous" schools won't spend two or three class periods watching it, because that doesn't seem like school work. Reading a play is hard: it's not meant to be read the way a novel is. Making children read Shakespeare before they've had multiple exposures to the joy of watching the plays is setting them up to dislike it.

In elementary school and middle school, we simply watched. Let the actors do the work. Many families read a short summary such as Edith Nesbit's *Beautiful Stories from Shakespeare* or Charles and Mary Lamb's *Tales from Shakespeare*, but for the most part, we haven't bothered, although it did help with *Hamlet* and *Macbeth*. We started off with the 1999 Michael Hoffman version of *A Midsummer Night's Dream* and later went to the BBC 1968 Peter Hall version of *A Midsummer Night's Dream* with subtitles. The BBC version of the *Tempest* and *Macbeth* followed. Because homeschooled children haven't been taught that Shakespeare is hard and stuffy, they simply enjoy it. Perhaps Helen and Anna don't enjoy it quite as much as they enjoy *Blackadder,* but it's close. Middle schoolers are the audience of "the Pit," where Shakespeare's working class audience came and enjoyed all the rude jokes. If you can watch half a dozen plays a few times each in middle school, you've paved the way for reading – and writing about – Shakespeare in high school. The more Shakespeare you watch, the more you "get your ear in" and can understand the dialogue. This is far easier to do than make it out in print on the page.

In middle school, we watched:

A Midsummer Night's Dream
The Tempest
Hamlet
Macbeth
Twelfth Night
Much Ado About Nothing
A Merchant of Venice
As You Like It
Romeo and Juliet
Henry V

The easiest way to do it is start with a cinematic version (usually cut down slightly), and then follow up with a version that uses every word (and if you watch it with subtitles, you can even claim that your children have "read" Shakespeare if you are so inclined). There has never been such a good time to study Shakespeare. Dozens of versions of the plays are available for purchase or rent and can be watched at home. (We found many versions were easier to find in the UK, including Trevor Nunn's incomparable *Twelfth Night* (1990). Software programs such as VLC Media player can cope with the multi-region problem.) Even when Shakespeare himself was on stage, theater-goers didn't have such a wide-ranging access to his works.

When your students are strong readers (high school level) and have seen a play several times, Marjorie Garber's excellent *Shakespeare After All* has substantial essays about all the plays, drawing from historical, social, humorous, and poetic background, to take you much further into understanding the play and appreciating the humor and the language.

The third step, which can easily wait until high school, is to read the actual play. Pick one that your children enjoy, and buy the Modern Library edition, which is the version used by the Royal Shakespeare Company, and is usually the basis for the "every word" versions you see in the theater or in DVD versions. The Modern Library editions contain footnotes, but they are not as overwhelming as the footnotes in the Arden Edition, which is better saved for college-level work. (The Oxford Editions are also a good choice if you use an actual print book.) Reading the Modern Library edition on a Kindle makes it very easy to flip back and forth between footnotes and text, and what I find myself doing is reading a page or so of footnotes, explaining the text, and then returning to the text and reading straight through. There is absolutely no need to understand every joke, every reference at this stage.

Whatever you do, stay away from SparkNotes' *No Fear Shakespeare*. This version has Shakespeare's words on the left-hand page, and a "translation" on the right-hand page. *No Fear Shakespeare* teaches students that they are too stupid to understand Shakespeare and overlooks the point that reading Shakespeare is not about the plots, it is about the language.

From *Romeo and Juliet*, for example:

It was the lark, the herald of the morn,
No nightingale. Look, love, what envious streaks
Do lace the severing clouds in yonder east.
Night's candles are burnt out, and jocund day
Stands tiptoe on the misty mountain tops.
I must be gone and live, or stay and die.

The SparkNotes' version:

It was the lark, the bird that sings at dawn, not the
nightingale. Look, my love, what are those streaks of light
in the clouds parting in the east? Night is over, and day is
coming. If I want to live, I must go. If I stay, I'll die.

The horror, the horror. If your children aren't ready to read it in the original, then they should keep watching the movie versions and keep reading other easier books and poetry, and wait to tackle reading Shakespeare when they know it better. No one is going to attend to the magic of the words on the left, when the right-hand page is so easy and so pallid.

As I looked up from the computer to have a rant about *No Fear Shakespeare*, Helen told me a story about when she had just turned thirteen. She'd been given a gift certificate to Barnes and Noble and went to the bookstore to pick out a book. We'd just watched the 1990 Trevor Nunn *Twelfth Night*, and she wanted to read it; all she could find was *No Fear Shakespeare* (this was before I'd heard of it, so she hadn't yet been exposed to my condemnation of it). She flipped through the book, and said she rejected it, because the "No Fear" in the title was "annoying – why should you be afraid of Shakespeare?" She continued: "All you could see was the translations because they were on the easy side to read." We now have a copy of *Twelfth Night* which belonged to Hamish at school, and the text is on the right hand page and the notes are on the left hand page. Without Helen's comment, I wouldn't have noticed how we are primed to read on the right hand page, and how much easier it is to read the words of Shakespeare when his words are on the right.

As Marjorie Garber points out,

> Shakespeare is the defining figure of the English Renaissance, and the most cited and quoted author of every era since . . . . The world in which we live and think and philosophize is, to use Ralph Waldo Emerson's word, 'Shakespearized.'
>
> . . . But if Shakespeare seems to us in a surprising way so 'modern,' it's because in a sense his language and his characters have created a lexicon of modernity.[94]

Our expressions, our way of thinking is informed by Shakespeare, whether we have seen / read his plays or not. His works deserve to be studied for appreciation and delight, not battered through one scene at a time in a mind-numbing marathon of translation.

What About an English Textbook?

After the success of Susan Wise Bauer's *Story of the World* series which we used in history, I was keen to follow the rest of her curriculum, set out in *The Well-Trained Mind*. One of the things she and her mother highlight is the importance of explicit grammar and composition instruction, so we started in with *First Language Lessons for the Well-Trained Mind* by Jessie Wise.

I began Helen on the *Language Lessons* for Grade 3, and Anna on the introductory book for Grades 1 and 2. I think we lasted two weeks with these. None of us enjoyed the time. Both Helen and Anna's spoken grammar is excellent (they've been correcting me for years on me/I, which is sometimes gratifying, sometimes annoying), and so I couldn't see the grammar lessons as time well spent. I haven't memorized the list of 15 Prepositional phrases, and I have survived. Knowing what a preposition and all the other grammar terms mean will make learning a second language easier (I had to learn what all the parts of speech were when I started French in the 9th Grade, and it doubled the struggle). We have met people who have used these *Language Lessons* and others who have used the Saxon Grammar Program, but formal grammar-only lessons did not work for us.

While we were slogging through these grammar lessons, we visited Hamish's school friend, Nick Oulton, then-publisher of the Galore Park series of school books which are aimed largely at the independent (aka private) school market in the UK. He gave us a copy of *So You Really Want to Learn: Junior English Book 1 for Year 3,* which is more of a mixed approach, with reading comprehension exercises, a sprinkling of grammar, and a concentration on writing.

American English textbooks for this age group seem to have an emphasis on fill in the blank answers; English students are asked to write their answers in full sentences right from the beginning. This achieves many objectives at the same time, which always makes me feel I am saving time, and thus, things are going well. The Galore Park text books are reusable for younger children and all the written work is done in a separate notebook. This practices penmanship, grammar, spelling, and working in complete sentences, plus of course, the work on reading comprehension.

Each Galore Park book has ten chapters, usually with two excerpts, a grammar lesson, and writing suggestions. I started out assigning the excerpts with the reading comprehension, but gradually gave up. If I could find the whole book where the excerpt came from, I'd assign that, if not I'd skip it (poems and articles are usually reproduced in their entirety). You could go far towards producing a good library by buying (or borrowing) copies of all the excerpted books, plus all the recommended reading at the end of each chapter. It is probably better for children to meet these books as books, rather than as reading comprehension exercises, although you can certainly use the questions to guide your discussion about the books. As Thomas Newkirk points out in "When Reading Becomes Work," encountering a story in a textbook changes a student's engagement with the writing:

> The change of venue to school anthologies usually involves surrounding the selection with a teaching apparatus — comprehension questions, extended writing activities, vocabulary lessons, etc. In this era of No Child Left Behind, any reading passage will be aligned with some reading standard. There is an agenda, beyond the engagement of the reader. The reader no longer feels that he or she can attend to issues of personal interest; rather key ideas are predetermined by the reading skills specialists. Reading is transformed from an experience to a task. It concludes not with that special feeling of literary closure — but with a set of comprehension assignments. Readers lose the sense of autonomy they experience when reading texts in the original venue, on their own terms.[95]

Or as Carol Jago says in *With Rigor For All*: "I hate excerpts."[96]

I'd recommend the Galore Park textbooks to any homeschool teacher contemplating purchasing a grammar textbook, and concerned about his or her ability to teach grammar. I realized after a while that I could teach this grammar more effectively through their writing, but not every parent may be comfortable with that approach, and *So You Really Want to Learn English* would make an excellent base to make sure the grammar issues are covered. Many of the questions and grammar constructions are very like the mini-lessons described in Donald Graves's *A Fresh Look at Writing*, and while professional teachers should be able to make sure grammar is covered in context, parents may not be as confident.

Perhaps, the true beneficiary of your child working through a grammar book will be your teaching. I certainly found this with spelling. Not only did Anna practice her spelling in the *All About Spelling* program, but I learned dozens of spelling rules I'd never known, and I was a much better teacher as a result, because I could remind her the fifty times it took for the lesson to stick.

Advanced Reading – Textbooks (Grades 4-8)

We are what we have read and how we read it, and no other single activity has the capacity to yield so much educational value.

– Doug Lemov in *Teach Like a Champion*[97]

In advanced reading, the one-on-one component of home-schooling can really pay off. Many homeschooling programs are aimed at having the student do most of the work himself, and while independent work is important, actively teaching can allow you to push the level of the reading assignment considerably. Assigned readings across the curriculum, from literature, history, and science should vary in their difficulty. A grade level below reading level may allow students to think harder about the material and draw connections and make inferences about the material. The reading portion is easy, so students can think hard. Reading at the reading level is going to mean quick acquisition of facts, but perhaps not allow the sort of advanced inferences that easy reading can allow.

When you weight lift, sometimes you want to do fast and numerous repetitions with a light weight, sometimes you want to do the standard 3 sets of 15 at your working weight, but every few weeks you increase the weight and lower the repetitions, otherwise your training will stagnate. It is the same with reading. Upping the reading level to a grade or so higher than a student's independent level is a very good way of boosting reading level efficiently, but like a weight lifter, the student will need a spotter, someone to support the reading and make sure the vocabulary is understood and the content assimilated.

Reading aloud together is a great way to achieve this boost in reading level. A parent can sit with one or two children and take turns reading from the book. The two children do not need to be at exactly the same reading level; the more advanced reader will help support the weaker reader and model pronunciation and diction.

I have been using this system of reading aloud with Helen and Anna in all their subjects (in fact, I rather thought I had invented it). As a result, they've pursued their studies at a much higher level than they would have without my assistance and, more importantly, they have acquired higher level reading skills faster than they would have without this practice. In history, for example, I started off by reading to them from the Susan Wise Bauer's *Story of the World* series. When Helen was in fifth grade, Anna in fourth, I introduced the high school-level textbook, William Duiker and Jackson Spielvogel's *Essential World History*.[98] That first year, I read Duiker and Spielvogel aloud, modeling how to read that sort of dense history textbook and demonstrating how to take notes and summarize the material. The next year, I listened while they read aloud from Duiker and Spielvogel, pausing to hold them accountable for vocabulary and understanding, and by halfway through the second year with this textbook, Helen and Anna were easily reading the material by themselves and able to write a coherent and accurate summary in their own words.

In this case, although I didn't quite realize what I was doing at the time, I made good use of the "I / We / You" technique described by Doug Lemov. "I" means the teacher reads, does the problem, explains, then "we" is the students working with the teacher at their shoulder, a coach to point out errors immediately, and make suggestions, and finally "you" is the students working alone. Unlike mathematics, where the "I / We / You" takes place in a single day or two, with reading levels, it takes place over several months. In the two years that we used Duiker and Spielvogel, Helen and Anna's comprehension improved, and they were able to grapple with more of the whys and wherefores.

Lemov recommends this technique to classroom teachers, but it is far, far easier to implement with only two or three children. It's one of the easiest "lessons" a parent can teach (no prep time; just open the book), and the benefits in increased vocabulary and reading level will be marked.

In addition to modeling how to read it, you can model what to do when you come to a word you don't understand (or perhaps understand well enough to use it, but not enough to define it for your children). In the early years, I did all the looking words up in the dictionary, gradually explaining what I was doing by pointing out that I was looking at the guide words, and sometimes quoting snatches of the alphabet song. Later on, students can look up the words themselves, but in the early years I think it's more important that they see you respect and use the dictionary, rather than interrupting the flow of the reading completely while they go through the laborious chore of finding the words themselves. We have never had a children's dictionary on board, just Hamish's old school *Concise Oxford Dictionary*.

When reading literature, ebook readers with built-in dictionaries are a marvelous advance: students (and teachers!) can click on the word and reach a dictionary definition immediately.

Because Helen and Anna read literature so much on their own, I have stayed out of the teaching of reading through literature, and focused my energy on reading history and, once they were in middle school, reading science. By asking yourself what your students need most, you can maximize the return on the investment of your time. I figured my children would get far more return from the direct tutoring in history than they would in literature; a child who struggles with literature or simply does not enjoy reading might benefit more from a focus on fiction.

Lemov asks his teachers to:

> Imagine, for a moment, a hypothetical school. This school values reading above all other endeavors – to an exaggerated degree .... It has recently decided to ensure that its students spend almost all their time in school reading. In science classes, they read chapters from articles and textbooks. In history class, they read primary and secondary source materials, often for the entire class period. They do write, but usually summaries and analyses of what they've read.

That sounds an awful lot like our school. Part of the problem that classroom teachers face is not being able to ensure that students are actually reading, but with your own children, as long as you're in the room, you can tell whether they're reading or staring off into space, and you can read every summary they write, immediately, and know whether or not they have understood what they've read.

Previewing

In both William Armstrong's *Study is Hard Work* and Harvard librarian Susan Gilroy's "Interrogating Texts: 6 Reading Habits to Develop in Your First Year at Harvard," previewing the text is given top priority. I don't explicitly do this in a book anymore myself – the scan happens without me realizing it, but older students can benefit from explicit instructions in how to preview a text. (And younger ones coming to grips with the busy format of Joy Hakim's *The Story of US* will also benefit from a lesson in previewing.)

Obviously, knowing the author and title is important, but that can be disturbingly hard to remember if you are reading an ebook. The next important thing to know, and judge, is the date of publication. Is it likely that the information is up to date, or is it an old text? Hamish had a marvelous Encyclopedia of Science, but we've had to retire it, even though we don't have a viable substitute, because so much of the information is out of date. If the student is reading fiction, the date of the original publication can inform the reading: what was happening in the world around the author while he or she was writing – for example, knowing George Orwell wrote 1984 in 1948, and a bit of historical background can help the reading. Is it historical fiction like Walter Scott's *Ivanhoe*, written about a fairly distant past, or is it set in the author's present day, like Jane Austen's books?

I don't encourage Helen and Anna to read the introductions on classical fiction that they read, preferring they make their first encounter with the book unencumbered by literary theory. In a history book, however, it is very useful to read the introduction. For example, William Duiker and Jackson Spielvogel's *Essential World History* begins with a single page explanation called "Themes for Understanding World History." Reading this page provides a context and an organizational system for thinking about all the pages that follow.

Trade books normally have chapter titles, and perhaps maps and illustrations (and viewing maps on a tablet or computer instead of an ebook reader can make them much more legible, even though for endurance reading, I vastly prefer a non-backlit screen). Textbooks have subheadings, maps, illustrations, and sidebars, and if students have a quick look through before tackling the prose, they will have situated themselves in the book, and answered some of their questions already, at very little effort.

When we are reading history books on the Kindle, I sometimes use screen capture on the Kindle for PC version to print out the maps and have a hard copy to hand while reading. This is even better than flipping back and forth with a real book version. Scott Anderson's *Lawrence in Arabia* became much easier with a folded paper map tucked into my Kindle cover.

Service Writing

Many elementary and middle school textbooks provide fill in the blank questions to test reading comprehension. Fill in the blanks, multiple choice answers, and so on are an excellent way for a teacher with thirty students to know whether or not a baseline of understanding has been reached, but for a pure measure of comprehension, restating the main idea or ideas in one's own words is what works.

Rewriting ideas in one's own words is also the fastest, most reliable method of learning. Occasionally, one hears of people who can listen to a lecture and retain it all, simply by hearing it. Or of readers who can make a single reading of a text and learn the content. But most people need to take in the information, mull it over, write it down, probably write it down again, and, in my case, write it down again.

In *Holding on to Good Ideas in a Time of Bad Ones* Thomas Newkirk writes, "when curriculum is defined as covering 'content,' writing in particular is the activity that gets crowded out,"[99] which is doubtless the case in places with over-complicated standards and a rigid focus on standardized testing, but when your goal is a content-rich study, with long-term retention, writing and content are far from mutually exclusive. Writing and analyzing facts and ideas is the best way of retaining the information.

David Sousa in *How the Brain Learns: A Classroom Teacher's Guide,* describes twenty-four hour retention rates as follows:

Lecture: 5%
Reading: 10%

Audio-visual: 20%
Demonstration: 30%
Discussion Group: 50%
Practice by Doing: 75%
Teach others / immediate use of learning: 90%[100]

Lectures and assigned reading, the two most common ways of imparting information to the next generation of students are the worst value in terms of retention. However, note-taking, summarizing, and thinking in writing and discussion after the reading can dramatically increase the uptake of material.[101]

My Harvard roommate has gorgeous handwriting. Every term at finals time, troops of less diligent students would come to the door, begging her for a quick read-through or a photocopy session with her notes. (The advantage of rotten handwriting: no one ever asked to borrow my notes.) But reading through her notes in no way replicated the learning process that went into the act of writing those notes.

We both went to all our lectures (okay, she did; I went to nearly all of mine), took notes, and when it came time for review, we rewrote our notes as part of the process of studying. It worked. There's one thing we could have done better, however, but I didn't figure out the trick until long after college. Had we gone to the lecture, taken our notes, retreated immediately to a quiet place and written down a half page summary of the lecture in our own words every day without fail, we would have had a lot less studying to do at finals time, and we'd remember more of it now.

This is what I call *service writing* – it's not meant to be a masterpiece, or even a particularly coherent essay, but rather an exercise to increase one's retention of the material under study. If you can carefully think about the material and write down a summary and an analysis (elementary students will probably emphasize summary over analysis, but that doesn't mean they can't be encouraged to explore analysis), you have the potential to enter the 75% zone of retention described by Sousa. Medical schools have long known the use of this kind of learning: student doctors often joke about "watch one, do one, teach one." A terrific way to increase retention in homeschool is by asking the student to do a reading, write a summary and analysis, and then a few hours later, explain it to a sibling or a parent.

These are the skills we can teach our children as we push them towards difficult reading. So much of school assumes that students know how to learn, but in fact, our job as homeschool teachers is to break down the steps towards learning. Merely providing the material to be learned is not enough. Whether it is French verbs, math facts, the complicated ideas behind a time in history, the methods of algebra, or the deep time of our universe, there are steps you can teach your students to go through to reach toward that knowledge.

At first, I worried a bit that this continued reading with Helen and Anna (say, after the third grade) was babying them in some way, and that they wouldn't learn to do the work on their own, but that has proved not to be the case. They read books well beyond grade level and restate them in their own words, and make connections from those readings to other readings and other times in history. Reading at a level that is often slightly too difficult and writing about that reading is a way of learning the core facts of a subject; meanwhile, students learn how to read better and more productively, how to maximize the retention of what they do read, how to learn, and the steps they need to take to master a subject.

I wish that William Armstrong's *Study Is Hard Work*[102] had been available when I was beginning high school (or anytime before I finished formal education); it would have saved me a lot of wasted time and inefficient reading and studying. It will probably be too advanced for your fifth and sixth grade students to read, but I recommend buying it at the end of elementary school / beginning of middle school to read yourself. With Armstrong's advice in your mind, you will be better able to target your instruction on how to cope with difficult books, how to take notes, and glean the most important information from a passage.

Note-taking and Outlining

The *service writing* described above – drawing at first, summarizing later on, and summarizing and analyzing by the beginning of middle school – is a useful technique for all levels of study. Once your students reach late middle school (Grades 7 or 8), they may need to add note-taking and outlining to their reading process.

The formal outline, written with indents (and always at least two points at every level) does not need to be belabored.

Sample Outline

I.

  A.

    1.

      a.

      b.

    2.

  B.

II. (and so on)

A couple of rounds of formal outlining, with a bit of harping on the format, will familiarize your students with the form, should anyone ask for it down the line. I have always found informal outlining and note-taking to be more useful. In real life, there are not always two points at every level.

Ideally, each student would have his or her own hard copy of the difficult books of middle school – science texts, literature, history books – and read them with a pen in hand, but that is not always possible. The expense of equipping all your children with new fresh copies of books can be an obstacle, library books can't be written in, and ebooks are a great way of reading and increasing vocabulary. The harder the book, the higher the stakes of the studying, the more important it is to have an individual paper copy of the book. I didn't teach annotating and marking up books until high school for purely logistical reasons.

If students do have their own books to annotate, I agree wholeheartedly with the Harvard University librarian Susan Gilroy's advice to students: "Throw away your highlighter."[103] Reading with a pen in hand is much more interactive, and allows you to write in the margin, underline key points as you need to, and creates more involvement than highlighting. It took me a while to figure this out when I was at school: I had long seen the rows of bright highlighters in the local university store as a mark of scholarship, but they simply got in the way. Highlighting is passive, annotating is active, and the active work is much more likely to be remembered.

Reading ebooks pushes students into virtual highlighting, because it's the easiest strategy. On tablets, students can generally annotate more quickly than on the lower tech ebook readers. Sometimes, you can add a keyboard and type notes in addition to highlighting. PDF versions allow you to write notes with a finger or stylus on a touch screen device.

A version of the Cornell Notes system works well for reading as well as lectures. I don't take my notes this formally myself, but it gives students a starting point they can deviate from as they get better at note taking. In the Cornell system, students mark off a vertical line a quarter of the way across the page, and then a horizontal line about a fifth of the way up from the bottom. The big space on the right is for direct notes, the column on the left is for writing questions or cue words about the notes after class or finishing the reading, and the space on the bottom is for summarizing the content of your notes from that page, after class or finishing the reading. The questions and the summary should be done as close to the time of the reading or lecture as possible.

It is critical that students draw a distinction between their own thoughts and ideas and those of the author. The Cornell system solves this problems by isolating the ideas of the author on the right, and saving space for the student's ideas and summary around it. Another way I do it is to put a squiggly cloud around my ideas, like a thought bubble in a cartoon, to distinguish my ideas from paraphrases of the author. (If it is a direct quotation from the author, I set it off with quotation marks.) When taking notes on reading, students should keep track of what page in the original book the notes are coming from. With an ebook, this can be done by noting the location number if the ebook does not provide the page numbers of the original volume.

In an informal outline, the student can copy the indenting for sub-ideas format from the formal outline, but it doesn't have to be so pretty. Another way to set off main ideas is to draw a box around the idea. However the notes are taken, it is worth summarizing them, either at the end of the notes or at the bottom of each page as in the Cornell system.

Table 8: Cornell Notes Sample Page

Vocab Keywords Questions Dates	**Cornell Notes** note-taking on book / lecture / discussion goes here in the main body of the page use code words and symbols for important ideas * ! ? "Put exact words in quotation marks." Put your own ideas in Thought bubbles
	After the lecture / reading / discussion is over, write a concise summary at the bottom of each page of notes.

Reading Summary

- Develop both a love for reading and stamina by averaging one hour per day or more of free-choice reading for pleasure, without record keeping, summarizing or other busy work
- In general, avoid simplified versions of the classics
- Read challenging subject-area books with your students through the end of middle school to help develop their skills
- Use service writing (summaries and note-taking, including informal outlines) to help with understanding and retention in assigned history, science, and literature readings

About Writing

After early reading, writing is the most important topic you will teach your students, and as such, writing and its related skills make up the biggest portion of this book. It's not especially difficult to teach writing, but it's distressingly easy (even for a former writing teacher and professional writer!) to push aside writing for the content subjects such as math, history, and science. Your biggest task is to carve out enough time for the children to develop writing stamina; this is true whether you create your own program, follow a boxed curriculum, or help your children after school.

The writing section of this book is divided into four chapters. This chapter explains the terms I use for thinking about writing, how to structure writing instruction across the curriculum and through the years, and describes the invested writing process. "Writing Assignment Ideas" offers specific ideas on what kind of writing your students can do once they've mastered putting words down on paper. "Writing and Revision Toolbox" pulls the ideas of the first two chapters together to give you suggestions to make to your students as they work through their writing assignments. Finally, "Writing-related Skills" is a chapter on penmanship, spelling, and keyboarding. Obviously, those skills are how we eventually transmit writing, but competence in writing and mechanical skills will naturally progress at different rates, and a lag in one shouldn't hold the rest of the process back.

In my early years of homeschooling, I failed to use the words "writing class" when speaking to Helen and Anna. Every day in history class, they drew pictures and wrote summaries of the readings, and they did the same every couple of weeks in science, but I called that writing time "history" or "science." When I wanted to back off a bit on the summaries and have Helen and Anna work on a longer piece of writing, they both felt it was unfair of me to add on an extra school subject. It was a failure of nomenclature rather than teaching.

There is nothing particularly novel in my methods of teaching writing – my ways of helping Helen and Anna develop as writers have a long tradition behind them. What is new, I believe, is the way I describe the different types of writing, emphasizing the similarities of writing across the curriculum, rather than teaching writing as part of "English Language Arts" and merely requiring the product in other subjects as is often the case in schools or homeschooling curricula.

To teach writing in the early years, you need notebooks, pencils, drawing paper, and time. Between ages eight and twelve, you can add a computer and a printer. The program is essentially the same for all grades: high volume of writing to develop stamina and practice of the three main types of writing, which I call *service writing, draft and a half,* and *invested writing.*

Service Writing, Draft & a Half, and Invested Writing

I introduced the idea of s*ervice writing* in the Reading chapter, as a way of understanding and learning content. Service writing can be used for any type of incoming information – reading, lectures, book or field research – and for outgoing information, refining and developing ideas and understanding for one's own pieces of writing. Service writing is generally not meant to be read by other people and generally not revised (although parts of it may find a home in a piece of invested writing). Service writing can be coherent sentences and paragraphs, formal or informal outlines, sketches and diagrams, or jumbled, exploratory ramblings.

Draft and a half writing is exactly that – the author writes a single draft and then polishes it slightly. We used to call these "one draft wonders" or "first draft finals" in school. They are not as good as they could be, but they are efficient, develop writing skills, and hone thinking. Most adult writing falls into the draft and a half category: letters, emails, daily news journalism, blogs, online discussions, reviews, tweets, memos, work reports, and so on. These types of writing are generally composed in one go, but now with computers, it is possible to write the text, and then spend time going through it on the screen, tweaking and adjusting, making sure that the words say what one wishes, and that the spelling, grammar, and punctuation are accurate.

This is a marked change from thirty years ago, when most of these forms didn't exist, and letters and journalism were written in one single draft, composed on a typewriter or in longhand, although it was still possible to make small changes to the text. Hand-written exams are a throwback to this old fashioned type of writing: students must compose under time pressure and have one chance to get it right. (Exams composed on a computer are an example of more modern draft and a half writing, for students can usually re-write paragraphs and tweak the language during the exam.)

Finally, *invested writing* describes the lengthy projects that can occur at any age, where the author has significant investment in the writing, whether it be fiction, non-fiction, a research essay, or another format. Invested writing consists of writing multiple drafts, revising the work to make it as good as it possibly can be. (I don't consider a long-term project such as a blog as *invested writing*, despite the copious number of words it may contain, because the individual entries are usually not revised after they are posted.) I will discuss the general steps for invested writing at the end of this chapter.

Many schools and homeschooling books stress either draft and a half or invested writing to the exclusion of the other, and most do not formally teach service writing. However, students need a lot of practice in all three types of writing. Each style feeds into each other – every word written counts, just as every word read counts towards making better readers. A thorough program will train students in each of the three ways of writing instead of relying on chance transfer from one favored style to the others.

Three of the books that I recommend for learning about studying and writing are William Armstrong's *Study is Hard Work;* Gregory Colomb and Joseph Williams's revision of Kate Turabian's *Student's Guide to Writing College Papers;* and Peter Elbow's *Writing with Power.*

Armstrong is a draft and a half man:

> To write well, you must think correctly. You cannot hope to write clearly unless you first have clearly in mind what you are going to write. Before you attempt to write anything, even the the answer to the simplest question on a daily quiz, you must have something to say.[104]

Colomb and Williams are invested writing men:

> Have you ever heard the tale of the one-draft wonder? That's the student who starts writing a paper at midnight before the deadline, knocks out one quick yet perfect draft, and then receives the best grade in the class. The one-draft wonder is one of the more enduring school-based urban legends ... but we've never seen the real thing.[105]

They're all three completely right and completely wrong (and, I suspect, they developed their theories of writing before composing on a computer was commonplace). There is a time and a place for both kinds of writing, and both are supported by service writing, as explained in Peter Elbow's *Writing with Power*. Though he doesn't use the term, the author, known to his students as "Write-it-Wrong Elbow,"[106] uses service writing extensively in developing writing. He is certainly an advocate of invested writing, but he is open enough to admit that sometimes writing needs to be done in a hurry: a draft and a half.

> [H]ow *do* we encourage excellence? There is no sure fire method, but one thing is clear: we have little hope of producing excellent writing unless we write a *great deal*. Plenty will be bad. If we want lots of practice and experience, we can't limit our writing to times when our mind is operating well, [n]or can we write a lot unless we get some *pleasure* from it, and pleasure is unavailable if we wince at everything bad that comes out and stop and try to fix it. If we write *enough*, we will have at least a chance of producing some excellent bits.[107]

There is a fine line between draft and a half and invested writing. Many draft and a half essays could easily be worked into a longer or more involved piece of writing, many of the prompts that work to start students off in draft and a half writing assignments work well as invested writing topics. I do find that invested writing projects work better if the topic comes from the student himself, rather than an outside prompt. But some students figure out paper topics with ease, and others spend valuable writing time tearing their hair out trying to find the perfect topic. I'm not shy about nudging topic finding along if necessary, and sometimes that means resorting to writing prompts.

In elementary school, I let invested writing happen organically – if there was a topic the children were interested in developing further, then they did, if not, they moved on to something new after a draft and a half. As a very loose rule of thumb, students might be encouraged to write as many invested writing essays (of any style or subject) as their grade in school – four essays for a fourth grader, eight for an eighth grader, and so on, but that is a flexible guideline – if a student is putting a tremendous amount of work into one project, then that project could easily count for two or three of those essays. The grade / essay number requirement would be better used to encourage reluctant writers and to curb (slightly) very enthusiastic writers, who might write dozens of draft and a half pieces, but never slow down to bring any of those papers to their potential.

By middle school, I explicitly assigned draft deadlines and "final deadlines," usually a week later, so that there were a specific number of pieces in a year that had gone through at least a draft and a half (or maybe even two draft) process. However, because I use *portfolio evaluation* (discussed further in the next section) that "final deadline" may not be the end of the writing process on a particular piece of writing. With fiction, non-fiction essays, research papers and so on, students often benefit from some time off – after they have worked on a piece for several weeks, they may find it helpful to put it aside for a month or two, and revisit it when preparing their end of term or end of year portfolios. With history essays, however, Helen and Anna tend not to be interested in revising them at a later date because we've moved on to a new time period in our study of history. Any additional work they do for the portfolio version of their history papers tends to be line by line proofreading and editing, rather than a true revision of the ideas and structure of the essay.

A strict invested writing / portfolio evaluation classroom would not require intermediate "final" drafts of the papers, and only require the portfolio, but I think it is good practice for Helen and Anna to turn in the papers that are merely draft and a half, because it gives them experience of deadlines and polishing. We also found that if the assignments were too open-ended, the writing would be pushed aside by other subjects with daily assignments, such as math, history reading, or science experiments.

As you go through other homeschooling books, or perhaps your boxed curriculum or children's homework, you'll find a host of terms for writing that I don't use, because I find them artificial distinctions. You may need these terms, however, in order to craft an evaluation or report to local authorities.

Schools and commercial writing programs divide writing into *genres* – for example, the Common Core uses the genres "narrative," "informative/explanatory," and "opinion," which is upgraded to "argument" in the fifth grade.[108] When most school teachers and standards writers use "narrative" they mean a fiction or non-fiction piece of writing that describes characters and events. In the real world, narrative fiction is called short stories, novellas and novels. Narrative non-fiction makes up the rest of our pleasure reading: biography, autobiography, popular histories, true-life adventures, and informative books about specific subjects.

Schools divide the world of non-fiction into narrative and informative/explanatory, but published books do not – there are usually elements of both, and probably some opinion and argument as well in every non-fiction book.

In most homeschooling books, however, *narration* means something quite different. Charlotte Mason, a British educator in the early twentieth century, uses the term to mean a child telling back a story after hearing it read (either by dictating to a parent or writing it down). I will instead use the word *summary* to describe this sort of writing, and I class it as a kind of *service writing* to support reading comprehension and retention.

Portfolio Evaluation

After stamina and explicit training in different types of writing, the third element of my writing program is *portfolio evaluation,* which takes the pressure off writing and allows children the chance to experiment and explore. Letter grades or even the simple check, check plus, check minus on returned papers discourages experimentation and the wobbly "I'm not sure what I think yet" writing that is so important to students' development as both thinkers and writers.

With portfolio evaluation, students themselves choose the best pieces of writing – usually invested writing, but it doesn't have to be – from the school year or semester, and spend a couple of weeks revising their work for the portfolio. Students learn to be selective and judgmental about their work, making decisions about both what writing is the best now and what writing has the most potential. Saving the grade or evaluation pressure for the portfolio frees students from perfectionism during most of the school year, which gives them a chance to experiment and bring out the best in their writing.

A portfolio can be as simple as three cleanly written (or computer printed) papers turned in at the end of the school year or as complex as an illustrated book, with a sewn or commercially-made binding. Once we moved to Alaska, our homeschooling was far more supervised than in earlier years, and Helen and Anna turned in portfolios four times a year, in the form of PDF documents emailed to their contact teacher. This was about twice as often as I would have chosen for myself – the preparation of each portfolio took a full week of school time, or a month a year.

If I were evaluating portfolios without any responsibilities towards outside teachers, I would assign a final portfolio once or twice a year, probably twice a year in order to keep a little bit of pressure on (a whole year's assignment can seem too long at this age). If the students were self-motivated, once a year portfolios could certainly work.

Because of the four deadlines in Alaska each year, there is less true revising than I would like for each one. As a result, writing contests rather than portfolios have served as deadlines for revision, and I encourage Helen and Anna to enter writing contests several times a year. That is a great way to focus their energies, and occasionally earn some outside recognition for their work.

Developing Writing Stamina

Thomas Newkirk writes in *Holding on to Good Ideas in a Time of Bad Ones:*

> I am convinced that we overvalue feedback and undervalue practice. . . . Volume, to be sure, does not equate with quality, but young writers can't get to quality without volume. The good writers I see in college have often developed their skill in self-sponsored writing projects like journals or epic, book-length adventure stories they wrote on their own.[109]

As with reading, writing is about building stamina, gaining experience in different kinds of writing, and giving time to write a high priority in scheduling school. Writers learn to write by writing, not by completing workbook exercises.

Reading is itself a critical part of writing. Vocabulary, grammar, and style are all gained through reading. Later in *Holding on to Good Ideas in a Time of Bad Ones,* Newkirk explains how extensive reading complements writing:

> Avid readers develop intuitions about form, language, dialogue, voice, levels of formality, genre – indeed, I firmly believe that many of the 'mechanical' skills like spelling and punctuation are fostered more by reading than isolated skill work. We learn a writing vocabulary by seeing words *in context* where we can see how a particular word is used with other words. It is a truism among writing teachers that not all good readers are good writers . . . but all good writers are good readers . . . .[110]

My goal for Helen and Anna's writing has been roughly one hour per day, minimum. The advantage of homeschooling is that you can spread the load, because you know exactly what the teacher is assigning in each subject area. Writing assignments can be in the subject areas (history, science or literature) or as pure composition assignments. If a student is working on a self-motivated writing project, you could drop writing assignments completely. Anna went through a phase where she worked for a couple of hours a day on a *Lord of the Rings* fan fiction story. She published it online at a fan fiction site, and she was very motivated by the reviews and comments from readers. In addition, she learned a great deal about writing by reading other people's stories – learning what made them great, what made them awful.

During this phase, I didn't assign her a single invested writing project. She still had the responsibility of doing her subject area service writing, but I spent my time working with Helen and let Anna write her story undisturbed. Every word counts towards making students better writers.

When I do assign writing projects, it turns out that almost every paper becomes a research paper of some kind. They may start out with a personal narrative style paper, but the world intrudes as the draft develops. For example, Helen wrote an early draft about the litter in the water in Kosrae in the Federated States of Micronesia. In the beginning, it was a personal essay, but it turned into a huge research project about the Pacific Gyre, the problems of Laysan albatross feeding plastics to their chicks, and the length of time different garbage items persist in the environment.

I wish I'd emphasized creative writing more in elementary school. This is one of the cases where I relied too heavily on homeschooling guides and not enough on teaching guides. The few teaching guides that I looked at were simply discouraging: perfect child after perfect child composing away, and I couldn't figure out how to get started.

Instead, I concentrated on history and science service writing and let letters home suffice as personal narratives until about the fourth grade. This doesn't seem to have had any ill effects on Anna's enjoyment of writing, but I think Helen would have benefited from a more rounded program. With everything else going on in early homeschooling, invested writing was the subject that would be pushed aside for other things.

I bought the *Writing Strands* books two and three, but when Anna's first writing assignment was to describe a yellow pencil, I put them quietly on a shelf. It could be helpful to look at *Writing Strands* (maybe skip the yellow pencil assignment) if you are nervous about teaching writing, but I found Donald Graves's book *Writing: Teachers & Children at Work* to be far more useful in structuring a writing program – there are even some examples of children who don't like to do their writing, and wander around the classroom disrupting others, although all of the examples do seem to work out in the end. Other families enthusiastically recommend the Institute for Excellence in Writing or Bravewriter programs.

Donald Graves describes writing as a "craft." The more a student writes, the better, but it must be writing, not worksheets on correcting sentences, grammar, or spelling lists. Graves suggests that "at least four forty-five to fifty minute periods [per week] are necessary to provide a strong writing experience."[111]

Developing Writers

What is writing? In the earliest grades, it can be a story-drawing, with or without letters on it. By the end of fourth grade, students should be familiar with going through a multi-draft process, and choosing their best work to put into a portfolio. By late elementary school, the work in the portfolio should usually be hand-written or typed by the student, but in the early years, it can be dictated to a parent or an older sibling.

In the history service writing, I did not emphasize the writing process. In the fourth grade, Helen decided to type up her history summaries into a book, and rewrote as she went, but that was her initiative. I did not ask Anna to do the same thing. History writing was about thinking, about getting the ideas down on the page, rather than a finished product composition. If you choose to have students write about literature (we did not), Nancie Atwell's *letter-essays* for middle schoolers (discussed in the next chapter) are an example of draft and a half writing, which suits middle school literary writing. I would never discourage a student from writing an invested literary essay at any age, but I did not make any specific literary assignments in order to emphasize the pleasure of reading and develop stamina.

My real failing in the early years of our homeschool was not to model writing for them. I had never seen a teacher write in front of me, so it never occurred to me that it would help. Donald Graves wrote about the importance of teachers writing in front of their students back in 1983, but it was all news to me. I've since tried it, and it really works. You mustn't worry about not being a "good writer" or a "good teacher" – you're the best writer in the room.

Graves writes, "Teachers don't have to be expert writers to 'write' with the children. In fact, there may be an advantage in growing with them, learning together as both seek to find meaning in writing. However, it does take courage to show words to children who haven't seen an adult write before."[112] Let them see the struggles over topic choice, structure, and ideas.

Here are some steps to move through the parts. The speed (and even the order) at which you move through the steps will depend very much on the individual child.

Dictation

By dictation, I mean when a child who can't quite print or write well enough to capture his ideas dictates a fiction story, non-fiction essay, or summary of reading to a parent or sibling, who takes it down in clear printing or handwriting. We used this method a lot, both before and after Helen and Anna were ready to try some words on their own. It let them see themselves as writers, as producers of ideas in written words, before they could easily write. This gave them added motivation to work on the tedium of penmanship and, perhaps more important, gave them an extra year of practice in *writing*, by which I mean composing and discussing ideas in words, rather than the mechanical skill of putting them down on paper oneself. It's easy for homeschooling teachers to take the dictation of a paragraph a day. Afterschooling parents can easily fit in taking a short dictation from kindergarten and first grade students, to illustrate drawings, or tell a story. Classroom teachers would struggle to provide this opportunity for thirty students, but it doesn't take long to scribe a single paragraph.

Many dyslexic children have found success by using a computer dictation program such as Dragon Naturally Speaking to take down their words. I tried this with Anna in grade three when she was having a great deal of difficulty with the mechanics of writing, but it didn't work well with her hybrid English-

American accent. By fifth grade, she was touch typing, and began doing all her writing on a computer, which solved the problem of the mechanics of handwriting. A dictation program that recorded words in the Dyslexie font might work extremely well for some children, particularly if they had the patience to work with learning the program (and have the program learn their style of writing and speaking).

Some homeschooling books advocate having the parent read aloud to the child who takes the dictation, so the term *dictation* can be a bit ambiguous. We tried that direction of dictation, but it wasn't helpful for us. Helen and Anna were both better off working on their own writing once they reached the stage of being able to write legibly. Taking dictation doesn't help with the "silent errors" of grammar discussed in the "Writing and Rewriting Toolbox" chapter, so teacher to student dictations end up being an exercise in error-marking. Homeschooling books lured me down this path for a while, but I eventually retreated to find a more constructive way of teaching writing. A page festooned with grammar and spelling corrections merely gives students the conviction that they are bad at writing and doesn't give them the tools to improve.

Story-drawings

Most students start with story-drawings, perhaps with a few letters or words around them. Story-drawing is a typical first step, but it isn't necessarily an immature one; look at Art Spiegelman and the Maus graphic novels. In *More than Stories*, Thomas Newkirk observes that these story-drawings are not mere "rehearsal" for writing, but rather adoption of the picture-book genre.[113]

Helen and Anna still did story-drawings in middle school. Anna, while working on multi-chapter fiction, often takes time out to draw her characters. Helen drew lengthy cartoons in panels. (She also illustrated her math book, which I had less patience with.)

In history writing, I explicitly assigned these drawings in the first grade. I read Helen and Anna a chapter from Susan Wise Bauer's *Story of the World* and asked them to illustrate the story. Anna will never forget the second "defenestration of Prague," after drawing a huge pile of manure, with four booted feet sticking out and two flies buzzing past.

I next asked for a picture and a dictated caption; later, as handwriting became easier, Helen and Anna began to write captions. By third grade, they were writing half-page summaries of the history readings without any prompting.

In the early days it was helpful to have them start from an illustration in both the history service writing and creative writing. On a photocopier, I made them writing paper half lined and half blank with the idea of encouraging the drawing and writing connection, but I think I persisted with this too long. It worked well for history, where I wasn't concerned with them writing multiple drafts, but in creative writing, having the illustration and the writing on the same page backfired. They didn't want to edit the writing because it would mess up their drawings.

If I were doing it again, I would use the split pages for history, but ask them to keep the drawings and the creative writing on separate pages, once they were comfortable with basic handwriting and attempting spelling. The drawing can be included in the final draft, either glued in or scanned in and printed out as part of a final portfolio draft. (I am not sure this would have appealed to Helen, who often wrote first and illustrated afterwards, like an illuminated manuscript.)

We kept drawing and writing separate on a lengthy science project when Helen and Anna were in second and third grade, and it worked well to encourage (or at least not stifle) revision. We were planning a trip, and I asked our hostess for a list of forty animals and birds to research and draw. The drawings were separate from the writing, and glued in at the end, so that the writing could go through as many drafts as needed. (An amusing result of this was that once we arrived, Helen and Anna were only interested in "their" twenty animals and birds; the other twenty were disparaged.)

Individual Writing

Individual writing is when the child writes the words himself, using invented spelling where necessary. If you have begun using a spelling program, it's likely that paper writing will not be up to the same standard as the spelling tests. Encourage the child to skip lines, to leave room for additions and changes. Provide plenty of paper for drawing alongside writing, but encourage revision by keeping the two separate until the portfolio stage.

Writing Across the Curriculum (Grades 3-8)

The table on the following pages is a rough guide to writing across the curriculum in the later grades, once a student is writing individually. This list highlights the similarities between writing in the different subjects.

In schools, writing is typically divided into subjects of "English Language Arts," "Social Studies," and "Science." Homeschooling allows you to break writing into more categories, and what is usually crammed into "English Language Arts" is instead divided here into five sections, personal-memoir, personal interest (often including subjects that would normally be taught in a Social Studies curriculum, such as current events and argument), fiction, poetry, and literary.

Although it's usually combined in one "English Language Arts" class, literary writing actually has far more in common with the other subject matter writing such as history and scientific writing because it involves understanding and analyzing events outside the self, what could be called *world-referential* as opposed to *self-referential*. In the case of literature, this can be writing about other people's novels, poems, short stories, and plays; in history, this means historical analysis (of general interest books and text books) and summary and analysis (of original sources). Science writing about others' ideas and researched-based writing falls into this category.

Table 9: Writing Across the Curriculum

	Service writing	Draft and a Half	Invested writing	With outside Research?
Personal-memoir	diary, free write	letters, emails, prompt responses, vignettes	recalling an incident and its effect	*usually not*
Personal interest	free write, vignette, idea mapping	polished vignette, op-ed argument	op-eds, researched writing, argument	*usually in invested writing*
Fiction	scenes, character sketches	early drafts	portfolio level	*for background*
Poetry	free writing	early drafts	portfolio level	*for background*
Literary	summaries, analysis, annotated bibliography	prompt responses, close-readings, compare-contrast	close readings, compare-contrast, reader effect	*generally not until college level*
Historical	summaries, analysis, annotated bibliography	summaries, analysis, prompt response, compare-contrast	analysis, comparison of sources, specifics to generalities	*generally middle school and beyond*

Table 10: Writing Across the Curriculum, cont.

	Service writing	Draft and a half	Invested writing	With outside Research?
Math	summaries, annotated glossary annotated formulas, math journals	complex problem analysis, real-life mathematics response	*generally not until college level*	*generally not until college level*
Scientific	summaries, lab notes, annotated bibliography	lab reports, experiment proposals, prompt response	*generally high school and beyond analytical papers describing research results*	*occasionally*
Second Language	learning tools, taking dictation, flashcards, reading summaries	short papers in personal memoir style or prompt response	*generally not until college level*	*generally not until college level*
Arts	summaries, analysis	close response to art or music work	*generally not until high school level*	*generally not until college level*

The Invested Writing Process

When I taught English 401, the required introductory writing course at the University of New Hampshire, I'd already taken the course four times. UNH was a pioneer in the teaching of writing as a process. Led by professors like Don Murray and Donald Graves (you will hear them mentioned in nearly every recent book about the teaching of writing), the English department at UNH studied teaching in local classrooms, experimented on their own students in English 401, and developed a program that has been emulated throughout the country.

I went to elementary school in Durham, where the teaching was deeply influenced by UNH on the other side of town, and in the eighth grade, I had my first teacher whose prior job had been teaching 401. I went on to Phillips Exeter, where two of my English teachers had previously taught 401, and again at Harvard, in their required freshman exposition class, my teacher had come from UNH, where she'd taught 401. Each of these classes emphasized the writing process and broke down the steps of writing, and gave us access to a tool box of solutions to common writing difficulties. (And it works through the grades – there isn't much difference in course structure at age ten, fifteen, or eighteen.)

This is in marked contrast to the old school style of teaching writing, where the teacher assigns the topic, the student thinks about it for a bit, develops a thesis sentence, writes a formal outline of the paragraphs (usually five) of the paper, and then follows the outline to write the paper. Because the thinking has happened (or hasn't, as is often the case) in the outline, the writing time is seen as the final draft, with attention and time given to choosing the right word and the right spelling and punctuation from the start. This paper is turned in, and the first teacher/student interaction is the teacher returning the final draft, with every spelling and punctuation error carefully marked in red ink and a grade on the bottom. If the grade is high, the student normally keeps it; if the grade is low, it usually goes in the trash.

As with math or music or reading, there are some students who have an initial talent for writing and do very well in this system, but the main thing about this method is that it is fairly closed. Most students will either do well at it or they won't, but there isn't a lot of opportunity for students to improve from one paper to another, because the only thing that is under consideration is their final product. Students were not taught how they might improve their techniques and practices. Don Murray changed all this.

The idea of the process of teaching writing seemed novel in the 1980s. Murray, in particular, examined his own process and habits of writing, and looked at the steps that he took to create writing. The "Process Approach" splits writing into three rough phases (with writers shifting back and forth between them, rather than always taking the straight route through the steps). Different books use different words to describe the three steps, but they usually fall into the following categories: *early writing, drafting and revision*, and *line-by-line editing*.

I cannot take credit for these ideas – this is my tuning of a process that has come to me and that I've worked with, but the ideas initially belonged to Don Murray, Donald Graves, Tom Newkirk, Bruce Ballenger, Nancie Atwell, Peter Elbow, Penny Kittle, Kelly Gallagher, and of course my father, whose writings and revisions went on all around me. It is impossible to believe that writing springs full blown from the writer when your childhood was surrounded by reams of paper revisions. Back before computers, my father's earliest drafts were written with a black Flair felt tip pen on yellow legal pads, with a plywood off-cut as a lap desk. The next draft was at the typewriter, on yellow typing paper. Several drafts of yellow paper might ensue, and my mother would read them, and then finally, my mother would get out her red and blue pencils and copy edit them for spelling and punctuation, missing words, and misunderstandings.

The only difference these days is the yellow legal pads are gone. (The same plywood off-cut still serves as a lap desk for editing computer printed drafts.) For his latest book, part memoir, part biography, part World War II history, the printed book sits slim atop a three foot stack of 2000 pages of drafts, research notes, and correspondence – and my parents still read the final draft aloud to each other to make sure what's on the page is what he wants to be on the page. (Although my father sometimes employs the Kindle Fire's robotic voice to read drafts aloud to him in the earlier stages.)

Here is my take on the stages of the writing process. I say "stages" because I do think of them as a progression, but I never march directly from point 1 to 2 to 3 in my own writing – the real steps loop around, sometimes progressing neatly down the track, sometimes going over and over old ground, until the final piece usually looks absolutely nothing like the ideas in the initial early writing stage. Each piece of writing is different – there is no particular virtue in following the steps one by one, although students need to know that successful writers do go through these steps. Sometimes it seems that the steps are not remotely linear, but rather a loop, from early writing to research to draft, around and around, until a gravity sling shot (or more usually a deadline) shoots it out of orbit and into line by line editing and completion.

As you read through my list, keep in mind that this process could take five years, five weeks, or a few hours, depending on the complexity of the writing project. Invested writing will go through many drafts, and hit most of these stages; draft and a half writing rushes through them in a day or so, and skips most of the revision stages, although writers may use some of the early writing steps to generate ideas and structure.

I call the first stage *early writing* (which I prefer over the often-used "Pre-Writing" because usually quite a bit of writing takes place in this stage, even if no word of it appears in the final draft). Often times, in what I call *service writing* where the student is using writing to help cement ideas, the whole writing project might exist in the confines of the *early writing* section.

The second stage is *drafting and revision*. Usually, the first draft is done rather quickly and is more of an exploration, where the author fine tunes his ideas as to exactly what the paper is about. If outside research is necessary, it takes place during both the first and second stages, as the subject is developed through the early writing and first draft. The earliest draft revisions will concentrate more on the ideas, and the later drafts on the language.

The final stage is the *line by line editing* where the author is concerned with her specific word choice and revising at the sentence level. (There is no point spending hours writing a paragraph perfectly in draft two if it gets cut in draft three.) Once the word choices are clear, then the author can go through and make sure that the spelling, punctuation, and grammar are all accurate.

Example of Invested Writing Steps

1. Early Writing
   a) Exploring possible topics and ideas
      • Brainstorming (generating a list by writing down words and phrases without stopping)

- Free-writing (picking an item on the brainstorming list and writing, without stopping, for five or ten minutes of free association about the topic)
- Return to old topics (there's nothing wrong with writing about old favorites, particularly if the student takes a slightly different angle or approach)

b) Preliminary Research[*] – write to engage the opinions/facts of the early research
- What do you know about the topic?
- What do you want to know?
- Where can you find that information?

c) Exploratory writing – write to discover what you think
- More free-writing and idea-directed paragraphs
- Summarizing research
- Analyzing research

d) Narrowing the topic

e) Secondary Research

2. Drafting and Revision
a) First Draft – write fast and with minimal reference to your notes
- Do not worry about the quality of the writing
- Do not worry about the links between ideas
- Do not worry about spelling, punctuation, and other matters of style

b) Dialogue with the First Draft
- What is your main idea?
- What are your secondary ideas?
- What is important to you? (if it isn't your main idea, perhaps you need to change the main idea)
- Where do you want to go next?
- Cross out (but don't destroy) parts that don't fit into the idea and a half of the essay

c) Tertiary Research
- Read through your notes. Is there anything that should be in your draft, but isn't?

---

[*] By *research*, I mean anything from formal academic research for a paper with citations and sources, to reading other people's view points to gain perspective on an opinion piece, or simply recalling bits of your own life or family history for a personal narrative essay.

- Make preliminary citations
- What do you still need to know?
- Exploratory writing to work with the new information

d) Later Drafts and Revisions

- Decide whether you need a second first draft (because the topic has shifted considerably or the order and organization needs a complete re-think) If so, return to step 2
- Is the first draft pretty solid? If so, begin the revision process
  - What works in the first draft? How can you expand on that?
  - Does the organization work? Would readjusting it help? (an outline of your paper can be helpful now if you are having organizational difficulties)
  - What is the main idea? Has it changed in the drafting?
  - Do you need any more research?
  - Repeat
- Share your work and ask for feedback – be clear that what you want at this time is feedback on the ideas/writing, not copy editing

3. Line by Line editing

a) Word choices and phrases

- Read the essay aloud (or have your computer read it aloud to you while you follow along)
  - Is it clear? Have you made any scenes vivid and strong?
  - Is the writing style suited to the genre? (in academic papers, students should generally avoid slang or contractions; for a more general audience slang and contractions could strengthen the writing)
- Work on the quality of language

b) Copy Editing
- Spell-check every piece of writing – computers make it easy now since even email programs have a spell-check
- Homophone check – check for misspelled homophones if you have difficulty with them
- Look for any other specific punctuation/grammar issues you find difficult
- Look for "Cut and Paste" blunders, where you've made an edit on the computer and failed to delete all of the old version
- Read what you've written, not what you wanted to write!
- For those with difficulties copy editing, it may be worth downloading the font Dyslexie to your computer and printing out preliminary drafts for editing in this font, even if your final drafts are in a standard font such as Times New Roman
- Share with another reader for a pair of fresh eyes on the copy editing. Be clear that what you want at this time is copy editing, not feedback on the writing

c) Corrections
- Key in any corrections you have made (being very careful not to make new "Cut and Paste" blunders)
- Read a final time (as a copy editor) before turning in your paper

In terms of this list, the final line-by-line editing takes up the most space, but that is not where the work happens; it's merely easier for me to be more specific about what needs to be done. Different pieces of writing use different percentages of time to capture these steps (and some seem quite endless).

Perhaps the biggest difference in the "Process Approach" compared with the "Product Approach" is that the writer is not expected to know the main idea of the essay when he begins writing. Writing is an intrinsic part of learning, rather than a triumphant demonstration of what one already knows. This helps cut out much of "writer's block" and the negative "I hate writing; I'm just not good at it" outlook which often comes from being required to know where you're going before you start.

Stuffing the writing process into an outline (which is one of the things this approach is trying to escape) is in some ways antithetical to the whole idea of the writing process, but I am merely providing it as reference. I do not recommend giving this list to elementary school students and sending them on their way; instead, it's more of a list of suggestions for the teacher to make as the students learn to write.

Writing Assignment Ideas

Service Writing

In addition to the service writing summaries used to support reading, described in Advanced Reading (page 104) and the History and Science chapters to follow, students will also find service writing helpful to support their longer creative writing projects. Service writing should never be graded, and probably never evaluated with any kind of comments, except perhaps a "this is interesting; I'd like to know more." In general, I ceased to read service writing after about fifth grade, although sometimes I glance at Helen and Anna's writing from across the room to see that it has indeed been done.

I would be more proactive with students I thought might not be doing the service writing assignments. When I taught English at UNH, I assigned a day book / journal, and once a week, students were to bring me a photocopy of one of their pages; however, they were free to black out anything they didn't want me to read.

Here are some ideas to get started:

Diary / Journal

For Christmas in their ninth years, we gave Helen and Anna five-year diaries, with a fifth of a page for each day. Every morning, they write a quick summary of what happened the day before, and they can read what happened last year on the same date. Although the exercise is very brief (an ideal start to the school day, so much so that it is sometimes tricky to remember on the non-school days), it serves as an *aide-mémoire* to the events of their lives, and I expect they will delight in going back through it when they are older. (They can also see real-time examples of improvement in their handwriting, grammar, and writing as they glance back through the years.)

Some children might prefer a less structured journal, where they can write up or draw their experiences. Whatever method they choose, encourage them to stick to it. This is where the five year diary format works well – it is so short that it can be required as part of school, without the risk that it expands to take over the entire day's work. The more writing they do in a day, the better. Unsupervised writing as in a diary is an important part of learning to write.

Writing Journal / Day Book

Writing teacher and writer Don Murray talks a lot about his use of a Day Book. Often, this takes the form of a spiral bound notebook (a 7 X 9.5 inch notebook will travel better than a full-sized one), or in the days of digitalization it can be a folder on the computer or tablet. Don Murray describes how he writes:

> [E]very day – well, almost every day – in a 10 X 8 spiral notebook filled with greenish paper, narrow ruled, and with a margin down the left. This worked for me. I write in my lap, in the living room or on the porch, in the car or an airplane, in meetings at the university, in bed, or stopping while I walk and sitting down on a rock wall.[114]

A day book (or a day folder on the computer) can be a place to store all these ideas and service writing, a place a student (or any writer) can return to when she is feeling a bit short on ideas, a place where she can doodle productively, map out papers, and store information or ideas that don't quite fit the current project, but might just be vital two or three projects down the road.

Free Writing

Free writing was developed by Peter Elbow.[115] The idea behind it is to free the writer from the constraints of perfection (all writers, not just students, can find this technique useful). *Free writes* are usually timed exercises – starting off perhaps with five minutes, continuing as long as thirty as the writer becomes more experienced. The only rule in a Free Write is don't stop moving the pen or hitting the keys, even if that means ten lines of *I don't know what to write. I don't know what to write. I don't know what to write.*

Late middle school students may benefit from reading Elbow's *Writing With Power: Techniques for Mastering the Writing Process.* Teachers of fourth to seventh grade students might prefer to read it themselves.

Elbow recommends the free writing technique as a daily warm-up and as a retreat when you don't know where to go while writing an essay. As a warm-up, it can be completely unfocused with no guiding topic, or it could be with a suggestion of a topic if you have a particular assignment (however, especially as a warm-up, the student shouldn't censor herself if the writing takes off in an unexpected direction. This could be the start of the next paper topic). Just keep the fingers moving, without stopping and correcting, censoring ideas, fixing punctuation or grammar. Don't stop until the buzzer rings.

Brainstorming & Mapping

Brainstorming and mapping are two ways into a paper. Brainstorming might be as simple as "write down a list of twenty issues you care about." Or once the student has narrowed that initial list into one or two items, "write down everything you can think about each item." Mapping can mean taking those items you know about and representing them on paper, with lines to describe the relationships and connections between the items. Mapping can now also be done easily on a tablet or computer using drawing functions in word processing programs.

Scenes & Character Sketches

Isolated scenes and character sketches can be a good way to practice writing, without the difficulty of making it into a memoir or fiction draft. There is very little difference in writing about characters and scenes in fiction or non-fiction, so you can invite students to imagine a character or to write about someone real in their lives. Many teachers think that all students should be required to write fiction and poetry; I'm not sure I agree. Some students will seem to have fiction or poetry pouring out of them, some have no interest (and that could be the same student, a year or two earlier or later). Forcing a student to write fiction or poetry when he doesn't want to is probably a waste of time, but he can and should sharpen the skills of character and scene in non-fiction writing.

Annotated Bibliography

An Annotated Bibliography can serve in place of or beside the chapter by chapter service writing described in the Reading Chapter above. I often request an Annotated Bibliography with the stated goal of "it will help you remember the book." For example, if I assign three general-reader history books over a month, I ask for an Annotated Bibliography at the end of it: the full citation (author, title, publisher, date, etc.) with one to three paragraphs sketching out the basic arguments and authority of the books. A bit more effort can turn this into a draft and a half piece of writing, worthy of going into a portfolio as an example of work and reading done. There's more detail about citations on page 149.

Note-taking

Note-taking (or outlining) is even more detailed than an Annotated Bibliography, for when you really want students to remember the content. It can help clarify difficult reading assignments, or merely put it a step further onto the road of long term memory. Note-taking and outlining on assigned readings is discussed in the chapter on Reading, page 106.

In addition, note-taking is an important skill when researching material for other writing, whether quickly for draft and a half writing, or thorough research for a personal, historic, or literary invested writing project. Kate Turabian's *Student's Guide to Writing College Papers*[116] has a good discussion of research note taking and writing about those notes, suitable for eighth graders and above.

Draft and a Half Writing

Vignettes

Another strategy I've used is assigning a daily "vignette." This can work well for students who are paralyzed by the desire for perfection. With Helen, I noticed that she would spend a great deal of time staring at a blank screen, not knowing where to begin, whereas Anna would plunge right in. I attributed some of this to a simple lack of practice. Anna writes fiction in her spare time, so by the time both children were in late middle school, Anna had a few hundred more pages of writing under her fingers.

The vignette assignment was to write a single double-spaced page on a single topic. (Helen was in 8th grade at the time; the assignment could be reduced for younger students.) This is a more focused and polished form than the "Free Write." In a university fiction writing class, our professor gave us an extra assignment in the form of a page or two writing about a kiss, due every Thursday, which freed us from the struggle of what to write about, and much of the concern about plot and characterization.

Prompt Response – Personal Writing

Ideally vignette topics would come from the student, but Helen found that extremely difficult. Specific prompts helped solve that problem, and since the goal for the vignette assignment is to put words down on the page, outside prompts are a good way of making sure more words go on the page. A friend gave her a birthday present of the "Family Dinner Box of Questions: Cards to Create Great Conversations," and this was quickly co-opted into a set of writing prompts for daily vignettes. Not all the questions were suitable for writing, but many make perfect starters for draft and a half writing, such as:

"What is one way your mom or dad embarrasses you?"

"Is it OK to tell a lie to protect someone's feelings?"

"What are your most and least favorite family activities?"[117]

In addition to prompts like these, some often used personal writing prompts include:

Time Expansion: Pick a ten minute moment in your life. Write down all the sensory detail you can remember, slowing down time.[118]

Time Machine: If you had a time machine, what person in the past would you go visit? Why?

Character sketch: Choose a person who has been important to you. Describe them both physically and illustrate their character to explain their importance to someone who does not know them.

Biggest mistake: Describe a mistake you've made and how it has changed or affected you.

Literary Writing

Book reports: Book reports are another way to introduce other sources and correct citation, although I almost never assigned them. Make sure each book report contains a correctly formatted bibliography, even if it is only for the one book. You want it to be second-nature for students to note down the key items from a book: author, title, edition, publisher, place of publication (I've never really understood why this is so important), and date of publication. This is particularly useful in the age of digital books, where the machine remembers your place, so you aren't exposed to the author's name every time you pick up the book and flip to your spot. It can take a real effort to remember the name of the author and sometimes even the title of the book you're reading.

Book reports can be simply an annotated bibliography, or they can be more creative, such as assignments that ask the reader to write a back story for the characters, write their college applications, create homepages or collages for them, and so on.[119] I generally considered book reports to be busy work, and did not assign them, because in my experience they don't evoke deep thinking about the book, and as such, I think the time could be better spent reading another book.

Novel v. Movie: Ask students to consider a novel where they've read the novel and watched a movie version. Ask them to compare and contrast the two versions and explain which they prefer. This is one of the examples of a "creative book report," that I'm usually unenthusiastic about, but the movie/film essay or conversation can often be a useful one, because it does inspire thinking about what can be achieved in the medium of writing versus that of a film, which is a way in to thinking about literature as an art form.

Letter Essays: Nancie Atwell's *The Reading Zone* describes the literary writing she assigns her middle school students. She uses the term "letter essay" to reinforce the informalness of the assignment, and now describes it as a "first draft final" (what I call draft and a half), although in her earlier years of teaching, she called it a "book letter" which was even less formal. Atwell's assignment asks her students to either do a close reading of an "essential" passage and what it shows about the book or the author, or to discuss their experiences as the readers of the book. The experiences discussion is not your typical reading comprehension assignment:

> Describe what you noticed about how the author wrote. Tell what you think the themes might be. Tell what surprised you. Pose your wonderings – your questions about the author, the characters, the structure, the voice, and yourself as a reader. . . .

> Be aware that a good letter-essay is one that teaches you something you didn't realize about your book, or yourself as a reader, before you wrote it.[120]

Atwell's comment here that the essay "teaches you something" is the crux of writing about literature. Too many literary writing assignments are "prove you've read it" work, questions that can be answered by SparkNotes and Wikipedia. For writing about literature to be worthwhile, it has to make students think. Independent reading, while critical for students enjoyment and stamina (and usually undervalued by curricula) is often shallow reading, where the reader takes everything at face value, concentrates on the plot, and passes the time. Reading that is followed by academic writing, however, is reading that requires careful thinking and making connections. I like Atwell's notion that these letter-essays are about "wonderings" – she does not ask her students to provide polished essays that regurgitate what the teacher thinks is the "deep hidden meaning" of the book, but rather to think about the books for themselves.

Literary Writing: Atwell's letter-essays are rougher versions of what is commonly required in high school English classes. In "Writing About Fiction" in *the Norton Anthology of Short Fiction,* editor R.V. Cassill divides literary writing into three types: that of a reviewer (writing for someone who hasn't read the book or story), a critic (writing for an audience who has read the book or story, but perhaps hasn't thought of it in the way or angle you're considering), or as a personal response (your audience may have read the book, but almost certainly hasn't had the same personal background and the same reaction).[121]

Since I didn't require literary writing in middle school, we did not do any of these strategies, but they could certainly be used as a way into more formal literary writing if you chose. Kelly Gallagher asks his high school students to write "Amazon Reviews" as a starter literature paper.[122] In high school English, I've asked Helen and Anna to write a "SparkNotes guide" themselves for their first literature essay, with a list of important characters, a plot summary, and a short critical discussion of some aspect they find intriguing.

Close Reading: Another good way into writing about literature is through *close readings* where students (or the teacher) choose a specific paragraph from the book, and go through it nearly word by word to explain why the paragraph is important to the book as a whole, the development of the character, or setting up the conflict or theme. Middle school students may benefit from the formal program of literary awareness set out in Kylene Beers and Robert Probst's *Notice and Note: Strategies for Close Reading.* Instead of using all the terms loved by English professors, Beers and Probst reduce it to six easily remembered terms, or "signposts:"

- Contrasts & Contradictions
- Aha Moment
- Tough Questions
- Words of the Wiser
- Again & Again
- Memory Moment[123]

These terms correlate with the "literary" terms of characterization, epiphany, conflict, theme, moral, didactic, motif, flashback, but they are perhaps easier for beginning literary analysts to comprehend and remember. The book is written for teachers covering the lessons in large classrooms, but it is easily adapted for one student.

Questions in an anthology or English textbook can help push students' thinking. Like other writing prompts, these questions can be helpful for students who collapse at the open-endedness of a more general assignment, but the best writing and thinking usually comes from problems or questions the student poses for himself.

Exam Writing

If you don't set exams for your students, you can teach exam writing by occasionally assigning exam-type questions as part of the regular English, history or science program. The important elements are legibility, working to the clock, outlining the ideas before writing, and following the outline in the writing. Exam writing is the vestigial remains of the old product writing style, before process writing came into schools. While process writing has more long-term value – most students will have some use for process writing in their later lives – exam writing is still an important school-skill, and indeed can help hone some of the process writing skills. Students should at least have a familiarity with the notion of the "five paragraph essay," that makes modern writing teachers cringe, but is often expected in exam writing and sometimes professional writing. Do you remember these from school? I used to describe them as: "Tell 'em what you're going to tell 'em. Then tell 'em. Then tell 'em what you've told them." The more formal way to describe this is a one paragraph introduction with a thesis statement, three paragraphs of support for the thesis, and finally, a conclusion that sums up how the support backs up the thesis.

To revisit the writing process outline from the previous section, exam writing follows similar steps:

1. Early Writing
   a) Lectures, classwork, oral discussions, reading assignments
   b) Writing summaries and interactions with class notes and reading assignments (service writing)
   c) Organizing notes and quotes while studying for the exam
2. Drafting and Revision
   a) Drafting answers to possible essay questions while studying for the exam
   b) Fast First Draft (brief outline/notes at the beginning of the page to organize the essay)
   c) Second draft – writing as polished (and tidy!) a piece as you can, given the time constraints, working from, but not slavishly to, the outline you prepared in the first page of the blue book or on the exam paper
3. Line by Line Editing
   a) Save the last five minutes or so for reading through your answer
   b) Proofread for spelling, punctuation, and clarity
   c) Make brief and neat corrections as necessary

What happens on an exam when you charge in with a thesis, write your supporting evidence, and suddenly decide you have the wrong answer? Fine. On an exam, there is usually no problem in writing a lengthy conclusion where you turn your initial thesis around. In an essay, this wouldn't be acceptable, but it's better than leaving the answer wrong in an exam.

Exam writing focuses less on the quality of the writing and emphasizes speed, decisiveness, and clarity. Eventually exam writing will be (nearly) as polished as multi-draft efforts, but in the early years it's more important to get the ideas neatly down on paper.

Students should begin by roughly outlining their answer at the top of the exam. This does not have to be a formal outline with Roman numerals and subpoints, but it should get across the idea of the introduction, the thesis, the supporting arguments, and the conclusion. Even universities sometimes give partial credit to a student who has written a clear outline, but failed to finish writing the essay in time.

University students generally write three hour exams, high school students one hour exams, and middle school students somewhere between thirty minutes and an hour. The time element is one of the most important parts of taking an exam.

In a half-hour exam, the student should spend five or ten minutes carefully reading the question and writing the outline of the response. The next fifteen minutes are used to write the exam, followed by a final five minutes of proofreading for spelling, punctuation, and logic. At first, you might wish to make these timings explicit, then gradually give your student the responsibility of managing the exam time.

Handwriting does matter. Imagine the university teaching assistant who has to grade a hundred three-hour essay exams. Clear handwriting will easily gain a grade over scrawl. You should start insisting on clear work now while your children are in middle school. Nowadays, it's easy to just concentrate on typing skills, but many university exams are still handwritten. The new Common Core standards in the US have eliminated cursive ("joined up") writing; it is still the standard in the UK. Most adults write in a hybrid style, joining up the letters that join up easily, printing those that don't, and this is probably the best handwriting for a written exam because it is both clear and fast.

Because exams are written under time pressure, you don't need to grade them to the same standard as a multi-draft essay. For a middle school student, look for how well they've answered the question, supported their arguments, and done it in clear handwriting in the time allowed. For the moment, it is okay if grammar and spelling are at a slightly lower level than you would expect in a multi-draft piece of invested writing.

Invested Writing

Personal Writing – Memoir

The classic way to teach "the writing process" to students is through a personal narrative essay. The idea is that students write about themselves, which saves the pesky research process. It can be a good way to start students writing, but at middle school age, Helen and Anna were fairly resistant to the idea. They were not yet at an age where they analyze what happens to them, and that makes a true essay difficult. The "dead grandmother" essay is the classic university freshman topic, and is very nearly a cliché. Teaching at UNH, I often wondered why the best essays were about death, trauma or tragedy. Was I simply privileging these stories in my mind or was I rewarding the students for having the courage to write about such things? Eventually, however, I came to the conclusion that these essays were actually *better*, and the reason they were better is because these awful experiences are the ones that we think about in a deep way. Mature students may be able to write meaningful essays about more trivial matters, but good writing requires good thinking, and a lot of middle schoolers aren't ready for that.

The only way I have been able to convince Helen and Anna to write about the events in their lives is in their diaries, or in letters to their grandparents, which they scrawl out reluctantly, and usually only because it's assigned. They love their grandparents, but Helen and Anna see their lives as ordinary – sailing to Antarctica and Tonga is just what they do. It is somehow easier for them to write an essay about history that is more remote from their day to day lives. This goes against the mantra of writing classes: "write what you know." But in these middle school years, assignments (or assigned letters) designed to capture the scene on paper can be valuable writing exercises, even if they are not particularly introspective.

Personal Writing – High Interest Topic

When you live remotely, it can be hard to expose your children to working in a large research library. If you find one, stop the rest of school and give them a research paper to write. (I say this, but when we reached our first English-language library in over two years, we were too busy checking out a rucksack full of novels every week.) When I taught at the University of New Hampshire, I found an enormous initial difference between the students from the local town and the other students from small towns with no university library. In those days, the local kids used the university library from kindergarten on, and it demystified the process of research.

But if your children miss a year (or two) of writing a formal research paper, it is not the end of the world. You can teach the same skills, apart from the library familiarization, wherever you are. Assign research projects using the books you have available. You might assign them the job of researching, writing, and illustrating a guide book to the local wildlife. Personal interviews (or interviews via email) are another way of broadening their sources. If you're studying modern history, why not assign them the job of collecting a family history by email? School teachers will cringe, but when you have access to the internet, let them use Wikipedia and other sources for a mini research essay. (Just keep an eye on them; I was surprised when, at age seven and five, Helen and Anna looked up "Harry Potter" and came up with a Google page of pornographic drawings.)

Apart from giving your children the experience of using a library, the main goal of writing research papers is to use sources. Students need to know how to correctly credit another person's work with either footnotes or endnotes, and they need to know how to collect the information and keep their sources straight. Whenever I'm researching (and I use a notebook rather than index cards), I am very careful to keep all the information underneath the author's heading, and note down which page it came from.

Historical Writing

Will Fitzhugh in "Meaningful Work: How the History Research Paper Prepares Students for College and Life" in *American Educator* magazine, suggests that busy high school teachers have given up assigning the research paper to their students, with the result that most of the student research papers published in his magazine, *Concord Review*, now come from private schools, where the research paper is still very much alive. When he described high school history teachers having five or six sections of thirty students each, so that a 20-page paper becomes perhaps a 3,600-page reading marathon, you can perhaps understand their reluctance, but with just a few students, you should assign many long papers a term, beginning at least in the sixth grade.

Fitzhugh writes:

> I suggest that our schools start assigning a page per year: each first-grader would be required to write a one-page paper on a subject other than himself or herself, with at least one source. At least one page and one source would be added each year to the required academic writing, so that fifth-graders, for example, would have to write a five-page paper with five sources, ninth graders would have to write a nine-page paper with nine sources, and so on, until each and every high school senior could be asked to prepare a 12-page history research paper with 12 sources.[124]

Helen and Anna have done roughly that over the years, working with citations and bibliographies from the second grade. I like the tidiness of the pages/sources/grade level, and it means your children won't be able to complain that the paper assignment is too long. It may be worth encouraging high school students to go beyond that page count, however. The papers in the *Concord Review* are usually about twenty pages long, and that seems a reasonable goal for the last two years of high school.

Knowing how to research and write (with several drafts) a long paper will stand your students in good stead, even if they decide not to go to college and never write another paper. In their future lives, the ability to collect and analyze information is useful for anything – as Will Fitzhugh writes:

By not preparing students for academic reading and writing, we set them up for failure in college and in the workplace. When we only ask that they read textbooks and write journal entries, we are not educating them. We are cheating them. We deny them the opportunity to see that *reading is the path to knowledge, and that writing is the way to make knowledge one's own.* The history research paper can help restore the importance of academic reading and writing in our schools, and in turn, refocus the purpose of education.[125] [emphasis mine]

Like Nancie Atwell's "wonderings," historical research writing is writing to aid learning and critical thinking, not simply an isolated academic task.

Citations

Works cited, bibliographies, footnotes, and endnotes must all be written to a standard format. Once students reach university, the individual departments will dictate what style to use.

There are four main ones to choose from, which are usually known by their abbreviations:

APA/Harvard Style:

for social sciences (American Psychological Association) [www.apastyle.org]

In text looks like:

(Smith, 2010, p. 14)

In Works Cited looks like:

Smith, J. (2010). *The book title.* New York, NY: Publishing House.

MLA:

for literature and languages (Modern Language Association) [www.mlahandbook.org]

In text looks like:

(Smith 14) or (Smith, *Book Title* 14)

In Works Cited looks like:

Smith, John. *The Book Title*. New York: Publishing House, 2010. Print.

CMS/Chicago:

for history (Chicago Manual of Style) [www.chicagomanual of style.org]

In text looks like[1]

and at the bottom of the page or collected at the end of the document:

[1] John Smith, *The Book Title* (New York: Publishing House, 2010), 14.

In Works Cited looks like:

Smith, John. *The Book Title*. New York: Publishing House, 2010.

CSE:

for science (Council of Science Editors; closely resembles APA) [www.scientificstyleandformat.org]

British students will probably find it useful to use the APA, as many British Universities use this as their default style (usually calling it "Harvard Style" rather than "APA"). American students may also find it useful, because it is far less intrusive in the writing process to simply write (Smith, 2010, 14) and carry on writing than to worry about formatting footnotes. At the end, the Works Cited list can be prepared with the style manual to hand, carefully copying the format. In high school, American students may want to match the style to the type of paper they are writing (MLA for literature, CMS for history, and so on), but it's more important that they are used to following a format, than which format they use. In university, they will find professors who really care about the difference between (Smith 2010) and (Smith, 2010), but in middle school and high school it just matters that they are consistent.

Links:

- [www.citethisforme.com]

- "Harvard Guide to Using Sources" at [usingsources.fas.harvard.edu/icb/icb.do]

- Purdue University's Online Writing Lab (OWL) [owl.english.purdue.edu]

The most economical way to check citation guidelines is using these online resources, or print them out if you don't have regular internet access.

Manuals for Late Middle School

General Grammar:

- William Strunk Jr. and E. B. White, *The Elements of Style*

With an emphasis on self-referential writing:

- Peter Elbow, *Writing With Power: Techniques for Mastering the Writing Process*
- Natalie Goldberg, *Writing Down the Bones: Freeing the Writer Within*

With an emphasis on world-referential writing:

- Kate L. Turabian, *Student's Guide to Writing College Papers,* University of Chicago Press
- Diana Hacker and Nancy Sommers, *A Writer's Reference,* Bedford/St. Martin's

Students probably only need one of the world-referential guides, but since Turabian and Hacker's books are written in such different styles, it may be worth asking middle school students to begin reading them in a library or bookstore to see if there is one they prefer, or buy both and see which gets used more. The *Student's Guide to Writing College Papers* is like having an older friend or sibling talk you through the aspects of writing a research paper. It is probably best to buy this book as a hard copy; we have it as an ebook, and while the introductory chapters are easy to read in this format, the final chapters about citation would be easier to read flipping through the actual pages. The Bedford/St. Martin's Handbook covers much of the same material, but with a very different voice. It is spiral bound, made for quick reference, and has colored tabs to help students find what they need quickly. The Bedford/St. Martin's Handbook is slightly more suitable for writing about literature; *Student's Guide* is aimed a bit more at history researchers, but either can be used successfully by any student.

Writing and Rewriting Toolbox

Plan the paper

In the sixth or seventh grade, students can start to take responsibility to plan their own essays. At this stage, writing about material they've read is easy – they can read a book or a chapter and do a summary. Now the next step is learning how to organize a bigger project with more depth. Don't assume they can figure this out on their own. It's okay to teach them the process.

The first step is to give your student a very specific assignment, for example, a narrow question (or perhaps a combination of questions from the end of a history chapter if using a textbook) or passage to discuss. Think about what the student can reasonably achieve in a week. As time goes on, the complexity, the independence in topic choice, and the length of project will all increase, but the more choices you can remove from this first project, the better.

The first paper might have a 10-day or a 7-day final deadline. For a paper without research, figure about 25% of the time for figuring out the ideas and the stance (you've already provided the question, so that saves time). The next 50% of the time goes to writing the first draft, which should be complete. If your student composed on a computer, print out the draft if you have a printer, or read the long-hand version if your student has written it out.

On this first paper, concentrate on the ideas rather than the grammar. See the writing conference section page 155 for tips on discussing the paper at this draft stage.

Finally, allow 25% of the assignment to re-write the paper, attend to grammar issues, and do any polishing before turning in a clean copy. We seldom used a printer when the children were in elementary school, and could easily have done without it, but in middle school, once they began composing on the computer, it became a frequent and useful tool.

Stick to your deadlines – I am not very good at this, but it will help your students in the future, and avoid some of the blankly staring at a page "writing," which isn't writing at all.

Sit beside your student as she plans a day-by-day schedule for accomplishing the paper. It might look something like this:

Preparation:
Day 1: Read the question, plan the paper and write summary of the chapter.

Day 2: Map out / brainstorm the analysis part of the paper.

Writing:
Day 3-5: Drafting – it can be helpful for students to write their introductory paragraph last, to avoid staring at a blank sheet of paper trying to come up with the perfect lead. A page a day is a good goal at first.

Day 6: Print and proofread the first draft. It should be in a professional format, looking like the final draft in presentation, even if the writing is not finalized. Writing Conference.

Revision:
Day 7: Revision.

Day 8: Print out final draft, proofread, and turn in.

(Day 9): Make sure you read and return it as soon as possible.

As the years and the complexity of the papers increase, add a few days to the project, but keep the draft deadline about ¾ of the way through the project, so as to increase the re-writing time. On a major term paper or assignment, what you the teacher will see as the "draft" should actually already have been through some drafting and revision, and might really be draft two or four.

I have had a great deal of difficulty making sure that the draft deadline was really perceived as a deadline, instead of a hint to start writing. I never had this problem with my UNH students, who turned their work in on time, but it is not something I have done particularly well as a homeschooling mother. It's the downside of being at home with the children – I know too well the other demands on their time, and so it can be hard to be the academic disciplinarian I would be if their home lives were invisible to me.

Since we moved to Alaska, we've had four firm deadlines a year for portfolios, and this threat of an outside evaluator has been extremely helpful in making up for my weakness when it comes to deadlines.

Advanced Work in Late Middle School

After a few papers, you will find you can back off on the structural help. By seventh and eighth grade, I stopped assigning such closely defined writing projects, and instead gave them six to eight week syllabi for history and literature. This would contain a blank calendar with the dates (and any commitments we had during that time), a reading list, and the paper assignments. I generally assigned a draft and a final due date for each paper, although the paper might be revised yet again for the portfolio.

When possible, I preferred it if Helen and Anna came up with their own writing topics, but I wasn't shy about suggesting topics as the deadline neared. If I were teaching a lot of students, I'd ask them to submit a written project proposal at the beginning, but with homeschooling, you can simply check up on progress at dinnertime.

After the First Draft

Writing Conferences

Writing Conferences are usually a big part of the process approach to teaching writing. It is a significant time commitment for classroom teachers, who must meet with each of their students individually, while coming up with something for the rest of the class to be doing, but it is quite effortless in a homeschooling situation, where nearly every student-teacher interaction has the feel of a conference.

However, merely meeting with students to discuss the writing isn't enough. The writing conference (which I call "Dialogue with the First Draft" in the section on the writing process), should guide the student towards making her own judgments about the writing, rather than be simply a time where the teacher tells the student what needs to happen to the paper – a writing conference is not teacher notes in another format, but rather a time where the student learns how to have an internal dialogue with the writing in order to see what needs work, what needs emphasis, and what indeed the writing is about.

Don Murray provides a list of starter questions for conferences. These questions work whether the student is 8 or 18.

"What did you learn from this piece of writing?"
"What do you intend to do in the next draft?"
"What surprised you in the draft?"
"Where is the piece of writing taking you?"
"What do you like best in the piece of writing?"
"What questions do you have of me?"[126]

As the students become accustomed to this type of questioning, they begin to internalize them. You don't have to think of yourself as a good writer to ask these questions, and the moments in conference are not something that can be replicated by a "Learn to Write" program. Murray calls the conference an "oral rehearsal draft" and notes, "I realize I'm teaching my students what they've just learned."

The key to the writing conference is that it takes place during the drafting process, not after the paper is turned in. In elementary and middle school, I assigned draft deadlines (which we have a "conference" about) and then provide another few days or a week for revision before the actual deadline. I generally write comments on the final papers, so they have it in writing.

Revision

The most important point to get across is that revision is not about punishment or correcting errors. Many of the writing process books aimed at early elementary school students strongly emphasize the importance of revision even in the early grades, but Helen and Anna both resisted it, and I didn't let it worry me, but instead let them move on to the next piece of writing. I could see their improvement in the new writing, even if they never improved the old.

Don Murray writes in his 1978 essay "Internal Revision:"

> I suspect the term rewriting has, even for many writers, an aura of failure about it. Rewriting is too often taught as punishment, not as an opportunity for discovery or even as an inevitable part of the writing process. Most [textbooks], in fact, confuse rewriting with editing, proofreading, or manuscript preparation. Yet rewriting almost always is the most exciting, satisfying part of the writing process.[127]

It's important to make a distinction between *revision*, where the writer is changing or tweaking the focus or structure or words of the writing in order to improve it, and *editing*, where the writer is working on line by line conventions of spelling, punctuation, and grammar. It is not necessary at this stage to go through the student's draft, mark every error in red pen and have them copy out a clean copy. That may have had virtue when I was in school, because it prepared us for writing in high school (my teachers in the 70s certainly didn't imagine that we would be writing our papers on a computer in ten short years), but most people will be doing their later writing on computers, which frees us from the drudgery of writing out a "clean copy" and makes corrections very simple.

I missed out on the useful step of writing with the children, but they did grow up watching me write articles and see the lengthy process between the first draft and the published piece in a magazine. The revision process wasn't invisible to them the way it is if you only read finished writing, but I wish I had written a personal essay or two alongside them in the early years.

Cut & Paste

Did you ever wonder why the processes are called "cut" and "paste" on the computer? In the old days, writers used to really cut up their manuscripts with scissors and paste or tape them out onto other sheets to rearrange them, and it can still be a valuable exercise. If a student is having trouble with an essay, and the individual paragraphs seem okay, but the essay as a whole isn't working, it can be helpful to print out a copy (or photocopy it, if it's longhand), and actually take scissors to the copy, slicing it up into paragraphs and then spreading them out on a table. This allows the writer to try different orders, shuffle the pieces, and see different versions very quickly. It sometimes helps to get away from the tyranny of the computer screen, where it is very difficult to re-envision the entire work.

Write it Again

Another technique for an almost-there paper is to have a print out by your side, open a brand new file, and begin writing again. This sounds old fashioned, but sometimes it is the only way out of a rut. One of the arguments against word processing is that writers are less likely to revise as ruthlessly as when they had to type the whole thing out again on a manual typewriter, and simply forcing oneself to re-type it gives that kind of pressure. The writer is more likely to improve or rewrite or delete a paragraph entirely when it must be typed anew than when it simply must be read and passed over on a computer screen.

Sharing Work

Writing process as taught in schools emphasizes the notion of the workshop. This isn't going to be practical in most homeschooling situations because of the lack of peers, but I wouldn't worry about not having peer workshops. Writing workshops are delicate things – the participants have a tendency to either praise too much or criticize too harshly, and neither helps the author very much. If you have two children who are close in age, it could be useful to try some workshops, but guide them initially, and make sure both children know how to comment on other people's work. It can be useful to give them specific quantities and questions: list three things you like about the (story/paper/essay/report) and three things that you want to know more about. (They can practice on sample papers from other students which are readily available on the internet, rather than cutting their critic's teeth on a sibling.)

Copy Editing

As the child becomes a better reader, ask him to go through the later drafts of a paper and circle any words he thinks are misspelled. Some children, like Helen, are able to immediately recognize when a word doesn't match what they've been reading, but others like Anna simply don't see it.

Silent Errors

For those considering going without an English textbook, the most concise summary of English grammar (aimed at an American audience) is William Strunk and E.B. White's *Elements of Style*. For most students, this is a high school level book, but you may find it a useful source as you help younger students with grammar.

Much of writing is simply a question of getting the words down on paper, but there are a few points of grammar which are invisible in spoken English, which makes them especially difficult for students to do accurately, and almost every student will need some direct instruction.

Silent errors include the comma splice, mistaking "its" and "it's," writing "alot" or "allot" instead of "a lot," and "would of" instead of "would've." You can't hear the difference between the correct and the incorrect versions, so a student can speak perfectly, never slip up with "me" and "I," yet still stumble on these points. They are worth attending to, however, because they are glaring in professional writing.

If I find these errors in Helen and Anna's writing, I pick and have a "grammar of the week" lesson (and some of them over and over again), to explain why the rule is the way it is, and we look directly at their writing to find the solution.

A **comma splice** is when you join two complete sentences with a comma; it's not strong enough. For example, *Bob went fishing, he didn't catch anything* is incorrect. You must substitute a semi-colon for the comma, or use a comma plus a conjunction such as *and* or *but*. *Bob went fishing; he didn't catch anything.* Equally correct is: *Bob went fishing, but he didn't catch anything.* Or get rid of the second subject and make it *Bob went fishing but didn't catch anything.* All three forms are correct; choose which ever one better emphasizes what you're trying to say. The first two sentences have a bit more emphasis on Bob's personal failure to catch a fish, whereas the third might be a better way of saying it if you wish to point out the perils of overfishing.

Common spelling mistakes include **using it's when you mean its.** Its, as in the dog wagged its tail, is a possessive pronoun and, like other possessive pronouns (his, hers, ours, theirs, or yours), it does not use an apostrophe. The confusion comes from the possessive of nouns, which do take an apostrophe s, for example, *The dog's tail wagged. The dog wagged its tail.* **It's** has nothing to do with possession; it's merely a contraction of **it is.**

Watch out for **a lot** and **all right** (in American). A lot is never one word (and means something completely different from allot, which will be suggested by your spell-checker). All right is always two words in American, but is frequently shortened to alright in books published in the the UK.

The "have" contractions: should've, could've, would've: it's very common for students to write "of" instead of "'ve" in these words. Not so long ago, contractions were virtually banned from academic text, but that's not such a strong rule anymore, and contractions riddle our casual writing – letters, emails, online talk, so it's important that students learn the right way to write these contractions.

The next two points aren't completely silent, but they're muffled. Even people who pride themselves on their spoken grammar tend to ignore these rules when they speak, but in writing, it is important that students understand the rules.

Me, myself and I: Nervous writers often substitute "myself" when they aren't sure whether they should use "me" or "I" in a sentence, and it can come across sounding either uncertain or pompous. Usually, students only have difficulty if there is more than one person involved: "Brett and me went to the movies." Removing Brett makes the error clear; you wouldn't say "me went to the movies." Likewise, "He gave the tickets to Brett and I" sounds wrong when you remove Brett and make it "gave tickets to I."

Adding on the missing verb can help too. "He likes football more than me." In this case, the sentence is inferring "He likes football more than me do" – instead, it should read, "He likes football more than I" (or "than I do").

Check for a **singular subject followed by a plural pronoun**. The generic word child is singular, but because it doesn't have a gender, you have to say either *he or she* afterward (or perhaps alternate between the two pronouns). You can't say "they" after child. (You of course can go back and change child to children, and then you get rid of the problem.) Saying the child ... he/she is awkward, so I prefer using the feminine pronoun sometimes and the masculine at others, but it is really a matter of personal preference.

Another common mistake is using pronouns without making the subject clear. Plenty of published authors make the same mistake with dialogue. Desperately trying to avoid a succession of *he said / she said,* they too frequently leave out tag lines all together, so the reader has to go find a pencil and label it himself. Simple tag lines are unobtrusive, and above all, the reader must know who said what.

If you're an indifferent speller, the easiest way to check a student's spelling is to open the file on your computer as most word processing programs will underline suspected misspellings in squiggly lines. You may wish to disable both the spell-check and "auto correct" on your child's program, however, so he gets into good writing habits now. If I type "alot" on this computer, it automatically fixes it to a lot, which is not necessarily a good thing, as the student doesn't realize the mistake and then repeats it on a written exam or when using a less sophisticated program. Middle school students should be doing most of their capitalization and punctuation correctly without thinking about it; a computer which sorts this out for them will slow down the learning process.

In Anna's case, since she has such extreme difficulties with spelling, I've disabled "auto correct," but left the spell-check on. She makes great use of it, and her computer-drafted papers are several grade-levels ahead of her hand-written work. It isn't simply the presentation: the ease of writing on a computer seems to actually free her mind for higher-level thinking.

Final Draft

Once the revision and rethinking is complete, students should print out their papers and take a final read-through of their work, checking for missing words, spelling, punctuation, and logic. Even if there isn't time to re-print or hand copy the final draft to make it perfect, it is better to hand in a correct copy than a clean copy. I never turned in a college or grad school paper without a correction or two. (More than that, and I'd correct them on the screen and reprint the paper.) Have the student make corrections as neatly as she can, using proofreader's marks.

The Portfolio style of evaluation promotes extensive revision in personal narrative essays, personal high interest research papers, and opinion pieces (which are the types of writing traditionally taught in a "Language Arts" classroom). In the subject-matter writing of history, literature, and science, however, we had usually moved on to new subjects, so Helen and Anna didn't have the drive for a true revision, although they would work on line by line editing before submitting the essays in their portfolios.

Evaluating Final Drafts/Portfolios

You should draw a distinction between early drafts and final drafts, which are turned in to you, usually by a specific deadline, as though you were going to grade them. In middle school you can choose to grade papers or not; you probably will not have to provide a graded transcript for middle school unless your child is applying to a competitive high school.

Final drafts should be keyed into a computer (some students will prefer to compose on the keyboard) and be laid out in a standard format. I like to have the name, subject and date in the upper right corner, the title a few lines down and centered, and all papers double spaced (easier for proofreading and making comments), indented at the beginning of each paragraph, and no extra lines between paragraphs. Students should know that much of the presentation is arbitrary – they will meet teachers who insist on paperclips and teachers who insist on staples, those who require title pages, those who forbid it, but they should learn that they must meet the teacher's standard, whatever it may be.

At the first reading of your student's essay, look for the big picture. Does the essay make sense? Are the arguments persuasive? Does the essay answer the question you posed? Does it use sources (literature, research or personal experience) to back up assertions?

Next reading, look to the style of the writing. One common phrase writing teachers always use is "show don't tell," meaning you achieve more with scenes or facts, particularly those that appeal to one or more of the senses, than by a summary statement. "The village was poor" is **telling**; a two-paragraph description of the pigs, the corrugated roofing shacks, discarded batteries on the ground, and the protruding ribs of starving dogs is **showing**. It's not simply a case of using fancy language – plain words often "show" better than erudite ones; your students' papers shouldn't sound like they've been pouring through a thesaurus. (I don't really approve of a thesaurus as a writing tool. Students should write with words in their working vocabularies; the best way to increase working vocabularies is by reading and looking up new words as they're encountered.)

Elementary school writing is often characterized by "and then, and then" structure. Middle school students should try to shake the "and then" habit, and experiment with writing out of chronological order, flashbacks, and shifting of sequence for effect. Sometimes a straight chronological order will best suit the essay, but in that case, the student should try to vary the transitions slightly from "and then." If students don't experiment with these devices on their own, assign a couple of short personal essay with a required flashback.

Finally, examine the writing for mistakes of grammar, spelling, and punctuation. Strunk and White, *The Elements of Style,* is a useful guide. Don't torture yourself too much about the placement of commas – a lot of comma work is a matter of preference. Reading the essay aloud is a good way to check the punctuation matches the tempo of the piece.

Teacher Comments

I don't think grades have a place in elementary school work, and I didn't grade papers in middle school, either. Most students in bricks and mortar schools in grades 6-8 will be graded by their teachers, but a mother's grades seem pretty meaningless to me. Helen and Anna know when they've done a good job on a paper, and when it could be better, but a grade seems so final, and so antithetical to future progress and revision that I've felt comfortable leaving them out of our homeschool.

Written comments are very good, and they train the student to look to the paper for the comments (which is the way it will be in future schools) rather than the teacher's words. (It's too easy for a parent to reflexively say "good" when they don't really mean it.) Use the red pen sparingly. At this age, it's important for a student not to be completely discouraged, but on the other hand, try to find some point where you can encourage improvement. With Anna, for example, in the early years, I restricted my comments to content, and ignored the dozens of spelling errors. There seemed no point in returning her papers blazoned with red marks. Helen, on the other hand, rarely makes spelling errors, so I am scrupulous about looking for them and marking them so that she can improve. (And since age thirteen, she has copy edited my work, so there is always a bit of schadenfreude when I can find errors in her paper, because she takes such unseemly delight in finding errors in my writing.)

Grade-level Samples

Understanding the steps in developing writing can help you teach the writing, but of course the isolated homeschool teacher is always going to worry, is the work good enough? Classroom teachers have years of experience and thirty students – or sometimes as many as four hundred a year in the later grades – and so develop an instant assessment of whether the writing is above average, on track, needs extra attention, or should be evaluated for learning difficulties. Fortunately, we now have the internet.

You can look online to find numerous grade-level writing samples to see how your students compare. (If you are making similar assignments, you might even find it helpful to show your children some of these samples, so they can have a bit of classroom experience – a writing workshop with invisible peers.) The US Common Core Appendix C has an example for each type of writing for each grade. This is a good place to start to see examples of different types of writing, but be warned that the samples here are exceptionally good. The goal of the Common Core standards is to have this be average work, but nearly every teacher I've spoken with or read confirms that they sound more like the best students at the end of the school year.

If you search "writing sample elementary school" you will find a wealth of sources online. Bricks and mortar school teachers frequently use anonymous writing samples in their classes as way to teach the writing process and writing workshops, so these samples are readily available.

Outside Assistance

The teaching of writing is one of the most important jobs you have as a homeschooling parent. If doing it alone seems overwhelming, you might take a look at **Writing Strands**, although that is a dedicated "learn to write" program, rather than mixing writing instruction in with the rest of the curriculum. We tried the earlier books in the series, but neither child could see the point of writing just to write, and they groaned every time they saw the books.

Bravewriter is another oft-recommended program. This curriculum takes students through the steps of writing, with programs available from kindergarten through high school; it is available as online classes or offline curriculum. A third popular program is the **Institute for Excellence in Writing,** which offers DVDs designed to teach the parent how to teach writing; and we have met quite a few homeschooling families who found it helpful. (Note: IEW is not a secular program.)

However, if you are still feeling unsure about teaching writing, it might be worth looking for an assistant, especially in the later middle school and high school years. Many universities have writing teachers on staff, usually graduate students working their way towards a PhD or Master's degree. Their stipends barely pay the rent, and most of them would be very glad to take on an extra student for a small fee. If you can find someone to help evaluate your student's work, provide a writing conference by email, and return essays promptly via email, it could be the help you need to keep homeschooling. (Insist on the promptness; it really matters to students, and it is not necessarily something teaching assistants are good at.)

A simpler option is to find an outside reader to help evaluate portfolios rather than each and every piece of writing. Relatives, friends, local teachers, and university graduate students may have the ability and time to help you, particularly if you stagger your portfolio deadlines so as to come at a quiet time in their work schedule.

Writing Summary

- Teach writing across the curriculum, using service writing, draft and a half, and invested writing
- Writing is a process
- Revision is not punishment or error correction; it's a way to discover what the writer thinks
- Develop writing stamina, with at least 20 hours a month devoted to writing

Writing-related Skills

As I discussed in the last chapter, I believe writing-related skills such as handwriting, keyboarding, spelling, (and to a certain extent, grammar), should be considered separately from *writing*. Writing is the art of crafting sentences – a very dyslexic student who must dictate papers into a computer program is writing – or composing if you prefer that term. Students will also need to study the writing-related skills, but to a large extent these two areas can be separated. Writing (composition) is a thoughtful subject; handwriting, keyboarding and spelling are automatic subjects, best developed through drill and practice.

Handwriting / Penmanship

There are a lot of theories out there about how to teach handwriting, and neither Helen nor Anna's writing can be described as beautiful, so I certainly don't hold up my way of doing it as the only way. Some programs teach lower case letters first, some teach capitals; some believe in beginning with cursive writing and skipping printing all together (most British schools do this, calling it "joined-up" writing); the new American Common Core leaves cursive off the syllabus all together, although some researchers maintain that's a mistake, as cursive writing may help brain development.[128]

Handwriting Without Tears is an American program, increasingly used in schools. It worked extremely well for Helen, but not very well for Anna. The handwriting itself is not very pretty – it is vertical, with no slant even in the cursive. But it's clear, and the letters are taught in the order that they are easiest to learn, not alphabetical order, and that does make things easier.

In retrospect, I wish that I had spent a lot more time on Anna's writing posture and pencil grip. (This is an important part of the *Handwriting Without Tears* program; I just didn't implement it very well.) I imagined Anna would correct her posture on her own, but by the end of elementary school, she was fixed in some bad writing habits, such as holding her head with her left hand while she wrote, or fiddling with something on her desk, and leaving her right hand to do all the work of penmanship and holding the paper.

I've read that it's better for dyslexic children to write in cursive, and as soon as one spots symptoms of dyslexia, it's worth switching to cursive writing, but with Anna, I missed so many years of symptoms that she really, really didn't want to change and her troubles were firmly entrenched by the time I realized they were a problem. So she still prints, slowly, and awkwardly, but after many years now, most of her letters are the right way around. She writes many of her letters in the reverse order from most people – for example, she begins a lowercase l at the bottom, whereas most people begin it at the top when printing and at the bottom when writing in joined up writing.

When you are choosing a handwriting program for your children, consider whether or not there is a possibility they will return to a school system in the future, and find out what type of writing is expected there. Most adults write in a sort of italic hybrid of printing and cursive, so that's probably where your students will end up, no matter how you begin.

Arguments for beginning with printing include:

- It reinforces learning to read because the letters look like those in books
- It is easier for parents to read, which is a positive reinforcement for children
- It is easier to learn

Arguments for learning cursive/joined-up writing include:

- It may help develop brain function (although researchers have not distinguished between learning cursive exclusively or learning it after printing)
- Cursive is faster, and thus better for note-taking and exam writing. (Writers of the Common Core presume that today's students will be doing all of this on the keyboard, but that may or may not be the case.)
- Reading cursive is a link to the past – reading grandmother's letters or historians going through journals. My children brush off the sight of a cursive letter as though it's Greek (no, I take that back; they're far more interested in learning to write their names in Greek).

Handwriting Without Tears follows the standard American schedule of beginning with capital letters in preschool and kindergarten (age 5-6) in a book called *Get Set For School,* followed by *Letters and Numbers for Me.* First graders (age 6-7) use *My Printing Book,* second graders *Printing Power.* Each of these books are self-contained, so there is no need to go through the whole sequence when starting with older children, although eight-year-olds might be better starting with *My Printing Book* rather than jumping straight into *Printing Power.*

In this program, children do not begin cursive handwriting until the third grade (ages 8-9) with *Cursive Handwriting,* followed by *Cursive Success* the next year. There are also two remedial programs for older children called *Can-Do Cursive* and *Can-Do Print.*

My children completed this cycle before the Common Core stopped recommending cursive. If I had young children in this cycle now, I would continue to teach them cursive, because we don't yet know how children who don't study cursive do in later life, in reading letters from other people, in taking notes in college, in writing exams. I'm willing to be proved wrong on this, but I wouldn't want my children to be in a position where they can't read letters from their English cousins. They may never receive a letter from their English cousins in later life – it could all be email – and I know that when I write letters to people who don't have email, I almost always compose it on the computer, print it out and mail it.

The Common Core's neglect of cursive has made me more relaxed about the state of Anna's handwriting, however. By twelve, she was doing almost all her composing on the computer, and in her thirteenth summer, she sat down at the computer every evening and churned out a 100-page novella in a month. She can certainly communicate in writing, which is after all the goal of handwriting.

There is a program called *Fix it Write* by Nan Jay Barchowsky, aimed at improving the handwriting of teenagers and adults. Helen did the entire program a few years ago and notes, "I hated the program while I was doing it, but actually it was very good." And I can now read her handwriting, and that's important, particularly in exam writing.

Whatever program you choose, it's unlikely to fill up an entire year of handwriting practice. I typically started the children with a Handwriting Without Tears workbook at the beginning of the school year, as a refresher after some time off. They worked through it for the first third of the school year or so, and for the rest of the year, I gave them *copy work* assignments. I picked selections from children's stories and poems, copied them out as neatly as I could, and asked Helen and Anna to copy them on lined paper. If you're using the Handwriting Without Tears program, it's worth buying their proprietary double-lined paper while your students learn to write; the more usual three line training paper is available world-wide.

Copy work exercises allow you to disassociate composition and handwriting practice. In the early grades, Helen and Anna's handwriting in independent writing was months behind their skill level in copying set pieces. They could see their handwriting improve, even though their handwriting in service of writing assignments juddered along behind. The quality gap between pure copying exercises and writing assignments is to be expected: a copy work assignment is asking the student to apply 100% of her brain and motor power to copying the text, whereas a composition assignment will co-opt most of the brain power towards choosing the right words, leaving only a small portion available to direct the transcription process.

Spelling

For some students, extensive reading (probably aided by phonetic instruction as they learned to read) will be enough. If your students spell accurately, you don't need a spelling program, and can simply teach the hard words as they come up in the child's writing. Helen spent a month or two twiddling her thumbs through the *Spelling Workout* series before I shelved it. She spelled everything correctly from the start, including "lettuce" which I have to spell-check every time. Her phonetic reading instruction, followed by a learn to type program at age nine, was all she needed to become a proficient speller.

The *Spelling Workout* series failed the *always difficult, but never impossible* test for both my children. It is a highly recommended, rules-based program, but Helen didn't need it, and Anna needed much more. It could work well for students somewhere in the middle, and was certainly better than the spelling program Helen and Anna met during their six week experience of a bricks and mortar school, where they were simply given a list of unrelated words to memorize each week. Neither child learned anything.

In the first few years of school, you don't need to jump immediately into a spelling program. Almost all students will use invented spelling in the first year or so, and many progress to spelling accurately without a lot of interference. If your child reads at grade level, but is still using invented spelling by age eight, it may be time to add a spelling program.

I didn't find *All About Spelling* until Anna was about nine and a half, but all students begin in Book 1, regardless of their age. It worked extremely well for us, and I learned a huge amount about spelling myself. I was shocked to discover that English has many set rules that I'd never learned. When I was in elementary school, for example, I was taught that "love" is an exception. (Why doesn't the e at the end make it lōve?) There is a rule! English words don't end in u or v. The only exception that I can think of is "you" which is a corruption of the French "vous" and so came at its ending u through a different route. I used to say to Helen and Anna that the u and v were cowardly letters and were absolutely terrified at being at the end of the word all alone and needed an e to protect them. English words also don't end in i or j. The words that do end in i, such as "ski" or "spaghetti" are direct imports from other languages. This was all news to me.

In fact, the improvement in my understanding of the spelling rules was an unforeseen benefit of the spelling program – it let me teach spelling through their writing much more effectively than my original plan of simply listing the misspelled words and having Helen and Anna copy them out a few times. I spelled poorly enough in school to be compared to Lois Lane, and since at that time I wanted to be Lois Lane, it didn't hurt enough to make me want to improve. Spell-check is a wonderful invention.

I enthusiastically recommend *All About Spelling* – despite its expense of $29 to $39 per book and materials. If you buy it second hand or re-use the program with another child, you will have to spend a tedious afternoon sorting the cards into the correct order. If you are teaching more than one child at one time, you can purchase additional student packets, but if there are a few years between them, the student materials are almost all reusable. (If they are only a year apart, you still might want to have two student packs, because the words, key cards, and so on, stay with a student until they are fully mastered – for example, when Anna was in Level 5, she continued to review many Level 4 words and a few Level 3s).

Anna's spelling is a good example of why writing skills should be distinct from writing. She still struggles with spelling (although now that she can type quickly and compose on a computer, spell-check helps enormously). In the seventh grade, she wrote a story which won a Silver Key in the Scholastic Writing Awards regional competition against an undifferentiated field of middle and high school students. Had her writing progress through the years been conditional on her spelling and handwriting success, or her writing assignments come back red with spelling corrections, I know she would not now think of herself as "a writer," and devote so much of her free time and energy to her stories. She would now be much more likely to say, "I hate writing." Remember, there are many dyslexic professional writers – they've just found a good proofreader.

Typing / Keyboarding

American guidelines suggest that typing begin very early. I think it is far better to wait until your child is ready to sit and work hard at a typing program and can spell at a fourth-grade level. Like learning to read, the most efficient way to learn to type is to have a dedicated program and work hard at it for several weeks. The program English Type suggests ten hours of practice as sufficient to reach 20 words a minute. We found it took a couple of months, practicing for half an hour, five days a week. Before and during this time, however, it is best not to have the child "fool around" on the computer keyboard, because that will encourage "hunt and peck" two-finger typing. Once the child reaches twenty-five words per minute (or maybe even twenty words per minute) it is fine to have him use a keyboard for typing up work, surfing the internet and so on, because he will naturally touch type.

Good readers "sight read," that is they process the words as whole words rather than as the individual sounds. Good typists are the same: initially one has to type out the individual letters and think about the fingering, but after a few years of touch typing, one has to merely think the word and the finger-memory does the rest for all but the most complicated words. That's why it's important to wait to allow free-typing until students spell at a fourth grade or even fifth grade level so that the words they train their fingers to type automatically are spelled correctly. If the child still writes "thier" for "their," then he will train his fingers to type it incorrectly, and it will be very hard to break the habit. (It is fine to begin typing training programs before children reach a fourth grade spelling level, and, in Helen's case, I think the typing program actually did far more to improve her spelling than any workbooks we tried.)

I don't see any need to introduce computer skills too early – the Common Core states as early as kindergarten:

> With guidance and support from adults, explore a variety of digital tools to produce and publish writing, including in collaboration with peers.[129]

I disagree. I feel children shouldn't begin using a keyboard until they are ready to learn to touch type, because it is so much easier to learn typing if you don't have bad habits to break. You can learn to touch type in a several weeks if you are starting from a blank slate; a recent innovation from Handwriting Without Tears called "Keyboarding Without Tears," takes *five years* to bring students to keyboarding proficiency. There is such a thing as starting too early.

Nine or ten is a good age to begin touch typing. This is an important skill for all students, and it is particularly useful for dyslexic children, because touch typing is like sight reading. You don't think T-H-E when you type "the" – instead, you think the word and your fingers make it without any deliberate instruction, as long as you have trained your fingers to type the correct sequence. It is more like playing the piano than writing.

Both Helen and Anna used a program called English Type. In addition to teaching typing, it did a good job of fine tuning Helen's spelling. For Helen, English Type was sufficient, and then in the fourth grade, she spend several months keying in her old history summaries. This was enough to get her typing speed up to an acceptable level. By the sixth grade (after beginning English type at eight), she preferred to compose on the keyboard, and wrote all her first drafts on the computer.

She's way ahead of where I was at her age, still working with masking tape over the keys on a manual typewriter. My father is a journalist, and so he started me off at nine on a manual typewriter, although I didn't really achieve speed and accuracy until writing papers in high school on a word processor.

With Anna, however, I took a very different route. She started English Type at about nine, but instead of letting her go straight into writing papers, I banned her from using the computer for composing until her spelling reached a fourth-grade level. Instead, I found her a shareware program called Amphetype, which creates typing drill based on any preset text that you put in (or download from an ebook) in unicode-8 text files. At the end of every *All About Spelling* book, I typed up all the dictation sentences (about twelve a lesson), put them into a notepad file, and then loaded them into Amphetype. Every day Anna practiced about twenty sentences. If she misspelled them, Amphetype turned the screen black, and she was unable to proceed until she corrected the spelling.

By sixth grade, her spelling had improved to the point where I encouraged her to compose on the keyboard, and by seventh grade she was able to write many-page essays and short stories on the keyboard.

I did recently discover it can be a mistake to rely entirely on typing programs: I watched Anna type the other day and realized she was using the same hand to hit the "shift key" and the letter, rather than simultaneously typing the letter with the appropriate finger, and using the pinkie of the opposite hand to hit the shift key. This bad habit will slow down her typing, but it had simply had escaped my notice. It will be very difficult to break the habit now that she's been typing that way for several years.

While students touch type, they should look at the computer screen, not the keyboard. This alerts them instantly to mistakes, and helps develop automaticity in their fingers. A cloth handkerchief makes an excellent hand-cover while practicing typing; unrepentant peekers may benefit from masking tape or stickers over the keys to hide them completely.

Back in the old days of secretarial school, typists were sometimes taught to type without looking at either the page or the keyboard, so that they would be able to type accurately without lifting their eyes from a handwritten letter their boss had composed. This is no longer necessary, as your students are learning to type in order to compose at the keyboard, not transcribe someone else's words. The writer needs to look over the words that he has written both for the ideas and logic and also TO MAKE SURE HE HASN'T HIT THE CAPS BUTTON BY MISTAKE.

The Common Core guidelines have an extremely ambitious program for keyboarding skills. They expect all fourth graders to type a page in one sitting, fifth graders two pages, sixth graders three pages. It doesn't say whether that is single or double spaced (presumably double), but that is a lot of typing for a beginning typist. At about 250-300 words a page, that is 750-900 words for the eleven-year-old sixth grader. For Helen, who by sixth grade was a true touch typist, who could type with all her fingers almost entirely without looking at the keyboard, that would take her twenty to twenty-five minutes of pure typing, with no time out to look out the window or be distracted by the tedium of the set typing exercise. This is a child who is dexterous, spells extremely well, has a mother who types at the rate of a fast professional, and a grandfather who gave her a computer at age eight just so that she could learn to type.

I'm presuming these exercises are targeted towards copying set pieces, not composing. If the guidelines are talking about composing 750-word essays at the computer at one sitting, then that's frankly ridiculous as a standard for all students. An article in *Author Magazine* notes that Stephen King writes 2000 words a day, Jack London wrote up to 1500, and Graham Greene "would stop for the day at 500, even if he were in the middle of a sentence."[130] And they aren't trying to learn algebra at the same time.

Keyboarding skills are very important, but the only way to get truly fast is not to cheat. Putting pressure on students to type up their papers before they can touch type will make them slip into bad habits which can make it impossible for them to break the 40 words a minute barrier later on. The reason the Common Core is so demanding of keyboarding skills is that the goal is for students to take standardized tests on the computer, using a keyboard to type the essay portions of those exams – it's for the benefit of the exam graders, not the students.

Your goal as a homeschool teacher should be to have your students typing at least 50 words a minute minimum (touch typing) by the time they are writing high school papers. Ideally, by then, they will be composing their papers directly on the computer and be able to type fluent letters and emails. Take care to insist on accuracy, ten-finger typing, and not looking at the keyboard in these early years, rather than emphasizing the page-length goals or pushing students to answer essay questions on the computer before they have the typing skills to do so.

Don't Be Afraid to Move On

These writing skills programs in handwriting, spelling, and keyboarding can be continued in middle school if your student needs them, but don't be afraid to make the decision to take them out of daily school. Homeschooling, even with rigorous academic goals, can be flexible. You can drop these subjects all together, or cut practice down to once a week, or introduce short "skills weeks" at different times in the school year where you review these skills.

Mathematics

Talking About Math

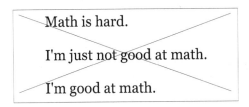

Math is hard.

I'm just not good at math.

I'm good at math.

Ban these three phrases from your conversations. All three imply that math ability is an innate talent, that students have or don't have. Remember what Salman Khan says about the tortoise and the hare in the How We Learn chapter? As Stanford mathematics education professor Jo Boaler asserts, *anyone* can learn high school math.[131] Obviously there are neuroatypical children who may not be able to finish algebra 2 and trigonometry, but in the present system, far too many students simply aren't given the chance, because they have internalized the idea that they aren't "good" at math because of their gender, their race, their parents' complaints about their own schooling, or simply not being as quick at answering questions back in grade four.

Programs

Math is the one subject where almost all but the most ardent unschoolers choose a pre-made curriculum. Although I've experimented with different programs in other subjects, I've ended up making my own programs in everything but math and second languages. Some families combine two math programs to have the benefits of different approaches.

After starting with a highly-recommended math curriculum that didn't work for us, I settled on Singapore Math for my children up through the end of 7b. (This is the level that most American schools consider the end of "middle school" math.) It worked extremely well for us, but that doesn't mean it's the only option out there. In this chapter, I will discuss different styles and theories of teaching math, the pros and cons of each, and a handful of the many, many options for homeschool math curricula.

I've also made a brief foray into discussing high school math, because choices in the elementary and middle school level do affect choices later on, and some fast-moving children may be doing high school level work in middle school, so I feel these programs fall into the scope of this book. Please don't let the talk of high school worry you if you're just starting out in elementary school. You can always skip that section.

Math and the Common Core

In the US, the Common Core is a hot topic in education. Parents of children in bricks and mortar schools and homeschoolers selecting curriculum often rage against "Common Core" math, and blame the Common Core program for all of their children's math ills.

It's important to remember there is nothing in the Common Core documents that specify *how* math should be taught. Instead, it specifies what topics should be covered in what year. Even then, there is flexibility, as the document suggests that high schools offer four tracks through high school, two of which have students completing calculus by the end of twelfth grade, two of which have students completing precalculus by that time.

Two popular homeschooling publishers, Singapore and Mammoth, have shuffled topics around in their books to meet the Common Core requirements. (Singapore still offers its older non-Common Core aligned programs.) The method of teaching is unchanged in both programs. Saxon Homeschool appears not to be Common Core aligned, although their books marketed to bricks and mortar schools are. The Art of Problem Solving Programs are generally in advance of what is required under the Common Core.

If you are planning to return your children to a US public school system, it's worth looking into a Common Core-aligned program, although students will likely be ahead of schedule if they are on the fast track in challenging programs like Saxon or the Art of Problem Solving. For most people, however, Common Core alignment should not be a major factor in your choice of a program for homeschooling. Some excellent programs are Common Core aligned; some excellent programs are not.

Types of Math Programs

There are two seemingly incompatible theories of teaching mathematics – *direct instruction* and *discovery learning*. Direct instruction programs are further divided into *spiral* (also called *incremental*) and *mastery* curricula. As you can imagine from the names, direct instruction focuses most on how teachers present material. Students usually learn a fixed routine or steps (an algorithm) to solve a problem, such as the procedure for multi-digit multiplication. Students go over worked examples and then practice the algorithm independently. Discovery learning is based on giving students (often groups of students working together) questions with real-life parameters, often including far more information than is necessary to do the problem. Students are to construct their own definitions and algorithms from working out the solutions.

Two years ago, I took a Stanford online course entitled "How to Learn Math: For Teachers and Parents" with Professor Jo Boaler. It was fascinating and turned many of my ideas on teaching math upside down. It was through Boaler's course that I discovered the writings of Carol Dweck, and her version of the "growth mindset" which is so important in teaching. This is discussed further in How We Learn (page 18).

One of the main assertions of Boaler's class was that students learn math better if they learn it through discovery problems. While taking the course, I became absolutely convinced of her thesis, but a year later, I found that it hadn't changed my teaching of math very much. It really depends on what sort of mathematical materials you are able to access, unless you are extremely confident of your ability to teach math without using a textbook (in which case, you can jump to the history chapter!).

Most textbooks follow the direct instruction model with varying degrees of clarity. My problem with discovery learning was, while I liked it in theory, I didn't have the confidence or energy to try to create a math syllabus from scratch. Under Boaler's influence, this is likely to be a fast-changing field, and there may soon be more options for elementary school discovery learning programs.

We tried a discovery learning program – Miquon Math – in the early years, and it didn't work at all for us, in part, because I didn't know how to implement it, and in part because the children were so new to the idea of school that they had no intrinsic motivation to figure out the puzzles. They didn't want to think about the problems because they had better things to do. At that age, direct instruction certainly worked better for us simply because the way to do it was clear to them, and they could imagine finishing the math for the day, rather than coming into a "problem solving" page, with no idea how to begin and no end in sight.

While Boaler's studies point decisively to the notion that discovery learning is vastly superior to traditional math programs, Richard E. Clark, Paul A. Kirschner, and John Sweller argue in *American Educator*,

> [M]inimally guided instruction is much less efficient than explicit guidance. What can be taught directly in a 25-minute demonstration and discussion, followed by 15 minutes of independent practice with corrective feedback by a teacher, may take several class periods to learn via minimally guided projects and/or problem solving.[132]

There is a lot of ill-feeling between different mathematical camps, just as there is in the teaching of beginning reading. In the end, I can only conclude (and I hope it isn't too much of a cop out) that every child is different, and one must follow a system that works for one's own family and not worry too much about the battles between different philosophies.

In fact, it is a bit freeing for the homeschooling teacher when educational researchers disagree so violently. Since I didn't have the confidence to create a full discovery learning program, nor was I satisfied with existing programs, that left me with direct instruction as my core math program. There were still decisions to make.

The *spiral* or *incremental* program is one where each math day has a large number of problems. Most of the problems are simple review problems, but a small portion are based on the day's lesson. Mathematical concepts are distributed throughout the school year, with constant built-in review.

Proponents of the spiral system maintain that it is a better one because students don't have the opportunity to forget how to do each type of problem; opponents of the spiral system maintain that the students never reach conceptual understanding because the concepts are buried in different algorithms taught weeks apart and never linked conceptually. Examples of spiral programs include Saxon, Teaching Textbooks, and Calvert Math.

A *mastery* program teaches different components of elementary math in units, with little review between sections. Examples of mastery programs include Singapore and Mammoth. Calvert, a widely-used homeschooling curriculum, used to offer its own math system based on a *spiral* system, but has recently begun offering a choice of the *spiral* Calvert Math or *mastery* Math in Focus (based on Singapore Math).

The Calvert website maintains that by using Singapore Math, "Your child will focus on fewer concepts that are taught to mastery, thereby eliminating the need to reteach concepts year after year."[133] Before Calvert changed to having a choice of math programs, we met a family who used the Calvert boxed curriculum, but had bought Singapore Math separately, and said they loved it, "because it has so much review."

This was not the case in our family! We'd finish a mastery chapter on fractions, say, and then move to another topic, and a month later, both Helen and Anna had entirely forgotten fractions. But I was also swayed by the arguments against a pure spiral program, such as Math Mammoth's Maria Miller's criticism of the Saxon algebra program. She writes:

> The problem with Saxon is not the content itself, but how the lessons are organized. Saxon mixes in the topics and does not have chapters on certain broad topics.... For example, one lesson is on range, mean, median, and mode. The next is on conjunctions, the next is on percents, and the next one on polynomials—and so on. I don't think that is the best way to learn.[134]

In the end, I chose a mastery program (from Singapore Math, Inc.*), but then found myself teaching fractions three times, and long division about four. I tried supplementing with Singapore Extra Practice books and Math Mammoth Review (Gold Series), but because both programs were also mastery-based, it didn't help. We did many years of math before I hit on a solution: combine a mastery program with five varied problems a day to keep the old subjects fresh. We didn't need a heavy drill program like Saxon – one long division problem, one fraction problem, one multi-digit multiplication problem, etc. a day were sufficient to keep the children from forgetting past topics. I found our version online from a public school website, but the *Evans Moor Daily Math Review* and *Use It, Don't Lose It!* series provide the same kind of refresher. We all wish we'd started using that from second grade onward – we could have saved ourselves from doing lots of review materials.

Consumables Versus Textbook

Most elementary school math programs include a write-in workbook for students; most middle school and high school programs do not. As students develop, they will improve their copying and transfer skills. Many elementary school students find it difficult to correctly copy problems into a notebook; copying errors will lead to math mistakes, which are really a writing

---

* There are many publishers who offer math based on the Singapore national curriculum. Our personal experience is limited to the US Edition from www.singaporemath.com.

problem, not a math problem. As you look through potential math programs for elementary schoolers, examine how much space is left for them to do the work. In many programs, there is a non-consumable textbook (reusable for younger children) and a consumable workbook, with space for them to write. Math Mammoth is an excellent program, but there is relatively little space for students to work out the problems; some students will find this very difficult – so they will think that math is difficult, whereas it's actually the amount of space alloted. (There are often workarounds: with Math Mammoth, for example, you can buy the PDF version, take a screen shot of each page, and chop that into smaller jpgs, which you paste into a document file. Print that out on plain paper or grid paper, and you may find that your student's difficulties disappear.) A lower tech option is to cut up the workbook or textbook and tape or glue it to plain or grid paper.

In many countries, math is routinely done on grid paper; in the US it tends not to be. Grid notebooks can be a boon to students who have difficulty lining up multiplication and long division; we found that lightly printed grid notebooks worked well, those with very bright distinct lines didn't help at all. One child worked very well with grid notebooks until middle school, then changed over to wide rule. Keep trying different options (including blank paper); a solution that works at one level may need to be adjusted as time goes on.

Sample Math Programs

These are not full curriculum reviews – the only program I have used year-in, year-out with my children is Singapore. Instead, I hope this can provide you with a head start as you research the options. There are many, many other programs out there. The programs listed are all available in hard copies for use without regular internet access.

Instruction Spectrum

Direct Instruction...........................Discovery Learning

Saxon	Mammoth	Singapore	Problem Solving		

Why are there two blank boxes at the end of the spectrum? I have yet to find a true discovery learning program which leads students through a sequence of problems, aimed at developing a comprehensive understanding of math. Supplementary problems abound on the internet, and Singapore and the Art of Problem Solving both include complex word problems that challenge students, but I wouldn't classify either as true discovery learning programs, as students are shown specific techniques for how to solve problems.

Singapore and the Art of Problem Solving do show multiple ways to solve different types of problem, which is important for students' mathematical development. A friend's daughter was presented with a problem like this: there are four groups of three apples. How many apples are there? In Singapore math, the connection is explicitly made that it doesn't matter whether you think of it as 4*3 or 3*4. This child's teacher marked her wrong for writing 3*4=12. One of the important takeaways from Jo Boaler's teaching math course is that there are many, many different ways to solve problems; children should never be marked off for not following the algorithm exactly, if their way leads to a correct answer.

Singapore Math (mastery)

Pros:

- While this is a direct instruction program, students are usually offered several ways of going about solving each type of problem, so while there are algorithms, there are no "right way/wrong ways" of solving problems
- This program is based on the Singapore Ministry of Education program, which turns out some of the highest

scoring math students in the world, and likely the highest for those with English-language text books

- These books emphasize conceptual understanding and work from a perspective of Concrete >> Pictorial >> Abstract
- The problems have a great variety of difficulty, to challenge both stronger and weaker students
- Available in 3 different versions (California Standards,* US Common Core, US Primary)
- Other enrichment books are available including Challenging Word problems, Extra Practice, Intensive Practice
- Online version available for levels 1-5

Cons:

- Students may find there is not enough review
- The American versions go through algebra 1 (book 8b, which can be used in 8th or 9th grade); students will need to find a new program after that, or transition into the Singapore New Elementary Mathematics books 3 and 4, which are not currently offered for sale in the US

Math Mammoth Light Blue Curriculum (mastery)

Pros:

- This is a rigorous program (resembling Singapore)
- The program may be bought as PDFs or as hard copy books
- The PDFs may be printed out for multiple children
- It matches Common Core pacing of topics
- There is a Spanish Language version
- This program is significantly less expensive than other options – each year is $37.50 to download, including tests and answer keys

---

* There are rumors that the Standards Edition may be on its way out. Singapore Math recommends that students not switch editions in the middle of the year (that is, finish the B level book before changing). In addition, be sure to use the same edition textbook and workbook at each level.

Cons:

- Many elementary students (especially dyslexic or dysgraphic students) will prefer a write-in workbook to avoid introducing copying errors (You can work around this; see page 182)
- Students who have trouble with remembering the last chapter's concepts may need to supplement with a Daily Math Review
- Students will need to find a new program in 8th or 9th grade for high school math
- It's expensive to print out if you choose to do that; using a laser printer or commercial printing service will often be less expensive than ink jet printers

Beast Academy / Art of Problem Solving (mastery)

Pros:

- Many children enjoy the comic book style of the textbook in the elementary series, Beast Academy
- It's aimed at having children self-teach
- It's for enthusiastic and intuitive students (the authors say for "good" math students)
- Other students might still enjoy the program and work successfully at a slower rate and still finish high school math requirements
- The program continues through middle school and high school with the Art of Problem Solving books
- For those with internet access, there is an active online community of students and teachers

Cons:

- In 2106, the series was not complete (additional books are planned for grades 2 and 5; series 3, 4, middle school and high school math are complete)
- You will need to teach math on your own without a textbook or use a different program for first and possibly

second grade math, although this does give you a chance to discover if your students are intrigued by and intuitive about math

- The mathematics is generally at a higher level than usually taught in schools, and some parents have difficulty teaching it
- Some children find the difficulty of the program discouraging rather than challenging

Saxon Math (spiral)

Pros:

- This is a comprehensive, well-tested program that is extremely popular with homeschool families
- It is available to buy as a complete Homeschool Kit, which includes scripted lessons for the teacher to read from in levels 1-3
- Teaching materials, workbooks, tests, and solution manuals are all available
- Saxon Math covers grades K-12, and success in one book means the student is ready for the next
- Books 5/4 and beyond emphasize self-teaching
- There's an alternate series for books 3-5 for students who don't do well with self-teaching
- There's an alternate series for high school, so that students working at a slower pace are still able to complete geometry by the time of college exams
- Book sequence can be matched to students' needs; see page 190 for details

Cons:

- This program is heavily algorithm-based, so students may not gain the conceptual understanding that they might with mastery-based programs
- There are a lot of drill and review problems each day; some students may find it too slow a pace
- The complete program is the most expensive of these four

Table 11: Sample Math Program Prices, 2016

	3rd Grade	Additional Student	Prealgebra	Additional Student	Includes tests?
Singapore Common Core	$76.30	$38.80	$107 (includes solution manuals)	$0	no
With teacher manuals*	$176.80	$38.80			no
Singapore US Edition	$60.30	$26.40			no
With home instructor manuals	$87.80	$26.40			no
Saxon Complete Kit	$126	$52.10	$112	$52.65	yes
Math Mammoth Complete	$37.50+	$0	$37.50	$0	yes
Art of Problem Solving	$108	$48	$54	$0	no

---

*   Home Instructor manuals are not yet available for the Common Core version.
\+   Factor in additional costs for printing at home or commercially.

Pacing

The important thing to remember about teaching math is to work at a pace that the student finds difficult, but not impossible. This may mean that your child's grade level doesn't correspond with the number on the front of the math book, but in a homeschooling situation, unlike a tracked school system, students can move faster and slower with the years. Some students find themselves a bit behind, and then suddenly "get it" and do two grades' worth in a year. It's more important that students understand their math than do the same math as their age cohort.

There's no need to be rigid about starting and finishing books "on time," either. Working at the correct pace may mean you're halfway through a book at the start of your summer vacation (if you choose to take one). It doesn't matter. In bricks and mortar schools, students are often rushed to finish a year's math in the time allowed or drag their heels because they could work faster. Homeschooling is ideal for many math students because they can truly work at their own pace without compromising understanding.

If you're beginning homeschooling in elementary school, thinking about high school and college right now might seem overwhelming, but I'm going to trace out the typical progression for most American schools, to illustrate that what matters most is mastery, not age/grade alignment.

There is a great deal of flexibility in math scheduling. Many bricks and mortar schools in the US use eighth grade as a catch up year. Advanced students move straight into algebra; slower students take another year over prealgebra. Usually skipping prealgebra is only offered to "fast track" students, but for homeschoolers it's also an option for students who have worked slowly and solidly through their elementary years, who really understand the math at the previous levels, and can move straight from the end of "seventh grade" math at the end of eighth grade into high school math in the ninth grade.

Saxon Homeschool Math Sequence

Most of the math programs I've mentioned here follow the same sequence no matter at what pace your child works, but the Saxon Homeschooling book order depends on how successful your student is at each step of the way.[135] Here are the possible courses of study:

Table 12: Saxon Sequences

Elementary School

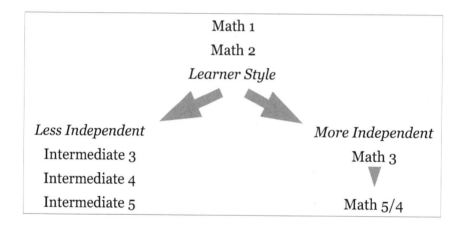

Math 1

Math 2

Learner Style

Less Independent

Intermediate 3

Intermediate 4

Intermediate 5

More Independent

Math 3

Math 5/4

Middle School

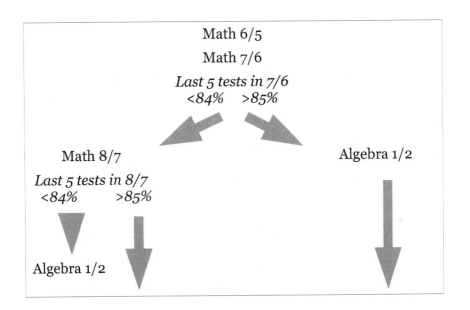

Math 6/5

Math 7/6

Last 5 tests in 7/6
<84%   >85%

Math 8/7

Last 5 tests in 8/7
<84%   >85%

Algebra 1/2

Algebra 1/2

High School

Begin 9th grade or older	*Begin 8th grade or younger*
Algebra 1 (4th ed)	Algebra 1 (3rd ed)
Geometry	Algebra 2 (3rd ed)
Algebra 2 (4th ed)	Advanced Math *(1st half)*
Advanced Math *(1st half)*	Advanced Math *(2nd half)*
	Calculus

College Expectations

- **Very selective colleges** for science, math, engineering majors: four years high school math, through calculus as a minimum

- **Very selective colleges** for liberal arts majors: four years high school math, through precalculus or calculus as a minimum

- **Most other colleges** for science, math, and engineering majors: four years high school math, through precalculus as a minimum

- **Most other colleges** for liberal arts majors: three years of high school math, through algebra 2 as a minimum

- **Many state universities** have more stringent requirements than their own state's high school graduation requirements – be sure your student understands college requirements before dropping math

- **Students who don't finish** requirements by the end of twelfth grade shouldn't feel themselves automatically disqualified from studying the sciences: if science is their passion, and colleges require precalculus, why not take an extra year to finish it up?

- **Drive, enthusiasm, and passion** for a subject will often take students farther than quickness, and many students discover the "point" of mathematics when it is in service of something they do care about, whether that be sciences or engineering

Table 13: Sample Math Sequences, Grades K-12

Grade	Singapore	Mammoth Light Blue	Beast/ AOPS	Saxon Traditional*	Saxon Integrated
1-2	1a, 1b	1a, 1b		1	1
2-3	2a, 2b	2a, 2b	2 a-d (due 2018)	2	2
3-4	3a, 3b	3a, 3b	3 a-d	3	3
4-5	4a, 4b	4a, 4b	4 a-d	5/4	5/4
5-6	5a, 5b	5a, 5b	5 a-d (due 2017)	6/5	6/5
6-7	6a, 6b	6a, 6b	Prealgebra	7/8	7/8
7-8	7a, 7b	7a, 7b	Intro to Algebra	8/7	8/7
8-9	8a, 8b (Algebra 1)	*Algebra 1 or Math 1*	Counting & Probability Geometry	Algebra ½	Algebra 1 (3rd E)
9-10	*Geometry or Math 2*$^{+}$	*Geometry or Math 2*	Intermed. Algebra	Algebra 1 (4th E)	Algebra 2 (3rd E)
10-11	*Algebra 2 / Trig or Math 3*	*Algebra 2 / Trig or Math 3*	Precalculus	Geometry	Advanced Math
11-12	*Precalculus*	*Precalculus*	Calculus	Algebra 2 (4th E)	Advanced Math
12	*Calculus*	*Calculus*	*Advanced Calculus*	Advanced Math	Calculus

---

* My name for the programs; not theirs. "Traditional Pathway" and "Integrated Pathway" reflect the terminology of the Common Core. Saxon's original program is "integrated;" the newer one is "traditional."

+ Singapore ends at 8b; Mammoth at 7b. Italicized titles in later grades reflect the US Common Core sequences rather than a particular program.

Notes on this Sample Schedule

- There are many other options for homeschool math, but I've limited my list to those which are both widely recommended and are available in hard copy books, as online materials are difficult for many rural homeschoolers with limited internet, and even families with fast broadband may wish to limit screen time.

- This sequence reflects the American system; British students will find that the end of US Math 3, AOPS's Intermediate Algebra, or halfway through Saxon's Advanced Math equates roughly to GCSE level; Calculus equates to A-level. Long-term British homeschoolers may find these programs helpful despite a slight difference in topic orders because of the teacher support; short-term homeschoolers may prefer to work with their local schools.

- Using the programs in either grade listed will complete the usual high school program and complete geometry in time for American college testing such as the PSAT, except for some Saxon students. See page 191 for the best Saxon path.

- To study math, science, or engineering at a very selective college, students would need to study each level at the earlier grade listed, apart from Beast Academy/Art of Problem Solving, where either track completes calculus in high school.

- Following a schedule a year behind the grades listed will complete most state requirements for high school graduation.

- Singapore's non-Common Core offerings 1a-6b, followed by New Elementary Math 1-4 (available in the UK, Singapore, and secondhand in the US) mesh up very well with the UK GCSE exams. (This Math 4 equates to the US Integrated Math 3. Confused yet?)

- Beast Academy and the Art of Problem Solving are aimed at students who are very intrigued by and intuitive about math. (They use the word "good" but I find that is too often equated to "quick.") In 2016, the Art of Problem Solving's Beast Academy only covered books 3a-d, 4a-d, and 5a. Other books in the series are due soon.

- Math curricula are not a long-term relationship. It is perfectly possible to switch back and forth between programs, as your children change and develop. Almost all the programs offer placement tests, which will help you find a suitable entry-point.

- Most high schoolers will find it easier to follow one pathway (Traditional US or Integrated), but it is always possible to change between publishers.

- Respectable programs will offer extensive samples online to help you choose. However nothing compares with actually trying the programs.

- Many programs also offer kindergarten math, but none assume prior math instruction in the level 1 books.

- Two other programs, Teaching Textbooks and Math-U-See, are also very popular among homeschoolers. Many students find these programs provide ample preparation, but it appears that their scope is not at the same level as the programs listed above. However, it is always possible to mix and match programs, so a core of Teaching Textbooks or Math-U-See could be easily supplemented in order to cover the full depth of the courses listed above. This extra depth may not be as important to students planning on studying liberal arts in college.

After finishing Singapore 7b, we moved across to Exeter Math, which covers high school math in four PDFs, Math 1 (mostly algebra), Math 2 (mostly geometry), Math 3 (algebra 2, trigonometry, and precalculus), and Math 4 (calculus). Most students will take more than a single school year over Math 3 and 4. Exeter Math teaches math in an unusual way – it's discovery learning problems, stacked in a logical way so that students learn ideas in order without realizing it. It's a hybrid of all the philosophies: discovery learning, direct instruction, mastery and spiral. There are no textbooks, no boxes of algorithms and formulas, and most important for homeschoolers, no answer key. This last may prove to be the deal breaker for us, and we will perhaps move across to the Art of Problem Solving or Saxon for the end of high school math. However, Exeter Math 1 and 2 have been very successful in our family.

Table 14: Common Core Math Schedules

US Grade	Traditional	Integrated	Accelerated Traditional	Accelerated Integrated
7	7th grade math	7th grade math	7th grade math plus	7th grade math plus
8	8th grade math	8th grade math	Algebra	Integrated I
9	Algebra	Integrated I	Geometry	Integrated II
10	Geometry	Integrated II	Algebra 2 & Trig	Integrated III
11	Algebra 2 & Trig	Integrated III	Precalculus	Calculus or Precalculus
12	Precalculus	Calculus or Precalculus	Calculus	Calculus

- Traditional programs include most mainstream American publishers and the new Saxon "traditional pathway" [*Algebra 1* (4th ed), *Geometry, Algebra 2* (4th ed)]

- Integrated programs include some mainstream American publishers, most international publishers, such as Singapore Math New Elementary Mathematics series and the original Saxon "integrated pathway" [*Algebra 1* (3rd ed),

Algebra 2 (3rd ed), *Advanced Mathematics* (1st half of the book)]

- Exeter Math and the Art of Problem Solving series are somewhere in the middle, with the overall emphasis following the "traditional pathway," but reinforcing concepts through integrated problems

With this much flexibility in late middle school and high school, there's no need to fret about grade-level math in elementary school. Students can easily work in a math book above or below their official grade level with no ill effects.

The More Years of Math, the Better

I believe strongly that all students should continue to study mathematics for at least three years, preferably four, of high school, regardless of their college aspirations. Many school models (A-Levels, for example) ask students to concentrate on three subjects after age sixteen, but I think this is too limiting. It means that students aren't free to change to other areas of studies later on, and I believe high school education is education for its own sake – if this is the last time your student will study mathematics, then the more math, the better.

Daniel Willingham in *Why Don't Students Like School* cites a study which shows students who continued to study math to the level of calculus remember considerably more algebra than students who merely took algebra. The key to retention is "continued practice." This effect continues fifty years out from the last math test. Willingham writes, " . . . a student who gets a C on his first algebra course but goes on to take several more math courses will remember his algebra, whereas a student who gets an A in his algebra course but doesn't take more math will forget it."[136]

Cutting off an element of education as soon as possible (usually about sixteen) may not harm students in the college /

university admissions process, but it will leave gaps later on in life. Even if your child has a strong focus towards the liberal arts or maths and sciences, she should be encouraged to study all topics throughout high school. If necessary, some subjects can be studied at a slightly slower rate or lower level to better match the student's abilities, which is far easier to achieve homeschooling than in a suburban school. I was encouraged to maintain my science and math studies, despite being one hundred percent certain at age thirteen that I would major in either history or literature. In my case, the pressure came from friends a few years ahead of me, who convinced me it was important. I studied both calculus and physics to AP level (roughly equivalent of A-Level) and majored in history at university, and I'm grateful that I kept up the math and sciences as long as I did.

Scientific and mathematical literacy are crucial in today's world. An understanding of history and appreciation of literature is equally important to science and mathematics students. High school is the big chance to gain a wide appreciation of knowledge; try not to let your students drop subjects early. Unfortunately for British students, the International Baccalaureate is not available for homeschoolers at the time of writing, as that exam rewards this sort of broad program of study.

PISA Scores & Mathematics Learning

There is always much lamentation about where the US falls in the mathematic section of the PISA exams – the international math, science, and reading tests given to fifteen-year-olds around the world. But when you look at the curricula around the world, this seems like an obvious result: countries like the UK and Singapore are a full year ahead of most American children at the age of fifteen, so it is unsurprising that they have higher scoring students, since they've had an extra year of practice.

It is far more important that your children understand math than reach a level at a certain age. Most adult math is algebra-level (usually taught in the US ninth grade) – even a physicist friend of mine reports that 95% of what he does is algebra. If your students have mastered that by the end of high school, you have prepared them for life. The more math courses they take, the better, and you should encourage them to keep taking math through high school, even if they (or you) don't love it. But if you have to slow down, slow down.

One of the important lessons in Professor Boaler's Teaching Mathematics course was that *slower in mathematics doesn't mean stupid*. She included inspirational interviews with Nobel prize winners who thought they were "bad at math" in elementary and middle school, because they were slower than their peers at understanding concepts. But once they did understand, they were the ones making the great scientific discoveries.

Teaching Mathematics

I have struggled with teaching mathematics, not because I find it a difficult subject, but probably because I don't. I find myself running out of patience in a way that I don't with foreign languages or reading and writing skills. I had trouble understanding how Helen and Anna can have difficulty understanding a concept that is so completely obvious to me. With our first math program, the assumption was that the students would figure out how to do the math on their own, to intuit their own ways of doing things. That didn't work at all. They ended up staring at the page for an hour, then I showed them how to do it, and then they did it, and the next day, they could remember nothing.

At first, I thought perhaps the fault was in Helen and Anna for not being able to figure out the ways of doing things on their own – so many authors promote "discovery learning" or "problem-based learning," and suggest that students will learn things better if they figure out the lesson on their own, but once we switched to direct instruction with Singapore Math, mathematics became much less of a battleground.

Techniques of Direct Instruction

Doug Lemov, in his book *Teach Like a Champion,* advocates direct instruction for teaching mathematics. He describes a technique he calls "I / We / You."[137] First, the teacher explains a concept. Singapore's text book has illustrations and examples to guide you through the explanation. Then, gradually, control is shifted towards the student. At the next example, the teacher can say, "what's the next step?" and take some input from the students. After that, the students do more and more, until the control shifts entirely to the student, and the final problems are done independently.

(In some homeschool programs, the teacher is replaced by a book, DVD or online lecture. The "I / We / You" still applies, whether the "I" is the parent, textbook sketches, or cartoon monsters.)

Elementary School and Early Middle School:

Independent work:

- Warm up: daily math review (5 easy problems, each acting as a refresher for prior concepts)
- Practice drill: math facts on an app, spread sheet, or flash cards

Together work:

- Lesson: go through the lesson in the Singapore textbook, using manipulatives to illustrate the ideas, child and parent discussing and doing the work together
- Practice: go through the practice problems in the Singapore textbook, with the student holding the pencil, parent watching to help with misunderstandings

Homework:

- Independent Practice: Student does exercises in the Singapore workbook over 1-2 days

- Parent corrects the work as soon as possible after completion
- Student reworks any problems that caused difficulty (on the same day, or the next day, depending on time and quantity of problems)

By Late Middle School

- Students work through math assignment on their own (1-2 hours)
- Morning meeting to go through problems and other ways of problem solving (This is optional, but it is a very good way of developing problem solving abilities, but it will work best with more than one person doing the problem set)
- Students work through review and math facts independently as necessary

Don't worry, I didn't latch onto this system of doing the work until rather late in elementary school. I did a lot of very ineffective teaching in the early days.

The Singapore textbook has explicitly done problems, followed by half-done problems, followed by practice exercises. I found it worked best if I watched my children work through the first couple of textbook exercises, so as to catch errors right away. A discovery learning advocate would certainly object to my looming over the children as they problem-solved, but when I left them to their own devices, they merely became frustrated. As Lemov points out elsewhere,[138] correction that happens right away is far more effective than correction that happens after a student's already done a sheet of problems the wrong way.

After the math lesson and once Helen and Anna had done and checked all the practice problems, I asked them to do another subject (or math review) before doing the day's workbook assignment. The idea here is to get some spacing between using the ideas. Homework isn't just because schools can't finish everything in the day (although sometimes it is used that way). The idea of homework is that you practice the concept in school, then several hours later have another go at it. This is far better than waiting until the next day, with a whole twenty-four hours to forget. When you're homeschooling, it doesn't make sense to assign homework – we want to get school done all in one chunk as much as possible – but I have found it is a help to take a bit of time between math instruction and the math exercises, to turn the exercises into "homework" that should be finished with no outside assistance if possible.

I made two big mistakes in early mathematics teaching. First, I moved to "abstract thinking" too early. Most younger children aren't ready to deal with learning what 8 + 4 equals. They should spend a long time simply solving the problems using manipulatives. Although I used the Cuisinare Rods (discussed on page 210) to explain the ideas to Helen and Anna, I pushed them to do the math workbook without the rods too soon.

The second mistake I made was more widely applicable to all grades. When a concept seemed easy to me, I didn't go through it in the textbook – I'd quickly show Helen and Anna how to do it, but then after a problem or two, they'd ask me for help, and I'd help them on one of their workbook problems, and maybe the next one too, and by that time they'd almost run out of problems to do. This affected Helen the most, and is probably why Anna was able to catch up with her in math. I was skipping the "I" and "We" part of the teaching and stealing from the "You."

After his description of the "I / We / You" method, Lemov writes:

> Often students are released to do independent work before they are ready to do so effectively. They are asked to solve a problem before they know how to do it on their own. They're asked to infer the best solution by "inquiry" when they have little hope of doing so in an effective and efficient way. . . . In other classrooms, by contrast, students get very good at watching their teacher demonstrate mastery without ever learning to do it on their own. . . . The answer of course, is not to choose between the poles of direct instruction and independent thinking but to progress from one to the other.[139]

Helen and Anna's early math instruction was just that – on the two poles, with no progress from one to another. The Miquon Math program asked them to figure it out, which didn't work, and my version of the Singapore Math was too much of my showing that I could do it, not gradually giving over responsibility to them.

One of the best tips I've received for teaching math is "don't hold the pencil" from Marina Koestler Ruben's book *How to Tutor Your Own Child*.[140] When a child asks you for clarification on something you've already explained (so she's on the "You" stage where she should be doing the problems herself), let her keep the pencil, and simply ask questions to lead her to the right answer. (It's a quick retreat to the "We" stage of instruction.) For years, when Helen or Anna would ask me for help in math, I'd seize the pencil, demonstrate the right way of doing it, and probably not do any better a job of explaining it than I did in the first place. The end result was simply to deprive them of one of their problems in the problem set, rather than to teach them anything.

Why Memorize Math Facts?

Having math facts in one's long term memory is critical for ease of mathematical processing and manipulation. Students' working memory has a relatively fixed capacity, and if it's filled with the hard work of figuring out math facts, there is not a lot of space remaining for complex mathematical manipulation. Students' long-term memory is almost infinitely expandable, so with regard to math facts, it's best to store them in long-term memory and *recall* them, rather than *calculate* them each time. I didn't really understand the reasoning behind this until we'd left elementary school behind and begun algebra: working through algebra presumes a great deal of background mathematics. Students who have math facts firmly in their long term memory will have an easier time with algebraic manipulation and *seeing* problems clearly.

One of my weaknesses as a teacher is spending too much energy on the "school" portion of the day, and not enough on the "parent" portion: I wasn't insistent enough on repetitive drill in the early years and Helen, particularly, is suffering from that now. If they'd been at school all day with someone else, I'm sure I would have drilled them mercilessly in the evenings, but it simply didn't happen.

Before your children start memorizing the multiplication tables, however, it is important that they understand the principle behind multiplication. Do a lot of multiplication with manipulatives before starting the memorization work. I don't remember ever studying the addition and subtraction facts myself – I think I picked them up through repetition – but it is worth studying addition, subtraction, and division as well as the multiplication tables.

By the end of fourth grade, students should know all their basic math facts. Anna achieved this, and Helen managed to escape fourth grade without having learned her times tables or basic addition facts. She understood the principles behind both, but the answers were not in her long-term memory. I didn't take this seriously enough at the time, and it made algebra much harder for her.

Make sure your children know their basic facts, whether you work with flash cards, Kumon books, or other methods. If you are using a computer to review, use either a program that allows mouse clicks on an on-screen numeric pad, or have the student work directly with a plug-in numeric pad if she hasn't learned to touch-type.

We tried all manner of drilling tricks for the multiplication tables, from magic squares (you make a 10 X 10 or 12 X 12 square with the numbers written in random order across the top and left side, and have the students fill in the products in each of the boxes), printed out sheets of problems (25-50 a day), commercial flashcards, the times tables set to rap music (none of us liked that), the spreadsheet program I wrote for them to generate random facts, a few online flash card programs, and a math facts app.

My second grade teacher, wise in the way of eight-year-olds, told us that when everyone in the class knew the times tables, she would cancel the afternoon's school, and we'd all walk downtown for an ice cream cone, her treat. Every student in the class was desperate to learn. The ones who picked it up easily drilled the others at recess, standing in line for lunch, and waiting for the bus.

Friends have found the Kumon math program very helpful. As a result of the half hour of daily drill, their boys are fabulous at mental math, and this gives them a big head start on other students, especially those who have been allowed to use calculators in their early school years.

Seeing their success, I tried to save money and copy this approach with a spreadsheet on the computer that randomly generated problems for Helen and Anna. This seemed to work with Anna, but failed completely with Helen. In retrospect, I would have done much better to stand over her with a stopwatch. I think there was too much daydreaming and not enough focus when I let her work on it unattended, with the result that every time she did a problem, she worked out the answer anew, without it going anywhere near her long-term memory. At twelve, Helen went back to the spread sheets, and this time worked better. In her case, it helped her to read about the effects of having the facts in her long-term memory versus figuring them out anew each time and cluttering up her working memory. But at thirteen, she still didn't know her times tables or math facts with enough automaticity, so we found an app to help her drill. It's been a slow struggle.

In order to quickly solve their math problems and manipulate algebraic problems with ease, students should memorize all their multiplication tables up to 12 * 12, plus all the division in reverse, all the addition facts up to 20 + 20, and all the subtraction from 25 – 25 on down.

Calculators?

I believe that students should not use calculators as part of math class until they are in higher level math, as it will harm the acquisition of the basic math facts. In order to progress in math, they need to know, instantly, the answer to 7 X 6, not how to punch in 7, X, 6, and = into a calculator. There is no benefit in "accustoming" them to using a calculator for these easy steps.

Once they get to precise square roots, log functions and trig functions, then a calculator is necessary. But the calculator should be saved for this sort of work, not the basic calculations, and it is not such a complicated tool that they need practice with it (at least until they begin using graphing calculators).

Many students enjoy playing with calculators and exploring their possibilities. This can help their understanding of math and shouldn't be discouraged.

Improving Your Mathematical Knowledge

Being able to teach math well requires conceptional knowledge – understanding the whys behind the systems or algorithms for doing the math, not just how to do it. For example, can you explain to your children why you need to stagger the columns in two-digit multiplication? In her recent book, *Knowing and Teaching Elementary Mathematics*, Liping Ma[141] describes a shocking number of American elementary school teachers who were unable to articulate why the second row of the solution needs to "step in one place" or even why a zero makes an appropriate placeholder.

Many American math programs teach the algorithm:

```
    23
x   34
----
    92
+69
----
   782
```

without using the placeholder 0

```
    23
x   34
----
    92
+690
----
   782
```

Of the teachers Ma interviewed, a large number thought the zero was confusing or didn't belong, and couldn't explain *why* the answer isn't:

```
    23
 x  34
 ----
    92
 +  69
 ----
   161
```

[The 0 does belong: you're not multiplying the 23 by 3; you're multiplying it by 30. And when you're multiplying 23 by 30, you can rewrite that to 23 X 3 X 10. And any number times 10 is the first number with an extra zero on the end.]

Liping Ma contrasts the approach of Chinese and American math teachers; the book's weakness is in very small survey samples (23 American teachers and 72 Chinese teachers). Although the American teachers were described as "better than average,"[142] a 23-teacher sample allows one or two teachers to significantly skew the results. Discussing "percentages" with such a small cohort is a bit dubious, but the anecdotal power of her discussion is certainly persuasive: her Chinese teachers are far more mathematically literate and flexible, which allows them to both explain ideas and resolve students' confusions far more efficiently.

I have searched for books and articles for parents, teachers, or tutors that breaks down the underlying mathematical concepts in a clear way, but I haven't found one that I absolutely love. There are numerous textbooks for aspiring teachers out there, but all are over $50, some considerably more. *Arithmetic for Parents* by Ron Aharoni is an economical option for teaching grades 1-6.

The best way I've found to refresh my memory is watching the Khan Academy videos. You can download them and save them to your computer for later viewing at [www.khanacademy.org]. Khan Academy covers math from kindergarten to college level in short, clear, low-tech videos. I found it even more useful in elementary math than middle school math, because it showed me how to teach ideas in an age-appropriate way.

Salman Khan does a good job of explaining the thinking behind the algorithms, and, for example, in the Basic Addition video, shows two important ways of demonstrating addition, using both counters (avocados in this case, but it could be anything) and a number line. This can be helpful if you're looking for different ways to teach what is 4+7. Cuisinare rods (accompanied by a ruler, which can double as a number line) are also helpful tools at this stage. Some students find watching the videos themselves helpful; in our case, I used it to help my teaching in the early years, and my children watched it directly when they had troubles in later years.

In the middle school years, you may also benefit from a reference book like *Everyday Math Demystified* by Stan Gibilisco, but, although the book is very good for discovering the reasoning behind all those laws and properties, it is laid out for someone who has already studied the math, rather than teaching it the first time.

When I started reading about the importance of explaining the concepts of math as well as the algorithms, I felt a frisson of fear: I've done it all wrong. Often, when faced by Helen and Anna's elementary school problems, I was unable to see them without the lens of algebra, and I didn't know how to teach them. One way I could have improved my teaching in late elementary school is by doing all the problems the day before, so I made sure I knew what was expected (and the age-appropriate way to solve it) before teaching. Having them simply get a wrong answer and my trying to solve it in front of them led to me to take algebraic short cuts that came to the right answer, but were way beyond their level. Making my own solution manual would have given me the time to explore simpler ways of solving the problems without the time pressure of trying to explain it to them.

On the other hand, using the very conceptual Singapore Math books worked well, even if I wasn't a particularly able teacher. I posed Ma's question about multiplication to Helen at age twelve, and she immediately answered that she was multiplying by "30" not "3" and that's why the zero was there, so it looks like I got away with it, at least as far as multiplication is concerned. Spiral programs, however, will require far more linking by the teacher, because the pieces of the concept appear at different times in the school year, and the teacher is the one who has to explain their connection.

If you choose to go with the Singapore Math US Edition, the one weakness I have found is it doesn't teach many of the common mathematical terms that will be found in US exams, such as the distributive law or isosceles triangle, and so on. (The new Common Core Singapore Math, now available for grades seven and eight, by contrast, has ample use of mathematical vocabulary, as does the Singapore-style Math Mammoth program.) Liping Ma notes that one of the strengths of the Chinese teachers in her study is their ability to weave ideas and vocabulary into the lessons, and their use of formal mathematical vocabulary and precise definitions when doing so.[143]

A look at the Common Core Standards will give you an idea of what vocabulary your students are expected to know in each grade, and a mathematical dictionary such as Thomas Sidebotham's *The A to Z of Mathematics: A Basic Guide*,[144] will help you with vocabulary and terms you'll encounter in teaching math.

Elementary School Math

The first step is play with math. Cuisenaire Rods were terrific – they're a set of wooden sticks in different lengths from one cm to ten cm, with a dedicated color for each length. It's worth buying a set per child if you have two in early elementary school at the same time, but if there's a couple of years between them, a single set will suffice. (Of course, they can built more interesting things with two sets.) In addition to teaching math, the sticks worked better than Lego in our family, because with Lego, it was always a struggle to convince the girls they should tear apart their masterpiece and put it away, whereas with the math sticks, it was simply a matter of shoveling them back into the box. These sticks are most useful in the early grades, but we continued to use them well into middle school to illustrate concepts like volume and area, although I did give away one of the sets to a younger cousin.

If you live remotely or are homeschooling while traveling, it's a good idea to stock up on math books. Every other subject can be delayed or created on the fly if you run out of material, but if you have the next year's worth of math stowed in a locker, then your children can go as fast as they want to. Once you know you like a program, it can be worthwhile to buy workbooks for younger siblings at the same time to protect yourself against future revisions that might mean buying new textbooks. (However, it may be that a different style of book or program will suit that younger child better, so bear that in mind as you make your shopping lists. If the extra workbook is a small additional price, then it can be worthwhile; if it's a significant dent in the budget, then it may be better to make sure your later children thrive with the same sort of instruction.)

If you hate a math program, change it. I tried to stay on too long with Miquon Math, and it simply did not work for us. Every book and article I read said it was marvelous and would turn my children into great mathematicians, and so I really wanted it to work. I'd invested money and time in the program, and it was hard to just throw it away. This is another strength of homeschooling: if your children are in a bricks and mortar school, they have to follow whichever textbook the district adopts; as a homeschooler you're free to choose between a hundred different programs. One will suit you. We had a very positive experience with Singapore. Some people hate it. The same goes for Saxon, Beast Academy, and Mammoth.

If we were going to do it again, I would still use Singapore, but I would begin a daily math review in the second grade, such as *Daily Common Core Math Practice* from Evans Moor Publishing. It will still be helpful even if you aren't doing a US Common Core curriculum, although you might have to skip an occasional problem if your children haven't covered the topic yet. For example, most of the US begins the use of negative numbers several grades ahead of the Singapore Primary Mathematics US Edition.

For math testing at this age, I tried using the Singapore placement tests, but they were long and hard, so I used past editions of the NY Regents Exam to keep an eye on Helen and Anna's progress. Later on, I switched to using the Saxon tests alongside Exeter Math.

Don't forget to keep using manipulatives when teaching math. They are very useful throughout elementary and middle school for illustrating concepts. If you don't have them already, I recommend:

- A set of colored poker chips
- 1 X Cuisenaire rods basic set

- ETA hand2mind Base Ten blocks (orange)
  - 20 X 10 rods
  - 10 X 100 flats
  - 1 X 1000 cube

(I've suggested orange, because the 10 rod in the basic set of Cuisenaire rods is orange, and that helps keep things consistent.) These rods, flats, and cubes allow the students to see numbers and understand them. They also have a place in study of history and other subjects: when we were reading about the Holocaust in fourth grade, we went out onto the road alongside the sea with chalk and bicycles and measured out how long a strip of thousand blocks we would need to get to 12 million people: 1.2 kilometers.

Middle School Math

Students may leave the manipulatives behind as they begin middle school math, but don't insist. Some students who found math easy in the early years will see a sharp transition at about fifth grade; some students will find it works the other way around. Usually problems become far more complex at about this age, and require a multi-step process. It could be time to revisit basic math facts, if they weren't firmly learned in the earlier grades, or it could be time to slow down, and make sure students understand the questions.

Middle school math is often when students transition to non-consumable textbooks and copying the work out into a separate notebook. Many students are ready for it at this stage, but some will still find that copying the problem leads to mistakes. Using a program such as Math Mammoth or Singapore's paperback textbooks mean students could cut out problems and paste them to a larger page to give themselves more space. This accommodation won't affect their college testing, as exams such as the SAT have space to work out the math on the test booklet, although the answers do have to be transferred to a scantron (fill in the bubble) answer sheet.

As time went on, Helen and Anna were able to transition from a direct instruction math "lesson" with me to working independently with the math book, checking a few practice problems in the answer book, and then working through the rest of the problems on their own. For a while, we ceased to have a math class scheduled in our day, as they worked independently through the books. I did find I had to keep tabs on what they were doing, otherwise they could easily go a week without doing math. When they changed to Exeter Math, without a solution manual, math class came back into the picture, as we met every morning to discuss the problems and work out solutions to the ones we couldn't answer alone.

Table 15: Math QUEST for Complex Problems

> **Q: Question.** What is being asked? Circle it in the problem.
> **U: Understand.** Understand the steps that will be needed. Are there any intermediate answers you'll need to solve the problem?
> **E: Estimate.** What's a logical answer to the question, roughly?
> **S: Sketch & Solve.** Sketch out a drawing of the problem if possible. Solve the problem.
> **T: Test.** Test your answer. Does it pass the logic test? Can you work backwards and come up with the original parameters?

On the Road Homeschoolers

Want to travel light? Math Mammoth Light Blue Curriculum followed by Exeter Math will give you a complete math syllabus entirely in PDF files for use on a tablet or laptop. Anna found it difficult to work from an onscreen PDF, so we printed out a couple of weeks' work at a time so she could use hard copies.

Singapore Math and Beast Academy also let students travel fairly light with paperback textbooks and workbooks. In elementary school you will need both the textbook and workbook ("guide and practice" in Beast Academy's terms), but in middle school both programs transition to a single textbook. Singapore continues to offer a "workbook," but these are supplements, rather than a core part of the program as they were in elementary school.

For those traveling with reliable internet, the Art of Problem Solving middle and high school books are all available as "online books," which makes carrying them around simple for anyone with a laptop or tablet (and it can even work on some phones).

Your student may work faster or slower than you expect. When we set sail, I made sure I always had the next year of Singapore Math on board so as not to run short when I was out of reach of the US mail. With the publication of Math Mammoth Light Blue, students who are working in other programs can easily have the next Math Mammoth or two stored on a computer or tablet, and at $37.50 a level, it's not a prohibitively expensive insurance policy.

Supplemental Math for Afterschoolers

As I warn in the introductory section about Afterschooling, parents will need to use some caution with proceeding ahead in mathematics. You don't want your child to spend day after day in school, bored in mathematics because you've sped ahead of the local school and there are no opportunities for advancement in its particular curriculum. Many schools now offer the possibility to advance in mathematics, particularly after seventh grade.

Even if your children don't have the chance to move ahead in mathematics, however, there are many opportunities for enrichment, so that they can learn more and understand more at each level, without spending the school day bored and miserable.

Basic math facts are probably the first and most important element of afterschooling mathematics. It is an enormous benefit for future mathematics to have these basic facts at one's immediate recall, because, as discussed elsewhere, it frees the working brain for processing and understanding. Kumon-style workbooks, a quick daily sheet on basic facts, flashcards, or simply quizzing on a car ride or while doing chores, can help elementary and middle school students with their math.

Find out as much as you can about the math program at your child's school. Look at the kinds of work they do in class: is the program based on discovery learning or direct instruction? If it's direct instruction, is it a spiral or a mastery program? (Discussed on page 179.)

Both discovery learning and spiral direct instruction programs can suffer from a lack of tying together conceptual ideas. You could balance their school programs with a conceptual review program such as Math Mammoth Gold review worksheets, offered when they are confused on various topics or as review during the holidays. Khan Academy videos can also help tie the concepts together.

Mastery direct instruction and sometimes discovery learning can suffer from a lack of skills practice: once a topic is left behind, many (most?) students forget the ideas of the old concept while trying to grapple with the new skill or idea. For students in this type of program, a daily math review with different kinds of problems such as Evan Moor's *Daily Math Review* or *Use It! Don't Lose It!* will help students retain ideas from previous units.

For children whose school programs seem to do a good job of blending conceptual understanding and daily review, logic and number puzzles, and discovery learning problems such as those offered on Dan Meyer's Three Act Tasks or in the Art of Problem Solving can help develop mathematical skills and understanding without making it difficult for students to fit in with the day to day math class. Teachers now call this *differentiating* instruction – a way of avoiding math tracking (which can make it impossible for students to ever move out of their tracks), yet still inspire and challenge those who understand the material quickly.

And if your child really wants to work ahead of grade level, like the ones who begin calculus at age 12? I'd strongly consider homeschooling, and if that's not possible, make sure they have a good book to read in math class, and a teacher who will let that happen.

Afterschooling Ideas

My math class is too hard: Look at individual topic reviews from Math Mammoth, either the Gold Series by grade or the Blue Series by topic. For a comprehensive summertime re-take, look at Mammoth Light Blue to cover the whole curriculum again. Another option is Teaching Textbooks or Math-U-See, which aren't as comprehensive as Math Mammoth, but could work extremely well for a summer or weekend course.

My math class is too easy: Look at Beast Academy/the Art of Problem Solving or Singapore Math's Challenging Word Problems.

I can't remember last month's topics: Look at Daily Math Review / Use it, Don't Lose it! Daily reviews or Mammoth Gold series by grade level for more comprehensive coverage of individual topics.

I can't remember the math facts: Flashcards are the old standby, apps do the same thing on a smartphone or tablet, and Kumon math pushes more complex mental calculations.

And for the early grades: at home play with manipulatives such as poker chips, Cuisenaire Rods and ETA Base Ten blocks.

Mathematics Summary

- Use manipulatives and sketching to illustrate mathematical concepts
- Use Daily Math Review to maintain learning and avoid the necessity of "relearning" concepts
- Memorize basic math facts to free the working memory for thinking about concepts
- Save calculators for 7th and 8th grade
- Don't rush – it's more important to understand than to be in the "right" math book

History

Why Study History?

History is our story, the record of our triumphs and tragedies. Our capacity to remember, describe and transmit our story is what makes us human. In the last 20,000 years, we have evolved slightly in important ways,[145] but we would recognize and know those people of the past if we met them, we could learn their language, we would have similar hopes and dreams and fears. Without history, everything is new and surprising. History is context; history does not predict the future, but it narrows the possibilities.

I have heard people suggest that it is unnecessary to know history now that we have Wikipedia, but how do you know you need to look something up if you don't know it ever happened?

The best way to learn history is to immerse yourself in the study of it – through historical television dramas, movies, historical novels, and by reading history, particularly one that takes both a social and political approach. Children love learning what other children's lives were like, and it can be a great way to introduce the study of history. But even older students (and adults) like their history to read like a novel.

In teaching history, remember the twenty-year rule: do you want your students to know this fact in twenty years? Vaguely from the past, I can remember a phrase on a history test: Harley-Smoot, probably because Smoot is such a fine name (or maybe I just remember it from *Ferris Bueller's Day Off*). I can't match it with any detail, however. It turns out to be Hawley-Smoot Tariff. Does it matter? I can always look up the name (as I did writing this paragraph). What is important is that a protectionist tariff after the 1929 crash contributed to the Depression. That information can have real value in times of future economic trouble. I'll save that for high school. In elementary school, the Depression is Dorothea Lange's haunting photograph of the "Migrant Mother." In middle school, it is *Cinderella Man* and *The Grapes of Wrath*.

The most important thing in elementary and middle school history is to encourage students to care about history, to see history as something that happened to real people whom they find interesting. That caring and that interest will fuel the hard work it takes to learn history at a more complex level, but chances are, your children won't find it hard work, because interest will turn the page for them.

Teach History as a Story

History is interesting. Remember that. I have heard countless teenagers drop out of history classes as soon as they can, moaning *history is boring!* If your students think history is boring, you're not teaching it right. In many countries, world history is often condensed to a single year of secondary school – no wonder far too many students hate it: endless memorizing of dates and key terms, thousand-page textbooks, dry, dreary accounts of dead men.

I became a student of history because:

I heard stories from one grandfather about World War II in the Pacific; I read the scrawled handwriting of my other grandfather of his days in the Irish Rebellion. My grandmother told me stories about her parents, gold and silver mining in Nevada. She showed me pictures of her mother in a long, flowing white dress amongst the dirt and dust of a mining camp.

I found gravestones in a field.

We drove past a house with a Trojan Horse in the lawn, and my father filled the next hour with a recap of the *Iliad* and the *Odyssey*.

My mother invariably made me go to bed in the middle of the Disney feel-good movies on Sunday night, but she would let me stay up and watch any of the British historical dramas on PBS: *The Flame Trees of Thika, A Town Like Alice, Danger UXB.*

My father read me stories of King Arthur, Finn MacCool, and Cuchulain.

I read books – *Little House on the Prairie, Carry on Mr. Bowditch, Tale of Two Cities.*

I accepted bribes – "We'll take you to see *Excalibur* if you first read *The Once and Future King* and a *Connecticut Yankee in King Arthur's Court.*"

Children's stories, television, books, and ivy-covered ruins: that is how I came to love history. Old photographs, journals, and a gold buckle I could mark with my fingernail made me a historian.

In addition to being a pleasure, learning about history through stories is also the best way to remember it. In *Why Don't Students Like School?* Daniel Willingham has an entire chapter entitled, "Why Do Students Remember Everything That's on Television and Forget Everything I Say?" The answer appears some pages later:

> The human mind seems exquisitely tuned to understand and remember stories – so much so that psychologists sometimes refer to stories as "psychologically privileged," meaning they are treated differently in memory than other types of material. . . . [S]tories are easy to comprehend . . . stories are interesting . . . stories are easy to remember.[146]

History is simply a collection of stories. In more advanced work, history is analysis and interpretation of these stories, but the story is always the basis: *what happened?*

Writing in *American Educator* magazine a few years prior, Willingham explains why textbooks aren't memorable:

> People find material presented in a story-format more engaging than if it is presented in expository text no matter what the topic. . . . History is a natural story; it has the four Cs —causality, conflicts, complications, and character —built in. Yet, history textbooks rarely use a narrative structure. For teachers, an important way to make use of story in history is through the generous use of [general

audience] books that treat history as biography, historical fiction, or a narrative.[147]

The study of history is a good example of *thoughtful learning*, discussed in the How We Learn chapter. It is far easier to learn material presented as a story – or as analytical history with a lot of story woven around it – than it is to learn the same material in the condensed, often dry language of the history encyclopedia or textbook, even if you have to read a hundred pages to learn what takes ten pages in a textbook. The hundred interesting pages will feel like nothing to those with reading stamina; those ten pages can be a slog for even the best readers.

Teach History Chronologically

As a child, I didn't realize that history was a school subject. Elementary and middle schoolers in the United States usually don't attend history classes; instead, it's jammed in with "Social Studies," which seems to give it carte blanche to be completely muddled. A tradition of sorts has arisen of what is studied when – listen to the Core Knowledge Standards for history:

First graders study early world history, modern Mexico, and early American history through the Revolution and westward expansion. Second graders jump back to Early Asia, followed by Modern Japan, followed by Ancient Greeks, then the US Constitution, the War of 1812, and onward to the Civil War in American history. Third graders study Ancient Rome, the Vikings, and in American history dive backwards to the Colonies. This makes no sense at all. It's almost as if someone took a deck of cards of "important historical moments" and shuffled them.

Even once I formally began studying history in high school and college, it was still scattered. I wound up with subway stop knowledge: a pretty good understanding of each station, but only in relationship to itself. I never came above ground to see the roads between. I never knew how closely tied the French Revolution was to the American Revolution, because I studied them years apart. We spent hours memorizing dates, but we never saw the whole timeline – maybe we were supposed to reshuffle it all in our heads with our solid knowledge of dates (but of course, we couldn't, because we forgot the dates right after the test).

English children generally study "history," but often that history is restricted to British or European history. The world is too interconnected these days for such a narrow view. From the National Curriculum:

Years 1-6:

- Stone Age/Iron Age Britain
- Rome and its impact on Britain
- Anglo Saxons and Scots
- Vikings in Britain
- Local history
- Ancient Civilizations
- Ancient Greece
- A non-European Society

Years 7-9

- Britain 1066 - Present (4 units)
- One non-British society or issue[148]

That's it. No grappling with world affairs, or with much of the histories of Asia, Africa, or the Americas, and little discussion of twentieth century history.

California does a bit better once students reach middle school, providing an integrated program:

- Ancient Civilizations (6th grade)
- Medieval / Early Modern Times (7th grade)
- US History and Geography (8th grade)
- No standards for 9th grade
- Modern World History (post 1800) (10th grade)
- US History & Geography (11th grade)
- American Democracy & Economics (12th grade).[149]

This is a good set of topics, although I object to US history being taught in a vacuum. As the US involves itself more and more with international affairs, the lack of understanding of the history and geography of the rest of the world is increasingly dangerous.

I much prefer Susan Wise Bauer and Jessie Wise's internationally-focused schedule described in *The Well-Trained Mind*. Students read about world history three times throughout their school days:

- Ancient History (to 500 CE) (grades 1, 5, 9)
- Medieval History (500 - 1650 CE) (grades 2, 6, 10)
- Early Modern History (1650 - 1850 CE) (grades 3, 7, 11)
- Modern History (1850 - 2000 CE) (grades 4, 8, 12)[150]

I do have some disagreements with Wise and Bauer on their techniques and methods of studying history, but the schedule and time frames are superb, although some students might benefit from holding off on adding history to the school schedule until second or third grades, or even later.

If you are completely free to schedule your own program, you can follow this with any number of students, because, as Wise and Bauer point out, it makes no difference where students are in the schedule at the end of high school. If you have to meet local secondary school requirements, or plan to return your children to conventional schooling for high school, you can tweak the schedule to allow you to mesh with that program. (Many places which allow homeschoolers considerable or complete freedom in the early years require more compliance in high school. Even so, it is usually possible to take classes in different years from the typical schedule as long as all the graduation requirements are met.)

It is of course impossible to fully appreciate world history in a mere four years (never mind the foolishness of trying to cram it into a single year of high school – usually age 15-16 in the US). But the three cycles of four years has a better chance of creating students who understand the sweep of history than, say, California's schedule of a single pass beginning in the sixth grade.

The Thomas B. Fordham Institute rated all the US states' history requirements in 2011, and amongst the 50 states and Washington DC, found only one that rated an "A" and eighteen which earned "Fs."[151] The authors write:

Whence do these follies and shortcomings arise? Mostly, it appears, from most states' ill-considered decision to embed history in "social studies".... [T]he single greatest failing of state standards in this field, even the best of them — is that history content remains obscured by the social studies fog.

This is a problem for two reasons. First, because social studies is a mix of several disciplines, and because social studies standards are organized according to themes or strands rather than content or chronology, teachers and students fail to grasp *why* history unfolded as it did. Second, because social studies practitioners focus more on skill acquisition than knowledge acquisition, students wind up with little true understanding of history.[152]

History happened in chronological order on our three-dimensional planet. Geography, climate, and the behavior of the country next door (or often on the other side of the world) has profound influence over the way history unfolds, and thus for the clearest understanding world history and geography must be studied as one overarching course, rather than splintered into either nations or themes.

Curriculum-setting adults seem to think that if it didn't happen next door, young children won't be interested, but that couldn't be further from the truth. American social studies standards usually begin with citizenship and national symbols. For example, California's Standards (and Fordham gives them an A-) for kindergarten cover learning to be a good citizen, the state flag, bald eagle, and Statue of Liberty, as well as "Thanksgiving, Independence Day, Washington's and Lincoln's Birthdays, Martin Luther King Jr. Day, Memorial Day, Labor Day, Columbus Day, Veterans Day, ... Pocahontas, George Washington, Booker T. Washington, Daniel Boone, and Benjamin Franklin."[153] Here begins the disjointed and scattered understanding of history, and the lack of connections which turn history into a boring collection of flash card facts instead of a rich, twisted story.

Young children are fascinated by the ancient past: hunter gatherer societies, early farming, the development of writing; they want to know how people used to live. Which would you rather do:

color in the state flag or look at dioramas of early humans and then try to recreate it in the park?

The secret to teaching history is to tell it like a story. Later on, in middle school and high school, there is room to add to (not replace) the stories with a textbook to link the ideas and stories, but for elementary school students, the story is everything. If you look back at the list of California standards for elementary school, the holidays and the examples of heroic people as explained at the first and second grade level can only be superficial. (We're talking about five to seven-year-olds, after all.) Studying the background of these US holidays provides fodder for first grade teachers counting down the days until the actual holiday, but what does it teach students?

The dire state of the standards for teaching history is to the advantage of homeschoolers however. In most places it is very easy to get around the standard requirements and do more than is required, if in fact homeschoolers are required to meet government standards.

Helen and Anna's first years of studying history were somewhere between the scattered knowledge of Columbus, Washington, and Pocahontas and a good story of history. At one stage, I did teach Helen and Anna about Columbus, reading to them from *The World of Columbus and Sons* by Genevieve Foster. Day after day we read, while they wriggled in boredom, and they wound up loathing Columbus and his entire century. I never did finish the book, and Helen and Anna invented a game where they would build elaborate driftwood ships, push them out into the bay and throw rocks at them for target practice. The game, to this day, is called Columbus Ships. I wish I could claim that it developed from my careful teaching of both sides of the story, but it was just bad teaching. I did learn something, however: if I was bored by part of their school, then it was long past time to change direction.

I adopted Wise and Bauer's strategy of teaching history three times after reading about it in Rebecca Rupp's *Home Learning Year by Year*,[154] and we did two years of history through a combination of texts before I found the third volume of Susan Wise Bauer's series *The Story of the World: History for the Classical Child*. The *Story of the World* series is, despite appearances, a textbook of sorts, and covers world history in four volumes, pitched roughly at grades one through four, although families with several children can easily use it a year or two later with some of the children, and a year earlier with others. Anna did find the fourth volume (*The Modern Age*) hard going in grade three. I was still reading the books aloud; it was difficult for her to comprehend rather than a challenge of her reading skills. Bauer recommends the book for fourth graders and above only.

If you don't want to use a textbook, you could easily organize a four year cycle of world history, reading trade books, organized around roughly chronological topics, especially if you have regular access to a good library. For example, you might choose to concentrate on nine or ten topics a year such as:

Table 16: Sample History Sequence

Developing Civilizations (to 500 CE)

- Becoming Human
- Human Migrations / Hunter Gatherers
- Early Farming
- Ancient Civilizations Mesopotamia & Egypt
- Ancient Civilizations China & India
- Mediterranean 2000 – 800 BCE
- Mediterranean 800 BCE – 500 CE
- Beginnings and spread of global religions (Hinduism, Confucianism, Buddhism, Judaism, and Christianity)
- Han China
- Your ancestors

Mobile vs. Sedentary Nations (500-1600 CE)

- Ancient Civilizations Americas
- Ancient Civilizations Sub Saharan Africa
- Nomadic Tribes invade Europe
- Origins and Spread of Islam
- Christian Empires / Crusades / Protestantism
- Tang / Song China
- Nomadic Tribes invade Asia / Yuan / Ming China

- European countries invade Americas ("Columbian Exchange")
- Renaissance Europe
- Your ancestors

Europe vs. the World (1600-1850)

- Sea Trade & Warfare: beginnings of a global world
- Qing China
- Mughal India
- European colonialism
- Africa enslaved
- US Revolution / Constitution
- French Revolution / Napoleonic Wars
- Industrial Revolution Europe
- Japanese Isolationism
- Your national history

The Global World (1850-2000)

- US Slavery / Civil War
- Social Effects of Industry
- WW I
- Economics: Capitalism and Communism (Great Depression / Ukraine Famines)
- WW II
- Cold War
- Middle East
- Latin America
- Cultural Changes: liberalism & fundamentalism
- Your national history

It was a struggle to limit this list to ten points each year. It is not a fixed list, of course; it is certainly biased, but I have tried to highlight cultures and ideas that still have influence in today's world. My own failing in history is usually to try to cover too much in a given year: I want Helen and Anna to know everything! But choosing to cover fewer topics in more depth can be a very good idea. Your local library, a book of timelines, and a historical atlas can help you put together a history of the world that will teach your children far more than jumping from ancient civilizations to Modern Mexico, and back again as the Core Knowledge Foundation (and many state standards) suggest. I have borrowed the dates from Wise and Bauer; the selections could be easily shifted by a few hundred years, especially if you fall behind or get ahead in the elementary school cycle.

Teach History and Geography Together

In the UK, students commonly take a geography course, which covers political geography and earth science. In the US, geography is seldom taught as a distinct subject, but it is nevertheless usually isolated from the study of history. I find political geography dull and hard to remember without the context of the people moving across it and interacting with it.

Instead, we studied political geography and terrain as part of history and separated geology into science. History makes a lot more sense if you look at the way the rivers, seas, mountains and prevailing winds intersect with the lives of people, and geography is easier to remember if it is studied in context.

However geography is taught, typical programs for young children will involve coloring in maps and labeling countries. I haven't found that coloring in teaches anything. The act of coloring takes up the mind; the shapes colored are meaningless. Instead, I asked Helen and Anna to copy maps right from the beginning. Often their sketch maps didn't bear much relationship to the world itself, but the act of drawing commits the copied map to memory far better than coloring it in.

Because we were using the *Story of the World* series as the basis for our history lessons in elementary school, Helen and Anna were able to copy the blackline maps from the book. If you choose not to use that series, you can find blackline maps online or purchase them as packets. We found that it was much easier in elementary school to copy blackline maps, but by middle school, both Helen and Anna were comfortable working from the more complex maps in the *Times Atlas of World History* or their textbooks.

Historical Sources

In history, we talk of three kinds of sources: *primary, secondary,* and, for lack of a better term, *tertiary.* Primary sources are what working historians rely on: the original documents, whether they are official (charters, agreements, constitutions), domestic (diaries, tax records, oral histories), or published books from the era (Homer, Plato, Shakespeare, Thomas Jefferson). Students should be encouraged to do some research and analysis of primary sources and most certainly to read some of the great books of our past.

Historians use the *primary* sources to produce *secondary* sources. These range from articles, to books for an adult audience, to monographs for other historians. These secondary sources are the best way to teach history, because they provide a wealth of details, personal stories, and interesting information that makes history memorable and important. The difficulty with these books is they usually require strong reading stamina. Many students won't be ready to read them until high school, which leaves middle school as the most difficult age to source good history materials. There is a new trend, however, of journalists writing secondary source histories, often based on historical monographs and their own primary research, or the research of others, creating very readable, exciting books about the past, which bring history alive for middle school and older students.

Tertiary sources are the third level, the least lively, the least readable, and often the least accurate. Here are your textbooks, which often are simply based on other people's (or other committee's) textbooks; here are your encyclopedia entries, your Wikipedia, and the summary histories of a region (or sometimes the entire world). These tertiary books have an important place in the study of history, but more as a spine, or a general reference book, rather than the sole source of information.

Historians know that every writer of history has an agenda; they are acutely tuned to perceiving bias. Students are seldom taught to take the same approach. It's obvious to most readers that primary source material will have biases, but it's important to remember that secondary and tertiary materials are also the product of the author's worldview, which is often simply better disguised than it might be in primary sources. Unfortunately, most sources of historical reading available to students fall into one of two poles: absolutism or relativism, with no guidance as to how to understand or even detect those biases. Most history books for children, particularly in the early grades, fall into the absolutist category: jingoistic platitudes about how marvelous one's own country happens to be. Adults who were brought up with absolutist history bristle with anger at relativistic history which asserts that all cultures and mores are equally valid. Real history takes a middle ground; it reports the good and the bad, and it evaluates and argues.

For his article, "On the Reading of Historical Texts," Samuel Wineburg analyzed the thinking process of professional historians versus that of strong American high school students, and discovered that this awareness of bias was one of the key differences in the way the two groups perceived historical writings. The students had not yet learned to mistrust their textbooks.[155] Without realizing it, I taught Helen and Anna this key skill early on, because many of their books were so biased that I couldn't let the notions stand.

Throughout our history program, I have emphasized broad conceptual knowledge over rote memorization of dates and people. I'm not convinced that *remembering* the minutiae of history is as important as having the global picture of the past ten thousand years. I do think that *reading* that minutiae is important, however. Too many history books take a "dates are boring" approach and it can be very difficult to figure out what date the author is talking about. Dates are important. They cost nothing to read, as they are a very fast shorthand to fixing events in your mind. Authors too often think that students will simply glaze over if they use a date, but I don't think that's true. Readers do not necessarily retain the dates, but knowing the date helps them make better sense of the paragraph, which may help them better remember the ideas in the paragraph. Remembering exact dates, however, has a high cost for most people: flash cards and drill.

It is obviously important to be able to access the exact dates of events (and probably even the name of the Hawley-Smoot tariff) if you are writing an essay about it or preparing for a high school or college level exam. But out in the real world, out at the twenty year test time frame, what most people need to know is roughly when the Depression was, what caused it, and how it affected people. John Steinbeck and Dorthea Lange will stay in your mind for those twenty years; Hawley-Smoot will not.

Polls of teenagers report a dire state of their historical knowledge. How many World Wars were there? And to American teenagers, "When was the Civil War?" (Of course many American students fail to know that most countries have their own civil wars to think about, because Americans often only study United States history, and that in isolation.)

I've focused on dates to within a thousand years before 1000 BCE, to within a century from 1000 BCE to 1700 CE, and a dozen exact dates for subsequent years. If students know a few exact dates by heart, they should be able to put other events in order around them. As with anything else, really remembering the dates does not happen without revisiting the information, again and again, year after year.

There is a card game called Timeline, with pictures of historical events on the cards – the object of the game is to put the cards in chronological order. One doesn't need to know the exact date, but one needs to know what event influenced others and how they fit together, which is pretty much my ideal. The dates your students remember will be memorable events, particularly ones that can be captured with a visual image. Other important events, ideas, and issues of the time can be organized around those key dates. For example, children can easily imagine themselves in the place of the African-American children taking tentative steps towards the Little Rock High School, while the National Guard kept back the screaming white protesters. Those experiences have more resonance with most children than the stories of adults from the same time period.

Of course students will need to know far more dates if they decided to take exams, such as the SAT Subject Tests or AP History in high school, but a dozen firmly known dates is more than most adults have. In many schools, there are so many dates that one needs to know, so many date tests, that students cram them all, then forget them all.

You can also ask students to choose their own dates. When speaking of the past century, what do they think will be remembered in one hundred more years? A thousand? You can choose to focus on inventors and technology when it is first discovered (through biographies) or you can look at a technology once it reaches a critical mass, perhaps when it affects roughly a million people. (After trying to do this, you will realize why most people focus on inventors: it's easy to say when Alexander Graham Bell invented the telephone (1876), but very difficult to pinpoint when it became ubiquitous technology that affected the entire country, although that is clearly more significant historically.) Sorting out which dates to remember can be a valuable exercise – it forces students to think about what is influential, what is important. There's no exact answers to what should be remembered, and the act of sorting will help them remember both the dates they choose and the ones they reject.

Teach Civics in the Present Tense

If you are teaching history chronologically, yet trying to meet local standards for social studies, you may find that you are missing out on civics and current events. Fortunately, these are the easiest subjects to *unschool.*

With elementary school students, for example, you can make sure you vote if you can, explain the reason you've chosen the way you have, yet try to explain why others might choose differently. Similarly, talk to them about current political issues, have an opinion, but see if you can work together to argue the other side of the issue. This will help students know what you believe, but also instill the idea that the other side has a valid point of view. This will help them later on when they need to write essays and debate, because an argument works best if you understand the reasoning on the other side.

In early middle school, I once asked Helen and Anna to make a list of five issues that they cared about. They made their list, did preliminary research on each one, and started working on what they thought was an argument for their side of the issue. But after a few days of exploratory writing and research, I gave them the actual paper assignment: write this paper arguing the other side. Their research ended up teaching them a great deal, and although neither changed her mind about the issue at hand, they could argue it far better with an understanding of the other side than without it.

Once students reach middle school, encourage them to follow current events in their own time (or school time if they aren't doing it on their own). We have found *The Week* magazine to be an excellent source of news, because it uses excerpts from a wide variety of newspapers and magazines, which ends up giving the reader a much more balanced viewpoint than most of the national media.

Learning History

While I don't worry too much about specific dates, I do want Helen and Anna to remember the general sweep of history. Sometimes it can be quite discouraging – I'll think that we went over something quite carefully, yet four years later, it seems as though we've never discussed it before.

However, re-learning the information a second time is more effective than simply learning it for the first time. It can drive the teacher nuts, of course, but according to the *What Works Clearinghouse*, the earlier study is not wasted. A second iteration of history makes the ideas much more likely to stick in the long term, more so than if you skip elementary school history and simply teach it once in middle school. As the US Department of Education's Practice Guide for "Organizing Instruction and Study to Improve Student Learning" notes, "Although this initial forgetting may be discouraging, ... research shows that even when students cannot recall previously learned material, reawakening of the knowledge through reviewing is more easily accomplished than was the original learning."[156]

It's never too late to start, though! Even if you miss the first iteration of history, teaching chronological, story-based history is far more likely to stick than scattered, fact-heavy history. For all teachers, but especially those who only have a couple of years to teach history, it is critical to revisit important events.

In elementary school, I did not worry too much about how much the children retained. I read them a selection aloud, and when I finished, they wrote a summary and copied a blackline map. Despite the detailed coverage, however, the only subjects that Helen and Anna remembered well four years later were the ones which they studied in other genres – especially reading novels or watching movies.

In middle school, I was more concerned that they remember the events. The daily reading remained much the same, although they transitioned to reading the selections themselves; the daily summaries, map sketching, and sometimes note-taking or outlining of complex material continued as before. Every six weeks or so, however, I added a paper-writing assignment to the mix. This achieved several things: improved memory of the history readings under discussion, a more nuanced view of history through the analysis, and finally, practice in paper-writing, citations, and so on.

Because we were in the wilderness much of the time, Helen and Anna did not do much in the way of individual research. Research can certainly benefit retention (children remember what they've discovered for themselves far better than what is told to them), and it is a useful skill on its own, but paper-writing and historical thinking can be taught without access to a research library or the internet.

Historical paper-writing without outside research uses the assigned books as sources. When using only assigned readings to write history papers, the writing can be broken down into two genres: describing and discussing. In the early days of middle school, I assigned one or the other; by late middle school, their papers both described events and discussed the results.

Description papers can be simply a more polished version of the daily summary. This type of paper teaches students how to describe events and acts as a revision of the information, which makes students more likely to remember the details. The US Department of Education's Practice Guide on "Organizing Instruction and Study to Improve Student Learning" recommends quizzes to help students retain information, but then notes that the best kind of quiz is either fill-in-the-blank or short answer (not multiple choice).[157] Description papers are like a short answer quiz, but they are perhaps a more powerful learning tool because the work is student-generated rather than a response to an outsider's question.

Discussion papers presume that the reader knows what happened and instead ask why or how it happened, or perhaps compare and contrast two different historical events and outcomes. I found I didn't need to teach comparisons and critical thinking; instead, when the children had a repertoire of historical stories, they naturally started comparing them. "This is like . . . ," "This is different from . . . " They started seeing trends and themes on their own. You can of course give students an example of this kind of thinking if they aren't doing it on their own, but once they have a good background, and if they've worked with the material on paper, they can often generate these comparisons on their own.

Another valuable suggestion in the above Practice Guide is to "space learning over time:"

> To help students remember key facts, concepts, and knowledge, we recommend that teachers arrange for students to be exposed to key course concepts on at least two occasions—separated by a period of several weeks to several months. Research has shown that delayed re-exposure to course material often markedly increases the amount of information that students remember.[158]

This revisiting can occur with quizzes, but it can also happen through short papers pulling together a week's reading, through a novel or movie about the time period. It can also occur over the dinner table, bringing the conversation back to events studied months before. Every act of recalling makes the memory more indelibly etched in the mind.[159]

Sample Stages of History Learning

Grades K-2: Teacher reads a history story aloud; students draw a picture and gradually transition to drawing a picture, writing a caption, and finally writing a short summary of the story and sketching a blackline map.

Grades 2-4: Teacher reads a history story aloud; students write a half a page summary and sketch a blackline map.

Grades 4-6: Teacher or student reads a history selection aloud; students either write a half page summary or take notes and make rough outlines of the material, make map sketches. Every six or eight weeks, students write 1-3 pages either describing what happened in a historical event, or discussing why and how something happened, or compare and contrast two events.

Grades 6-8: Students read assigned readings from textbook and adult-level history books. Textbook readings should be accompanied by notes or outlines, followed by a four or five line summary of the most important ideas. When working with longer books, students can take notes and annotations, and should write a short summary at the end of the book with a bibliographic entry (see page 149 for more on citations). Map sketches continue to be valuable learning tools in geography and understanding how and why events happened as they did. Every six or eight weeks, students should write a 3-5 page paper (topics can be assigned or free choice), with or without outside research. Most papers should contain description, discussion of the events and perhaps a comparison with another event in history. In addition to discussing the reading, papers could also discuss the relationship of historical novels or films to the actual events of history.

Questions at the End of the Chapter

Throughout history learning, I have generally not asked Helen and Anna to answer the questions at the end of the chapter in their textbooks, although I read them when prepping for discussions. We frequently end up talking about the same issues, or they discuss them on paper in their summaries and essays, but when the questions are self-generated they are much more likely to be remembered.

Writing about history is an excellent example of how writing can benefit and enhance learning. The old style school writing assignment – where students wrote an outline in response to a question, and then wrote down a five paragraph essay regurgitating what they already said in the outline – gives students the opportunity to show the teacher what they knew at the start of the paper writing project, but they don't have the chance to learn or puzzle out new ideas and problems. Tackling history questions as a paper, writing over several days allows students to pose tougher questions and then tease out the answer. Students should be *writing to learn*[160] rather than simply demonstrating knowledge. Grappling with ideas, and searching out evidence for those ideas is far more exciting than simply regurgitating the "right" answer to the questions at the end of the chapter, and students will remember far more of it several years down the line.

It can be tougher for the teacher to evaluate this sort of writing. (Teachers' manuals often come with multiple choice questions and answers to the fill in the blank questions; they can't help you with papers that answer student-generated questions.) The most important thing for the teacher to look for is *evidence*. Does the student support his statements with historical facts that have proper citations and come from reliable sources? It will be easier to evaluate the paper if you've also done the reading, but sometimes there's too much going on, or the student will be focused on an area of personal interest, and in that case you will simply have to make a judgment as to whether the evidence suitably backs up the statements.

History discussion papers are a good time to introduce students to the great secret of professional writers: they usually write the introduction last.

Choosing Historical Readings

For homeschool teachers who may have been heard to shout "history is boring!" themselves, teaching your children is a wonderful way to learn all of those stories that you missed out on in your own schooling. Read the stories along with your children, watch the movies, find out about your family's story, or one like it if your own is lost. Read historical novels.

Narrative history books (that is, books where history is presented as a story) often make the best-seller list. Try *Mayflower, 1776, Cod, Nathaniel's Nutmeg, Longitude,* and so on. After the success of *1776*, various authors have come out with books centered on a single year: *1491, 1492, 1493, 1927, 1968.* These books capture a moment in time and bring it alive to modern readers, adults and strong middle school readers alike.

Michael Maxwell's *Student's Friend* is a useful cheat-sheet to world history, including 188 key points and terms in world history. This is *not* the way to teach history to elementary and middle school students, but it can help focus your teaching. Unfortunately, it neglects the same regions that are missed out in most US and British curricula, but it can be a helpful starting point.

Reading through *The Student's Friend*, I have found several debatable ideas, however. Like too much of history, Maxwell's points are presented as absolutes, whereas in fact there is often much scholarly debate. For example, he describes Jericho's walls as being built to withstand raiding nomads. The walls of Jericho provide a classic example of how our understanding of history evolves over time. The Biblical story relates how Joshua and his people shouted and brought the wall down. Without those stories, the ruins of the city might never have been found. Archaeologists and historians hypothesized that the walls were for keeping out nomadic raiders, and most history books present that hypothesis as fact. Later archeology revealed that only the western side had evidence of fortification; the rest of the wall hadn't blown down, it simply never existed. Ofer Bar-Yosef was seemingly the first to ask the question *why* in 1986; he hypothesizes that the wall was defense against flood-waters and mud slides, not raiding tribes.[161]

Going further back in pre-history requires even more work of the teaching parent, because scientists' understanding of our pre-history is developing faster than the pace of children's books. Every one of Helen and Anna's early books (and their high school textbook published in 2004) maintained firmly that there was no interbreeding between humans and neanderthals; recent science shows that as much as twenty percent of the neanderthal genome is distributed through human populations today. But instead of fretting about these changes, I welcome them: it shows Helen and Anna that history is an ongoing discovery, just as much as biology or astronomy. When working at the edges of science and history, I try to bring up-to-date periodicals, such as *Scientific American*, into our study. In elementary school, reading *Scientific American* meant perusing the illustrations and maps; by middle school they were grappling with the articles.

I choose to teach prehistoric humans as part of "human history" rather than as science, for the most part because it is generally not included in the biology texts, and because Helen and Anna are so interested in it, it deserves more time than is alloted in a typical science program. Similarly, I teach the history of scientific discovery as part of history; many of the ideas are now discredited, so it seems more part of history than of science.

However, it is certainly possible to teach these topics as part of science instead, and simply points to some of the artificialness of subject-area divisions in school programs.

Books We Used

Elementary School:

- Usborne Time Traveler series [grades K-5]

- World History:
    - Story of the World series (4 volumes) by Susan Wise Bauer

- National History:
    - The Story of US (US history in 10 volumes) by Joy Hakim
    - Our Island Story (Britain)

Middle School:

- World History (began using in middle school; continued to use through high school)
    - Duiker & Spielvogel *Essential World History*
    - Felipe Fernández-Armesto, *The World*
    - Numerous adult-level popular histories and historians' monographs (7th and 8th grade)

- National History (middle school level)
    - The Story of US (US history in 10 volumes) by Joy Hakim
    - So You Really Want to Learn History (British history 1066-1900 in 3 volumes) by Pace & Oulton

K-8th Grade and beyond:

- Atlas
- Times Atlas of World History

- Timelines of World History
- Dorling Kindersley books

When we began high school history, Helen and Anna complained that we were only having our DVD history lectures twice a week. "Can't we have it three times a week? Or four?" I told them how my freshman ancient history class had bored me to tears. They looked amazed. "How can history be boring?"asked Anna. This is certainly not to say that there weren't times when they found history to be extremely dull. We started out very well with Usborne's Time Traveler series, *Ancient Egypt, Rome and Romans, Knights and Castles,* and *Viking Raiders.* Both children loved these books, and were bitterly disappointed there were no more in the series. Odds Bodkin's version of the *Odyssey* inspired them. Even *Columbus and Sons* failed to dim their enthusiasm for history.

Susan Wise Bauer's *Story of the World* series is an excellent introduction for elementary school.[162] I read them aloud to the children; other families we know have had good luck with having the children read along in the book while listening to Jim Weiss's audio version of the books. The first two volumes in particular have a noticeable Judeo-Christian bias to them and have a slightly mocking air towards all other religions, past and present. They also leave out some of the more unpleasant aspects of Christianity, such as the Inquisition. Overall, however, the books are marvelous, and so I simply made sure I discussed the biases with the children. I preferred reading aloud to the audio versions, because this let me point out the problematic points immediately. After listening to me read, Helen and Anna wrote summaries of each chapter and copied the maps, and that provided 80% of our history curriculum for two years.

In the beginning of middle school, we had a gap of a couple years where *Story of the World* was too simplistic, but Helen and Anna weren't strong enough readers to tackle adult histories. I filled in the time with assigning what I thought was a very interesting textbook, as far as textbooks go, (Duiker and Speilvogel's *Essential World History*), but they found it very hard going in the fifth and sixth grades. We've compared some of the alternatives, so I think, doing it again, I would still assign Duiker and Speilvogel, but perhaps something more age appropriate, yet still challenging, will be published soon. This time with *Essential*

World History proved to be an excellent point for them to learn the techniques of reading complicated texts, taking notes, and occasionally making outlines. Initially, I worked very closely with them, in what is called "scaffolding" by reading teachers. I've discussed this approach in greater depth in the Advanced Reading – Textbooks section, page 100.

If you're just beginning homeschooling in late elementary school, you could also begin with the *Ancient Times* book in the third or fourth grade and carry on from there, gradually adding complexity and additional readings in later grades. We didn't discover the *Story of the World* series until Helen was in third grade, so we began with *Early Modern Times*. They ended up reading *Ancient Times* in the fifth and fourth grades (with a lot of other material, including *Essential World History*), and by the time they were in sixth and fifth grades, I assigned *The Middle Ages* as a "summer reading" book, and only occasionally assigned readings from it during the school year, as they were doing very well with *Essential World History* by that point.

We started our study of history earlier in time than *Story of the World: Ancient Times*, spending weeks learning how people lived pre-farming, and about the gradual spread of farming. Bauer's history books (especially the first three volumes) bring a lot of history to life by presenting it through the eyes of a child – the industrial revolution and its effect on children's lives, a native boy mining silver for the Spanish in South America, and so on. The fourth volume is much more political, and was tough going for Anna in Grade 3 (age 8-9).

There is a set of workbooks to go with the *Story of the World* series, and I know people who have used them, but I never felt the need. There was plenty to do with just the stories themselves, and I've always (even when I was seven) failed to engage with the idea that baking bread like the ancient Greeks brought them any closer to me. I was gleeful to read Daniel Willingham's take on it, when he writes:

> A teacher once told me that for a fourth-grade unit on the Underground Railway, he had his students bake biscuits, because this was a staple food for runaway slaves. . . . I pointed out that his students probably thought for forty seconds about the relationship of biscuits to the Underground Railroad, and for forty minutes about

measuring flour, mixing shortening, and so on. Whatever students think about is what they will remember.[163]

No longer will I feel guilty about my reluctance to bring biscuit making and art projects into history lessons.

Dorling Kindersley's excellent Eyewitness books on various history topics are a bit too dense for most elementary schoolers, but they are worth buying or borrowing from the library to use as illustrations of the *Story of the World* books. It is extremely hard to read the Eyewitness books straight through because there are so many interesting sidebars and illustrations. This makes it difficult to follow the narrative, and makes it a far more "difficult book" than the plain text would be on its own. At the end of eighth grade, in a bid to make space, I gave away all our Dorling Kindersley books, and I regret it, as they are still suitable at the high school level. They make a good library for children for the twelve years of their study, and are well-worth as much as you're willing to spend on them. Most libraries have a good selection if you have access.

The *Story of US* by Joy Hakim makes for fairly difficult reading for elementary school students, but it's a little bit too easy for most middle school students. (Helen read most of them outside of school when she was in the fifth grade, which is probably the right age. So perhaps if you timed Modern History to match fifth grade you could make better use of the books than we did.)

Part of the difficulty with the *Story of US* lies in all the sidebars and well-captioned photographs. It is very, very hard to read the text straight through without getting side-tracked. We experimented with reading the text straight through, then returning to the side information, next with trying to do them both in the same reading, and third, with reading through all the sidebars and photos, and then returning to the main text. This third method was the most successful. We called it "reading the distractions first."* The other problem with it is Hakim's overwhelmingly positive take on American history that borders on jingoistic. This can be used to advantage, however, as a time to look at bias and agenda in writing. Helen particularly enjoyed skimming through the books in her own time, although she loathed using them as a source for classwork.

---

* We must not have been the only family to find this difficult; K-12 publishes a Concise Version of Hakim's series.

Throughout our study of history, I have made heavy use of historical novels and films. I generally don't call these movies or novels part of "school," but I make an effort to stock up with those that fit our time period. I don't stick to any particular rule about watching/reading them before or after we've studied the time period – watching them a bit early acts as a teaser for the next subject; watching them later acts as a review. I look for movies and novels that are written for the children's age groups, and generally avoid the junior versions of adult classics, as these are usually dismally bowdlerized, and of no particular value for the student, apart from giving them a dull, SparkNotes-like introduction to the plot.

You can check on the historical accuracy of novels and films online. I have found dozens of websites with rankings of "the best historical movies" with historians providing commentary about what's right and what's wrong in the films. Even if there are historical errors, the movies or books can be a valuable resource, provided the students have enough background to spot the mistakes, and you make a point to discuss them (this discussion doesn't have to happen during school time). Even Disney's delight in ahistorical, buxom heroines (Pocahontas, Mulan, Brave and so on) can be turned into a history lesson.

As your students begin middle school, choosing history readings can be more difficult, particularly if you don't have access to a strong library. A high school textbook can make a good spine to support topic readings (such as adult popular histories), novels, and films. If you are going to use a textbook for history, you need to choose very, very carefully. Most manage to utterly destroy the excitement and romance of history and bleed it dry. Middle school textbooks are usually written at fifth-grade level, and thus don't offer any possibility of advancing reading levels. Choosing a high school or AP level history book generally means the arguments will be more sophisticated, the vocabulary more challenging, and often there are fewer mistakes, although you will have to be prepared to spend more time helping students read the book than you would with easier texts.

In early middle school, we combined William Duiker and Jackson Spielvogel's *The Essential World History* with Bob Pace and Nicholas Oulton's *So You Really Want to Learn History Volumes 1-3* (British History from 1066 to 1900) and a lot of movies and novels. Dorling Kindersley books bought for the first round of studying world history came back out and again provided the illustrations, and we also made use of the *Times History of the World* (an atlas of historical maps and their significance) and John Teeple's *Timelines of World History*. When we reached time to add the history of the United States (annoyingly, most American textbooks of World History do not include the United States, as if it exists in a vacuum), the children were ready for more sophisticated reading. I turned to the many popular histories for adults; there are dozens available that fit my requirements of being well-researched, but not overly scholarly. I tried to buy as many of these as I could on the Kindle, so that we could each have a copy. It might have been better for our discussions to have hard copies that let us write in the book (although you can highlight and make notes in most ebook readers), but it would have been much more expensive.

When I started using Duiker and Spielvogel's *Essential World History*, I was too caught up in the notion that I had to have everything in chronological order, and I ended up spending a lot of time trying to order reading assignments that way. In retrospect, I should have just started at the beginning. Their telling of world history is not strictly chronological, but it's very close, and they have made careful choices about what goes where, and we should have followed their argument.

Essential World History is divided into Prehistory to 500 CE, 500-1400, 1400-1800, and 1800-1945 and 1945-present. Combining the last two chapters turns it into a four year survey of world history from fifth grade to eighth grade, although you may need to supplement it with your national history.

So You Really Want to Learn History is pitched at British Year Six through Year Eight, so it is a genuine middle school text. It is a lot easier reading than *Essential World History*, and the type of questions at the back are exactly the sort to be expected on the British exams (ISEBs and GCSEs), and indeed, Volumes I and III were written by the ISEB's chief exam setter. This is the only book which made me break my rule of never asking the questions at the end of the chapter, because they tended to be thorough and thought provoking. Like all textbooks, the *So You Really Want to Learn History* series suffers from too much condensing – it could easily have ten times as many pages – but the choice of material is thoughtful, and if one had access to a library for further research, it could prove a spark for studying in greater depth.

While I agree with much of the criticism lobbed at textbooks in general, I couldn't find another way of teaching the first two or three years of the middle school four year World History survey. I spent hours online, searching for historian's comments about textbooks, and in particular looking for a single or double author textbooks, not those written by a committee. Duiker and Spielvogel were well reviewed, and we've been pleased with the way it reads, although it is always good to take a break and read something like Bernard Cornwell's *Azincourt* (be warned, many historical novels have have adult situations; you might want to pre-read them). And it's worth noting that Helen and Anna remember far more about Agincourt than anything else we studied that year.

Before your students move on to lengthy adult-level popular history books, they need to have high reading stamina. If they can't read the book within a week or two, while keeping up with (most) of their other schoolwork, then it's too early to introduce it. The best way to develop this stamina is by open reading, where they read books of their own choice, at their own speed, without a lot of "school activities" tacked on to the reading.

Reading on a Kindle or some ebook readers has the advantage of the instant dictionary, where unfamiliar words can be looked up without budging from one's chair. Although we vastly prefer the non-backlit Kindles for reading in general, it is helpful to have a computer or tablet to view the maps and pictures, as the graphics don't do well in the small, non-backlit format.

The closer history books come to the present day, the more dry and crammed they feel. There is simply too much to say about recent centuries. A full chapter devoted to Mesopotamia can read well and have a good narrative flow, but when authors try to fit the twentieth century into a chapter, it feels like a rushed outline.

The other problem with world history textbooks published in the US is they tend to not mention the United States. Most Americans take US history in the 11th grade, and if they take world history, it is a one or two year survey in 9th and 10th grades. When Helen and Anna were in seventh and eighth grade, we changed to Felipe Fernández-Armesto's *The World* history text (which is considerably harder to read than Duiker and Spielvogel, but also more thematic, so it draws in more comparisons between the countries). Although *The World* is significantly easier than the rest of Fernández-Armesto's writing, it is tough going for seventh and eighth graders; I don't think I could have used it between fourth and sixth grade. It is organized for a one or two year survey course, and as such, it would be extremely hard to absorb all the information. Instead, we read a chapter every couple of months, and then follow up with an immersion in histories, novels, and movies, taking a month or so between chapters. This pace is far more manageable than the typical high school survey course covering a chapter a week.

Alan Brinkley's *The Unfinished Nation* is one of the better American History text books I've found, but like all the others it suffers from not having a global perspective. I dip into it occasionally while plotting out their history assignments, but I seldom actually give them reading from the book. I think it will be more useful in high school, however. (This is the first textbook since Joy Hakim's *Story of US* that I've found the girls reading on their own, dipping in at random for pleasure reading while we've been studying Ancient Greece in high school.)

By the time of seventh and eighth grade, when students are reading more trade books, the history textbook becomes the least important item. We spent a long time traveling without the textbooks during that time, and both Helen and Anna did just as well in their history reading and writing with trade-books on their Kindles, alongside a Kindle copy of *The New York Times Guide to Essential Knowledge,* which gave them a short sketch introduction of historical events before delving into the trade books.

GoodReads or Amazon reviews were my best sources for finding suitable novels and general audience history books for late middle school history. I emphasized finding well-researched, extremely readable, adult-complexity books, rather than trying to achieve a comprehensive coverage of world history.

Short-term Homeschooling

If you are homeschooling for only a year or two, you have a great deal of flexibility in how you approach history. Try to find out what history lessons are like in the school you left behind or the school your children will be returning to.

Does the school have a strong, detailed syllabus, so that missing out on a year or two will leave big gaps in history?

(Californians missing seventh grade will never have the opportunity to study the middle ages again.) If that's the case, then you will want to cover the same time period as the school you left behind, and your children's school may be able to provide you with some books and materials, which you can supplement with trade books, historical novels, and films.

Does it have little teaching of history at all? Or only an emphasis on national history? In that case, I would focus on world history, and make the decisions on what to cover based on how old the children will be. *Story of the World* has enough material to be a year's syllabus in each book for younger elementary school students; older elementary or early middle school students could read two books a year, and cover a comprehensive survey of world history in two years. Older middle school students may find the early volumes of those books too simplistic; they might appreciate something more difficult such as *Essential World History,* or perhaps a timeline of history, an atlas, and a good collection of historical trade books, biographies, novels, and films to tell the story.

If you are only homeschooling for a year or two, the most important thing in history class is to develop an interest. Of secondary importance is developing an understanding of the sweep of history and geography and how they fit together. Writing short summaries of textbook chapters and trade books will help students retain information, and is always valuable; the writing of history papers can be put off until your child returns to school.

For middle school students, however, it is worth having a conversation with the social studies or history teacher in the school they will be returning to if you can find one who is supportive of your plans to homeschool. If certain conventions of studying history, such as taking notes, outlining, or writing essays will be covered in the years you are missing and not be revisited, then your child will definitely benefit from covering those skills while you are homeschooling.

Afterschooling History

History is one of the best subjects for afterschooling, because there's no limit to the depth children can learn and still fit into the classroom. You can choose to either match your program to the years under study in school, or look at a completely different time period to avoid the risk of your children glazing over in class.

All of the books and movies suggested for homeschooling history work as afterschooling study, although depending on your child's school work load, it may be better to just read and watch, rather than doing the short summaries and history papers.

History Summary

- Teach elementary and middle school history chronologically
- Use writing to expand understanding
- Textbooks help with the big picture, but trade books are more memorable
- Use literature and film to complement historical readings

Science

Many homeschool parents find science the most daunting subject. We know how to read well enough to help our children learn to read, our math is good enough for helping with basic math, and in history, we can read along and answer questions, even if the region under study is new to us. But science? Even scientists sometimes have trouble answering some of the wild and wonderful questions posed by the average three-year-old.

Science is a topic where homeschoolers, afterschoolers, and parents of preschoolers can often benefit from doing their homework. A nature walk with a four-year-old is the easiest time to introduce the concepts of evolution, time and distance of space, the history of the earth, and the nuclear fusion powering the sun. When the children were young, I immersed myself in reading about science. It wasn't a conscious "I'd better mug up for homeschooling" decision, but perhaps unconsciously I'd realized that I was answering too many of their questions with "I don't know."

Every child is a scientist. The trick is retaining that interest and enthusiasm through the school years. The fill-in-the-blank worksheets found in many elementary schools, the rote memorization without the whys in middle school often serve to deaden scientific interest.

Very few elementary school teachers have a science degree – a mere *four percent* in one 2000 study had degrees in science or science education. The report continues: "Fewer than one-third of elementary teachers reported feeling very well qualified to teach each of the science disciplines. . . . Three quarters of science teachers in grades K–5 have had 15 or fewer hours of science-related professional development in the preceding three years."[164]

Fifteen hours. Can you devote twenty minutes a day to reading about science for the next month and a half? How much can you learn in that time? How many books can you read?

I had the answers to some of Helen and Anna's questions, but not all of them. I read Bill Bryson's *The Short History of Nearly Everything,* revisited early evolution with Carl Zimmer's *At the Water's Edge* and Neil Shubin's *Your Inner Fish.* Remembering that Carl Sagan's *Cosmos* on TV had taught me more about science than most of my elementary school science classes, I watched Neil deGrasse Tyson's remake. Richard Dawkins's *The Ancestor's Tale* is a lengthy foray through evolution. Gabrielle Walker's *An Ocean of Air* taught me about the atmosphere. While Helen and Anna were in elementary school, I watched two Great Courses programs, *How the Earth Works* and *Understanding the Universe,* filling in gaps that I hadn't studied in school. I was starting to have some answers to their questions. (I still haven't managed to get through Stephen Hawking's *A Brief History of Time.* Maybe by the time they graduate from high school?)

I bought over a dozen DK Eyewitness books, both for the children to look at the pictures, and for me to do my own reading: *Plant, Whale, Ocean, Rocks and Minerals, Dinosaurs, Prehistoric Life, Evolution, Universe, Human Body, Early Humans, Fish, Weather, Bird,* and *Insect.* A friend gave us an Atlas of the Night Skies. When they reached late elementary school, I started stocking high school level textbooks as reference material. (We usually didn't have internet access; it may not be necessary to have so many textbooks if you do.)

For older children, having a paper subscription to *Scientific American* or other adult-level science magazine is a great way for them to internalize the idea of the scientific method, and the way science advances in increments, with occasional overturnings of ideas, and the excitement of the advancement of knowledge. They don't even have to be avid readers of the magazine to have this effect. Read it yourself and leave the magazine lying around: just looking at the cover will help them understand how science works.

There were three strands to my teaching of science: unschooling, hands-on experimentation, and book and video learning. The three strands continued from pre-school to elementary school through middle and high school, although by high school they were doing less unschooling and more book and lecture learning; in elementary school the emphasis was reversed.

Jump ahead for your age group. The coverage is equally applicable to full-time homeschoolers and afterschoolers (although they may want to focus on a single strand at a time to lessen the time commitment). Science is an excellent topic for afterschooling, as the average US elementary school can only spare twenty-five minutes a day for science education.[165]

Early Elementary School

The basis of my plan for science education came from Jerome Bruner back in 1960: "We begin with the hypothesis that any subject can be taught effectively in some intellectually honest form to any child at any stage of development."[166] Nowhere is this truism more neglected than in the sciences. From the time I had preschoolers who could articulate words, I was surrounded by marvelous questions.

- Where did I come from?
- Why is it dark?
- Why do I have to sleep?
- What's a rainbow?
- Why is that animal dead?
- Why is the moon out in the day?

For the first few years of school, we did not study "science." Instead, we immersed the children in the natural world, learned about the animals and environments available nearby (including gazing at the night sky), and discussed evolution, space travel, black holes, the distant stars, dinosaurs, the birds at the birdfeeder, the ants in the park, snails in the garden. Why? How? We had a library of resources – natural history guides, identification guides, science encyclopedias, natural history television programs – but no fixed schedule as to when different subjects would be studied. We did no drill, no quizzes, yet the children learned vast amounts of science, terms, and comprehended the beginning ideas of complex scientific theories.

Improving your background knowledge will also help inspire those teaching moments, off-hand comments in the middle of discussing something else, that seem to stay with students far better than organized instruction. When Anna was about four, she complained that Helen was always older than she was. Hamish said patiently, "Well, she's always going to be your older sister."

Anna said optimistically, "Not if she goes off in a rocket."

Most adults struggle with the notion that time slows the closer to the speed of light one travels, but four-year-old Anna had no problem with it; indeed she'd even extrapolated how it could be turned to her advantage. I don't remember explicitly teaching her the idea, and it certainly wasn't on the syllabus (she hadn't even started school yet).

Early on, I tried to introduce the idea of a nature journal, where the children would draw items they found in nature, and later write about them. It never worked. For some children, this would be an ideal introduction into the world of a scientist; for mine, it got in the way of playing outside. But even without this formal documentation of their discoveries, they were learning a tremendous amount. I backed off. It was my first encounter with unschooling, and I didn't trust it: shouldn't they be doing worksheets? But I looked at some science workbooks and never even bought them. All worksheets and even mandatory drawing and writing would teach them was "science is boring."

Their science education began long before they were officially school-aged. Nighttime reading sometimes came from science picture books and every living creature we saw was a subject for discussion. Watching gray squirrels, red squirrels and chipmunks in the yard was the basis for discussing food webs, ecological niches, and evolution. Different dog breeds in the park led to a discussion of artificial selection, which fed back into the divisions between squirrels. We bought the entire Magic School Bus series on eBay (the original classic series by Joanna Cole and Bruce Degen is the best, though we read all of them). We read these aloud, over, and over, and it gave Helen and Anna an excellent introduction into the big ideas of science.

We were lucky enough to spend a great deal of time in the wild, where nature played out in front of us. Animals and birds died, mated, and gave birth and hatched in front of us. The children reassembled skeletons and found mouse femurs in owl pellets, sheep femurs in the hills, seal femurs on the beach. I bought them a twelve-inch plastic human skeleton model so they could compare their findings with the human versions. I taught them the names of the most commonly found bones: femur, scapula, humerus, tibia, fibula, and challenged them to figure out what they were looking at. For entertainment, they watched the *Blue Planet, Planet Earth,* and *Frozen Planet,* over and over. When they were a bit older, we watched *Cosmos* and *Your Inner Fish.* We caught fish and trolled through the organs, investigated the stomach contents. We asked why?

Karen Skidmore Rackliffe's *Wild Days: Creating Discovery Journals* has lots of advice on how to create nature journals if you want to go that route, but I felt the idea was most useful for children living in a suburban or city home, who had to struggle to see the natural world.

When Helen and Anna were a bit older, a botanist friend came over to where they were playing with bull kelp. "Let's see what it looks like inside," she said, and cut a piece up with her pocket knife. It was a wonderful glimpse into how a scientist thinks – I wouldn't have thought to cut it up.

The *only* reason I didn't study biology in high school was because I didn't want to cut up a fetal pig. There, I've said it. My daughter may never respect me again. I was a vegetarian and very squeamish. I did not want my daughters to be limited by that same squeamishness, so they have been dissecting fish since they were preschoolers, watching and poking when they were too young to wield a knife.

Identifying birds and learning to use the identification books effectively is another thing to do with young children. I was amazed when my zoologist cousins came on board the boat for a couple of weeks: after a short time, they knew more about the local birds than we did, even though we'd been sailing there for years. They were simply better at spotting the important bits of the bird, and then skimming through the book to find the right one, and this is something that comes with years of practice. We're getting better at it. The *Sibley Guide to Bird Life and Behavior* is a good book to have alongside the identification guides. It's about North American birds, but we've been able to use it in many parts of the world where there are similar families of birds.

Identifying the wildlife you see is a step towards making children aware of nature in a scientific way by classifying the different species. When Helen was about fourteen months old (before we moved on the boat), her grandmother paid a visit. "Look at the pretty yellow bird," said my mother.

"It's an American Goldfinch," said Helen with an air of condescension. Five years later, my botanist friend took them for a walk, and taught them the scientific names for grasses and flowers, and pointed out to me: "Why *shouldn't* they call it *Poa annua?*"

Late Elementary School

When the oldest was nearly nine, I added a series of experiments from the Young Scientist Club. The kits were excellent, although expensive at about $300 for the entire set (it took us several years to get through them). I bought several high school / college level textbooks, and we sketched drawings from them, and occasionally read sections. Science "class" was infrequent, low level, and missing out on many subjects. Science "learning" happened every day.

I couldn't find a curriculum I wanted my children to follow in elementary school, so I took another tack: I tried to learn as much as I could about the latest science, so I could seize learning opportunities, so I could explain, so I could be a talking textbook for them that reacted to the world around us.

A survey of public elementary schools in 2000 reported that the average elementary school spent two hours on science a week,[167] so it's easy for homeschoolers to do better. We found that our experiments were taking a long time, so I declared Friday to be science day, and we did nothing but an experiment, science reading, sketching and so on. We usually spent about four hours a week on classroom science, plus a huge amount of unschooling time out of doors.

I usually had a theme for the school year, but I didn't stick to it entirely. One year, we focused on earth science and astronomy, another year biology and evolution. We did chemistry experiments as part of the Young Scientist kits, but we didn't study it formally otherwise. I found that cooking and increasing independence in cooking was about the best chemistry I could do in the early days. When it came time for middle school labs, I was very confident of my daughters' abilities in the lab – they were used to boiling water and making tea and pasta, measuring for cookies, and re-tweaking recipes when we were out of ingredients, so without realizing it, they both knew a lot of chemistry, plus, their lab skills and care were excellent.

This didn't happen all at once: when they were in late elementary school, I wrote up the recipe for apple crumble on the white board. My handwriting wasn't clear enough, because my t for teaspoon had too much of a curve on it, so they read ½ t of salt as ½ c of salt. Fortunately, we didn't have half a cup of salt on hand, so they came to ask about it! But those moments are a great way to learn the techniques of a lab, following instructions, dealing with hot ovens, and so on, so you're confident of the children's abilities *before* they start measuring hydrochloric acid.

If I were teaching elementary school now, I would strongly consider using the resources from Pandia Press R.E.A.L. Science Odyssey. Coupled with tailored lab kits from the Homeschool Science Tools, these make a complete subject area science program, covering two days of science a week over four years: Life, Earth and Space, Physics, and Chemistry. I prefer the idea of the package of tools and equipment all in one box, for though we did many of the same experiments in the Young Scientist kits, tools and equipment arrived piecemeal over the months, so we couldn't diverge from the syllabus and design our own projects. The R.E.A.L. Science textbooks also have a read aloud section, which takes care of much of the science I had to learn myself and then translate. The programs emphasize scientific vocabulary – not rote memorization, but rather frequent use over the years, so the words become an authentic part of the child's repertoire, rather than remembered for Thursday's test and forgotten by Monday morning.

The R.E.A.L. Science books are available as both hard copy books and ebooks, and combined with lab tools, extra page options, and so on would run from about $100 to $200 a year, depending on the course and number of students. This sounds more expensive than what we did combining pure lab and textbooks, but given the high cost of textbooks and the background reading I did, it actually would come out less expensive in the long run.

Studying the same topic with multiple students is a great virtue of creating one's own curriculum. Life science could be studied with a couple of elementary school students, a middle schooler, and a high schooler all at the same time. It makes sense to target your subject towards whatever suits the oldest child. If you are traveling and planning to homeschool for only a year or two, it is probably worth prioritizing life science and earth science while you are away: they're easily transportable, will work into the changing environments you'll encounter, and are often under-taught in public schools.

Middle School

Middle school can be a tough time to homeschool science. It is a level that many non-scientist parents find daunting, and what is more, there is a dearth of academic scientific homeschooling materials. I expect things will improve dramatically in the next few years: Pandia Press has just published Blair Lee's excellent *Biology Level 2*, which is a rigorous middle years biology and lab program, and they are due to bring out the other components including physics, chemistry, and earth / space science in the next few years.

It can be worth taking the time to consider your high school plans while working out a middle school syllabus. If your children are following a US program, whether or not they plan to go to a bricks and mortar school, the most common high school sequence is currently biology, chemistry, physics. A mere seven percent study earth science at the high school level.[168] (This is a good reason for homeschooling high school, or, if you are going to send your children to school, making sure they have a thorough coverage of earth and space science in middle school.) A new program of study, promoted by the American Association of Physics Teachers is for "physics first" – physics, chemistry, biology. The Next Generation science standards calls for far more earth science, and recommends a three-year high school schedule follow the pattern of physical sciences (physics and chemistry), life sciences (biology and chemistry), and earth / space science. This schedule allows students to specialize in an advanced placement (AP) science in 12th grade.

Students following the GCSE program (or the International GCSE, which may better suit homeschoolers), can take up to three science programs for exams in the end of year 10 or 11. Students may do any combination of physics, chemistry, and biology, and may take them simultaneously. Students who want to specialize in science would then choose their subject(s) for A-level. (International Baccalaureate is another option, currently not available for homeschoolers.)

Table 17: US High School Science Paths

grade	Traditional US	Physics First	Next Generation
9	Biology	Physics	Physical Sciences
10	Chemistry	Chemistry	Life Sciences
11	(Physics) / (AP subjects)	Biology	Earth & Space Sciences
12	(Physics) / (AP subjects)	(Earth Science / AP subjects)	(AP Subjects)

So, there are many options for high school science, but it makes sense to consider them before scheduling middle school science. We didn't – I learned about the idea of "physics first" as I started to think about high school, which meant that our middle school program followed a path of earth and space, evolutionary biology, and physical science, and we're now on schedule to go in reverse through high school: physics, chemistry, biology, earth science. It would have been perhaps better to have meshed those two schedules so as not to do physical science and physics back to back.

There are essentially two traditional versions of high school physics – algebra (and minimal trigonometry) and calculus. The physics first idea takes the algebra version and simplifies it further for ninth graders who haven't finished algebra or taken any trigonometry. Looking at schools across the country, it seems that schools either are going for a narrow, mathy version of Newtonian physics (closely resembling the UK GCSE syllabus) or a broad, minimal math version of all physics, such as Paul Hewitt's *Conceptual Physics*. Neither program will adequately prepare students for the US SAT Physics exam, but either will give students a solid base in physics which could be extended with a SAT Subject or AP Physics in 11th or 12th grade. Biology has become much more complicated in the last hundred years, and physics and chemistry help lay the foundation. In addition, physics reinforces math learning by making the abstract real, and for many students this can be the difference between loving math and hating it as irrelevant.

In middle school, although I named each year with a single science "subject," I stayed flexible on individual topics. My course titles reflected my overall emphasis during the school year, but we dipped into other areas during each school year for a change of scene. During the "Physics" year, for example, we had a post office box in the US, so I ordered up fetal pigs and pregnant rat specimens for Helen and Anna to dissect. We also visited several glaciers and learned more about earthquakes and tsunamis because we were living in Alaska. The skies were clear at night a few times during the winter, so we watched the northern lights and other astronomy highlights. During our "Chemistry" year, we watched Neil deGrasse Tyson's *Cosmos,* Neil Shubin's *Your Inner Fish,* and a dozen lectures from the Great Courses program *Understanding Physics.*

After a strong element of experimental science in the elementary years, I cut back a bit on the experiments in the first two years of middle school science. Earth Sciences and Astronomy are easily brought to life by observations of the world around us, and the lab component of Evolutionary Biology can be observation and dissection. We have not done as much as I would like with growing plants and related experiments because we were traveling for so much of these years. When we were settled, it was a good time to focus on experimental chemistry when they were in 7th and 8th grades. I bought the high school honors kit from the Home Scientist Ltd. (please note, this kit is recommended for students sixteen and up), and did a full-on immersion in lab techniques and experiments, without much background reading.

I have bought numerous high school and introductory university textbooks on the sciences. From the fourth grade, in Anna's case, she has been reading sophisticated science texts and watching complicated programs on DVD. Her experiments were what one would expect for someone her age, but the thinking and reading behind it went far beyond what is usually required. As a result, I trust when she comes to read the big text books in high school, they will hold no fear for her, since she has been handling them since she was nine.

A good science textbook is a treasure trove of fascinating information. A caveat: when buying second hand, take care not to buy one of the bowdlerized "custom curriculum" versions. It can be hard to figure out as chances are the students re-selling them aren't aware they were taught from a censored edition. One way is to look for teachers' editions or compare the table of contents with a list on the publisher's website.

High school and college textbooks are usually written by specialists in the field; the same is not true of textbooks published for middle school science. In fact, the American Association for the Advancement of Science in Project 2061 evaluated the most popular middle school science textbooks for life, physical, and earth sciences – the evaluation charts make grim reading: only a single textbook receives an "excellent" rating in *anything*. The University of Michigan's free *Matter and Molecules* earns an "excellent" in six categories, and "very good" in an additional six. Few other books even merit a single "very good" across the range of all three science subjects.[169] I was not aware of this free PDF-based textbook when making my plans for middle school physical science; I wish we had explored it.

For the parent, teaching with high school science books can be incredibly daunting. Maybe similar textbooks to these are what put you off science in the first place. But you can learn the material along with your students, and this will give you more confidence to teach high school science when it comes. A popularized introduction to science, such as Bill Bryson's *A Short History of Nearly Everything* can be a good starting point for you as the teacher, although it is likely too complex for the average fifth or sixth grader. (Helen read it for pleasure at age twelve, but her factual retention is not that high, although she does now have a broad familiarity with the history of science.)

Bryson mixes current thinking in science with the history of science. I prefer to teach the history of science as part of history, rather than science, but that is a matter of personal preference. My choice is based on our chronological study of history, and the history of science naturally fits in there and gives a window in to the philosophy and the interests of the people of the time, so it seems to me to be part of history. Others prefer to include the history of science as part of science because it teaches students about the scientific method.

Joy Hakim's three-volume history of science series is a good way to introduce middle school students to the history of science, wherever you compartmentalize it. Ancient, Renaissance, and Modern history both have large sections of history of science, but the Medieval period rates only a couple of entries. This by itself teaches a great deal to students of history. Like Hakim's American History series, however, the science books suffer from excessive busy-ness, with far too many distracting sidebars and illustrations. This makes them considerably harder to read than the reading level of the words themselves would suggest.

Fifth through eight graders can cope with a lot more Latin words and complex ideas than most curricula give them credit for. I don't worry about teaching all the material – my goal is that they get a taster, an overview of the subject. At first, I read aloud from the more difficult sections; by seventh grade, they read aloud themselves most of the time, and I paused them on difficult words and concepts to make sure Helen and Anna understand them. By eighth grade they read silently to themselves.

Students won't remember every word; they won't even remember half. When I study something, I find that it takes at least three times for an idea to really sink in. Students who cram for tests may be able to shine at exam time, but will they remember it six months later? After the reading, Helen and Anna write a very short summary of what was discussed and usually draw the illustrations in the text. Drawing is an incredibly powerful tool for memory. If you merely study a diagram, your retention will not be nearly as good as if you copy it out and label it.

Many science textbooks are now available as ebooks, and while I celebrate reading literature (and scientific articles) on an ebook reader, it seems that the scope of a science textbook is better suited to a hard copy. There's something about flipping through it that doesn't happen with an ebook. The cost of a secondhand textbook is usually about the same as the ebook version. If you're doing a lot of traveling, however, science texts read on a tablet could be a very good (although expensive) option.

Many digital textbooks can now be rented from Amazon, which saves money but means you can't refer back to them in later years. In addition, you can find free downloads of open source textbooks at [www.ck12.org].

In a regular school, the teachers can't help each student individually; reading has to be simplified so that almost every student can read it without outside assistance. There is nothing wrong with reading aloud with your students, having them read aloud to you, and working with them to figure out the text of a complicated subject. We aren't used to that, because it doesn't happen in schools, but it can be very valuable in a homeschooling environment – in addition to teaching the subject matter, you're teaching them how to read and how to study. Typically, these things are not taught in school, and good students figure it out on their own (or their parents teach them). By reading aloud with your children, especially on a subject that is a bit unfamiliar, you have the opportunity to model when to try to figure out a word from context, and when to go to the glossary, and when it's so complicated that you need to go to an additional source such as the Khan Academy YouTube lectures.

This early association with the complex words of science will help enormously in high school science. As sociologist Donald Hayes notes, scientific texts have increased significantly in complexity over the last hundred years, yet the preparation of students has declined. In his research he ranks the difficulty of texts, using English language newspapers as a baseline of 0 (and their reading level has remained remarkably consistent over the years). His analysis shows modern high school science text books rank at a 19, more difficult than a peer-reviewed article about DNA in the 1958 scientific journal *Nature*. (By 1994, *Nature's* vocabulary was near the top of the charts with a vocabulary difficulty of 40.) Meanwhile, the vocabulary of a sixth grade reading textbook has dropped from 8 in 1896 to a -7 in 2000. [170] Reading science textbooks together in middle school, combined with high level independent reading, will help prepare your students for the rigor of high school science classes.

The other important element of science is experiments and writing up lab reports. There are no end of experimental texts and science fair projects for middle schoolers (I'm just having problem finding background materials). I either make up the experiments or use or modify ones from the Nuffield Foundation website.

Robert Bruce and Barbara Thompson's lab books, *Illustrated Guide to Home Chemistry Experiments* and *Illustrated Guide to Home Biology Experiments*, are good sources of labs for high school and careful, methodical seventh and eighth graders.

Equipment

I am trying to build up a good "supply locker" of science materials. Everything I buy is with an eye to high school science – for example, there is no point in buying a lot of plastic beakers for middle school when we'll need glass in high school.

Carolina Biological is the best place I've found for buying dissection and lab supplies [www.carolina.com], and the Home Scientist LLC [www.thehomescientist.com] provides excellent comprehensive kits and experiments within the US (all 50 states), and will ship the biology and chemistry kits internationally. The Home Scientist offers an excellent way to buy discounted chemicals for chemistry and biology, because they come in small "family sized" quantities, rather than the "school sized" versions available at Carolina. In addition, the kits have a thoughtful division between plastic and glassware, in order to keep the prices down, but with enough glass to do high school level chemistry.

In 2015, their Honors Chemistry kit, which should see both my children through two years of chemistry, cost $184. I bought a few extra glass 250 ml beakers, which have come in handy, but are not necessary to do all the "High School Honors" lab work. And for the same price as two glass beakers, I purchased a dozen tempered glass wide-mouth pint canning jars, which don't pour as well, but can be used for many projects.

Helen is very interested in dissection, so I've outfitted them both with college-level dissection kits. I didn't skimp, despite the high cost. The basic tools for each student cost about $40 – and they easily could have shared the tools, but I knew if I did that, Helen would do all the cutting, and Anna would watch with her mind elsewhere. You can buy single-use kits for far less, but I wanted this to be equipment we would use many times a year through high school and perhaps college.

To that end, I spent an additional $90 on 100-piece boxes of two sizes of scalpel blades and 350 T-pins. If you have a student with a serious interest in biology, buying blades and pins in bulk will be cheaper in the long run, and using fresh sharp scalpel blades is safer than old dull blades which can lead to careless hacking. (In 2015, 10-pack blades were available for about $7; 100-packs were about $33.) Even some of the best pre-made kits include disposable scalpels which only last through a couple of dissections, and they often include many different types of scissor and scalpel blades, which are unnecessary at this level. Middle school students don't need the variety of say a No. 21, 22 and 23 blade, but they need more serious tools than a single disposable No. 22. (With scalpel blades, the bigger the number, the smaller the blade or handle.) A pair of teasing needles is often included in the pre-packaged sets, but you can just use a T-pin. A mall probe is nice, but we've used a kitchen skewer to good effect.

This may seem like a huge expense, especially coming from someone who doesn't want to spend the extra $50 to have two history textbooks, but in this case, the extra costs really seemed to affect their educational experiences, whereas a few squabbles over where the book sits in history class does not have as much effect (and might even teach them something about sharing).

Sample Dissection Kit

- Dissection tray aluminum with vinyl pad (for pinning)
- Handi-Pins, 2 inch, box of 350
- Case for dissection tools
- Scalpel Blades, Economy, No. 22, Fits Handle No. 4, box of 100
- Scalpel Blades, Economy, No. 11, Fits Handle No. 3, box of 100
- Scalpel Handle, Economy, No. 3, Stainless Steel, Uses Blades No. 10-15
- Scalpel Handle, Economy, No. 4, Stainless Steel, Uses Blades No. 20-25
- Dissecting forceps, fine point
- Dissecting scissors
- Mall probe and seeker

Of course most of what we do could be handled with a well-sharpened paring knife, a pair of tweezers, and a cutting board, but I want to emphasize that we are doing science, not filleting dinner, so I have tried to outfit them with the type of equipment they'd have in a good school science lab.

Middle School Science options

A four year program might look like Earth Sciences and Astronomy, Evolutionary Biology, Physics, and Chemistry. The State of California standards break it down into three years: Earth Science, Biology, and Physical Sciences (Physics and Chemistry). If I were homeschooling for only two years of middle school, I'd teach Earth Sciences and Astronomy one year and Evolutionary Biology the next, but I'd try to incorporate as much physics and chemistry as possible into those two courses. For a single year of middle school, I'd teach Evolutionary Biology instead: most school districts gloss over it, so merely by teaching it, you're doing a better job than many bricks and mortar schools.

Later in this chapter, you will find a list of the textbooks we found valuable, and would be good resources even if you are teaching from a boxed curriculum. The titles listed are American, but can be purchased both through Amazon.com and Amazon.co.uk (shipping from the US to the UK at reasonable rates). I don't list British science books as I have no direct experience of any of them, but there is a wide selection available at Amazon.co.uk and other vendors.

Use caution when shopping for used textbooks. For example, Pearson sells three versions of its Miller and Levine Biology books: on level, foundation, and core. *On level* is written for ninth and tenth graders in a standard high school class. *Foundation* is written for struggling readers or English as a Second Language learners. *Core* is a reduced textbook, designed for use with online resources, and should be avoided in the second hand market, because the access to online materials may not be still valid.

When I am confident of the subject matter, I buy second-hand textbooks; when I am not, I buy full price new materials directly from the publisher as an official school, in order to have access to the answer keys. For me, this means I spend $150 for physics and chemistry textbooks and $20 for biology and earth sciences textbooks.

The video courses from the Great Courses [www.thegreat courses.com] are excellent for advanced middle school students. While they are exceedingly expensive, all of the courses go on sale once a year (at different times, however, so you have to pay attention), which makes them much more manageable. Many public libraries carry the popular courses. They also have a UK website [www.thegreatcourses.co.uk] and an Australian website [www.thegreatcourses.com.au].

You can find free, downloadable textbooks from the CK-12 Foundation at [www.ck12.org] and online lectures from the Khan Academy [www.khanacademy.org]. The CK-12 textbooks are not as polished as the ones from mainstream publishers, and it is hard for a non-specialist to evaluate their quality, but they are a marvelous option if cost or mailing address is an issue, because all you need is a good internet access to download them.

Other excellent free resources include the *Molecules and Matter* mentioned above, the American Chemical Society's Middle School Chemistry program, and E.O. Wilson's biology textbooks, *Life on Earth*. Unfortunately, *Life on Earth* is available only for those who have iPads, and when I inquired, they had no plans to bring it out on other platforms. The Howard Hughes Medical Institute offers an extraordinary array of free materials, both online and mailed to schools (including homeschoolers). Pandia Press and the Home Scientist offer commercial homeschooling programs with academic science.

Links:

- *Molecules and Matter*
  [ed-web3.educ.msu.edu/reports/matter-molecules/]
- *Middle School Chemistry*
  [www.middleschoolchemistry.com]
- *Life on Earth* [eowilsonfoundation.org/]
- HHMI [www.hhmi.org/educational-materials]
- *Biology Level 2* [www.pandiapress.com]
- Home Scientist Kits [www.thehomescientist.com]

Neutral Science

There are a great many homeschooling science packages out there, complete kits with lab materials, tests, answer keys, and lesson plans. It can be very hard for a non-scientist to evaluate them, however. Homeschooling science curricula can be divided into three categories: academic science (the sort practiced in major research universities and labs around the world); "neutral" science, which includes most of the major elements of academic science, but omits some key components, such as evolution, the age of the universe, climate science, and so on in order to reach a wider market; and religious science, which explicitly teaches young earth creationism.

It's easy enough for me to determine that I don't want to teach my children "science" through programs with titles like Apologia's *Land Animals of the Sixth Day* and *Exploring Creation through Biology,* or Answers in Genesis's *God's Design for Heaven and Earth*. The difficulty comes with science programs that sound academic, but aren't. Blair Lee, author of R.E.A.L Science Odyssey Biology 2 and Chemistry 1 (both of which teach academic science), writes:

> Many of the so-called "neutral" science courses omit the parts that provide the evidence supporting these facts and theories. If you use these "neutral" science courses for your middle school or high school chemistry and physics, your child will be left without the necessary science background to understand evolution, the Big Bang Theory, climate change, and other key science principles.[171]

This is not simply a homeschooling problem: a 2011 study in *Science* reported that seventy-three percent of American biology teachers do not include evolution in their courses. Thirteen percent teach creationism, and the "cautious sixty-percent" simply don't mention it either way. In high school science, it is possible to buy college textbooks, so the lack of academic scientific curricula is most acute for elementary and middle school science materials, for both homeschoolers and the *ninety-six percent* of public elementary school teachers without a science background.[172]

Lab Reports & Lab Notebooks

In addition to taking notes and summarizing readings and lectures, middle school students should make careful records of their experiments and demonstrations, using either lab reports or lab notebooks.

When I was in school, we always did lab reports, but keeping a cohesive lab notebook can be even more valuable, in terms of tracing projects over time, and having a valid record of time in the lab (which may be useful for homeschooled high school students looking to prove that they did actual lab science, since colleges sometimes disregard homeschool lab work). We used both methods so Helen and Anna would have experience of both, although, we didn't do much with formal lab reports until they could work easily on the computer, so they could concentrate on the science, rather than the handwriting.

Lab Reports

Writing up middle school science experiments follows a set pattern. Each experiment can be written up in three sections: "hypothesis," "experiment," and "conclusions." The experiment section is in turn broken up into a further three sections: "materials," "procedure," and "results."

Where liberal arts essays blend the different sections together, science lab reports usually have each section labeled and separated. Most experiments start with a question (*what happens if I grow mung bean sprouts in the sun?*), but by the time it reaches the hypothesis stage, it should be written as a statement that can be tested. In science, having a negative result on an experiment is an equally valuable result. Science is all about **evidence,** so unexpected results must never be rewritten to match expectations, nor the hypothesis rewritten to match the results.

Middle school lab reports can be either handwritten or keyed into a computer. Computers are great for tidiness, but you have to be careful that early middle school students don't get too caught up in the pleasures of graphic design and spend more energy on the layout than the science. Middle school students typically keep a lab notebook in pencil, but formal lab reports should be turned in copied out in ink or keyed into the computer, at least in seventh and eighth grade.

Instruction Sheet for Lab Reports

Lab reports should be neatly handwritten / typewritten.

Name
Date
Title of Experiment

Hypothesis: Your idea of what will happen in the experiment, written in statement form.

Experiment:

- Materials: This section should include a detailed list of all the materials needed to do the experiment. The main objective of the Materials and Procedure sections of the lab report is to make the experiment **repeatable** by someone else who wishes to test the results. Scientific evidence must always stand up to repeated tests before being accepted. Be very detailed in your materials section; for example, a plastic beaker might yield different results from a glass beaker, and a flared water glass still different results. Include illustrations if appropriate.

- Procedure: Again, this section is about repeatability. Be as careful as you can with listing the steps, so that someone else could do the same experiment. Illustrations can be very helpful here.

- Results: Figure out a way to display your results (a graph? a table?) and draw them as carefully as possible. Note any possibilities of error (for example, if you are using a tape measure, a ruler, or a micrometer, your results will have a different margin of error). Include illustrations if appropriate. (Pie charts can be fun, but are often misleading and are not recommended for formal academic work.)[173]

Conclusions: The beginning of the conclusion should restate the hypothesis as proved or disproved by the results. You should also add a discussion of possibilities for further experiments to fine tune your results. This can include suggesting a new hypothesis for another experiment, a more refined procedure to remove ambiguous test results, and improvements in the materials portion.

Bibliography: This section should list any readings or references that you used to gain background knowledge for your hypothesis, gain ideas for materials and procedures, or analyze your results.

Lab Notebooks

Another option for middle school students is to work out of a formal lab notebook instead of submitting polished "Lab Reports." We've switched to this method for Chemistry, after reading about it in Robert Bruce Thompson's *Illustrated Guide to Home Chemistry Experiments*.

Thompson writes:

> If you're just starting to learn about chemistry lab work, keeping a detailed lab notebook may seem to be overkill, but it's not. The habit of recording observations in an organized manner is crucial for any would-be scientist.[174]

The formal lab notebook is written in pen, on pre-numbered pages (so that it is an authentic record of work), and contains both the introduction and the conclusions/discussions of the lab report, and also contains the field notes from the actual lab, written at the time of observation. Beginning this in middle school can be good practice for high school work, particularly if your homeschooled students are preparing for university science. Many colleges and universities will request lab notebooks to go with Advanced Placement exam scores when considering whether to give university credit to incoming students. (The APs are roughly equivalent to the British A-Level.) It might be a good idea for homeschoolers to have similar evidence of their lab work, even if they are not preparing for the APs.

The usual components of a lab report listed in the section above are included in the lab notebook, but in addition to being more "real world scientist," I suspect my daughters prefer the lab notebook format because it means they don't have to type up a clean copy.

If your students are working on observational science, such as dissections or investigations, you can ask them to do it in the same way, but simply leave out the hypothesis section. In all science work, student-drawn illustrations can be a valuable component of learning, whether it is sketching the chemistry lab set-up or pausing in a dissection to draw what is seen.

Useful Science Textbooks

- *Earth: An Introduction to Physical Geology*
  Edward J. Tarbuck and Frederick K. Lutgens

- *The Atmosphere: An Introduction to Meteorology*
  Frederick K. Lutgens and Edward J. Tarbuck

- *Essentials of Oceanography*
  Alan P. Trujillo and Harold V. Thurman

- *The Cosmos: Astronomy in the New Millennium*
  Jay M. Pasachoff and Alex Filippenko

- *History of Life* Richard Cowe

- *Campbell Biology* Jane B. Reece and Lisa A. Urry

- *Conceptual Physics* Paul G. Hewitt

- *Conceptual Chemistry* John A. Suchocki

Science Summary

- Start off with observational nature studies and an appreciation for the natural world
- Infuse home life with big science ideas – evolution, earth science, astronomy
- Bring high school level science into the middle school – look for big ideas and overall understanding of concepts, not endless memorization of small details
- Use labs and observations when you can; use videos and DVDs when doing it yourself is too complex or expensive
- Shop ahead for high school level tools and lab equipment if there is any chance you will be homeschooling high school science

Second (or Third) Languages

Second Language studies is the "learn from my mistakes" chapter. In our homeschool, we've studied Spanish, French, and Japanese, and I studied French in high school, Chinese in college, and spent many years unsuccessfully trying to "pick up" Spanish. The early homeschool years were completely unsuccessful; I'm fairly sure that the children would know more Spanish if I hadn't taught them at all.

My problem stemmed entirely from listening to advertising. I believed the blurb on Rosetta Stone that it taught "immersion-style" and that all I had to do was plunk my children in front of the computer. I have met parents of high school children who found Rosetta Stone successful, but for younger students without the ambition to speak a second language, it doesn't make sense.

(I use the term *second* language instead of *foreign*, following William Armstrong's advice in *Study is Hard Work;* he recommends banning the expression "foreign language" from your speech, arguing that the very word puts up an unnecessary obstacle to your learning.)[175]

There are three ways to learn a second language:

- True immersion with a native speaker parent
- Partial immersion in all-day school or day care
- Academic study

I believed all the articles and sales pitches on language tapes that young children will easily pick up languages. I believed the Rosetta Stone and Muzzy blurbs that suggest you can simply park your children in front of the screen, and they'll learn the language. It's false advertising. *Immersion learning,* a term popularized by the programs at the Middlebury Language schools, means you're completely surrounded by the language for many hours a day, as children do with a fluent parent or in all-day school.

Many of the language programs aimed at elementary and middle school homeschoolers call themselves *immersion* programs, but what they mean is *target language* programs. A target language program has no English instructions; all the words and explanations are in the target language. While this is a very useful component of any language program, it is not true immersion.

Through the years, I gradually became better at organizing language instruction. After a disastrous two years with Rosetta Stone Spanish, I took four months to give Helen and Anna a crash course in French. It went much better, though they don't remember much of it. We went back to Spanish briefly, and then spent six months learning Japanese. That worked the best of all, because I'd already done everything wrong the first few times. In every other subject, I could remember my own struggles with that topic at a similar age, but since I didn't begin second language studies until high school I was missing that background when designing programs for Helen and Anna.

True Immersion

The best way to learn a second language is to have a parent fluent in the language who speaks nothing but that language to the child. (We did meet someone who was trying to speak only French to his child, despite being not particularly articulate in French; I am not sure how that experiment worked out.)

If you are fortunate enough to be able to raise truly bilingual children, beware that not every college will regard this as a "second language." In the US, very selective colleges will sometimes expect *non-native* language studies in addition to those learned at home, so while English would count for a student raised in a home without English, true bilinguals would need an additional language.

On the other hand, many US colleges work on a strict point system, and do not consider how the language was learned. In these cases, a SAT Subject or AP language exams can offer an excellent admissions boost for bilingual students.

Partial Immersion

Friends who spent as much time as we did in Argentina and Chile have completely bilingual children. I always had an excuse: friends sent their children to daycare, but ours were too old when we arrived, we were moving too quickly to put them into school, I didn't want to give up on their academic schooling, etc. A young friend of ours is French, spent much of her time in Argentina up to the age of 13, then her family moved to the Falkland Islands, and she has just finished secondary school in New Zealand. She speaks French, Spanish, and English like a native.

So, the second best way is to put your children into day care or school for a year or more in the country with your target language. I feel guilty that we didn't do that in Argentina, because I would really like Helen and Anna to be fluent, but I am not sure that I wouldn't have made the same decision if we were back suddenly at age eight and I had the chance to do it all over again. We didn't want to be tied down to one location, and I wanted them to do their academic work in English. In retrospect, missing a year of early elementary school would have been a small price to pay for fluency, but I didn't have the gift of hindsight.

Academic Study

The third way is to teach it as an academic subject. When you learned English (or whatever was your first language), you were constantly immersed in it. Before you said a word, you were listening to people talk around you for almost a year. You were bombarded with your first language non-stop, and everyone around you spoke to you in simple phrases, and your ear was full of more complex language as they spoke to each other over you.

Even an hour a day (and young children aren't going to manage that) on Rosetta Stone or other target-language programs will not give you that quality of immersion. I was lured by the notion that children are predisposed to learn language and that language instruction is far more effective before the age of eight. I thought that they would just *learn it* because they were under eight, but that only applies for true or partial immersions.

Eventually, I added Galore Park's *So You Really Want to Learn Spanish*. This worked to a point, but it is aimed at much older children (it is recommended for British Years 7-8, and there is now a third volume for Year 9, or advanced students in middle school). Since then, Galore Park has introduced a new series called *Skoldo* for French and Spanish and *Latin Prep*, aimed at younger children.

The fundamental problem, however, is that I did not drill the subject sufficiently. Had I treated the vocabulary and the verb conjugations like math facts and worked on those, rather than hoping Rosetta Stone would do it for me (or, once we added *So You Really Want to Learn Spanish*, that the text exercises would be sufficient), they (and I) would have learned more Spanish. I was so taken in by the notion that they would find it easy to learn languages at their age that I didn't do the academic drilling that had been absolutely required of my language studies in high school.

Most of the mistakes I made in Helen and Anna's Spanish and French lessons were from assuming that they would have a basic understanding of how to learn. What they needed was far, far more explicit, broken-down to the details instruction to teach them both the language and the ways of learning languages in general. (See A Better Way to Drill, page 40.)

You don't need to know the language yourself to be an acceptable teacher, but if you don't know it, you will probably need to study it alongside your children. We know people with high school-aged children who are independently using Rosetta Stone (a different language for each child) and speak very favorably of it, but for us, it proved to be enormously frustrating, because we were in a Spanish speaking country and the Rosetta Stone progress was unbearably slow. Months went by, and we still didn't know how to have even the most basic playground conversation. Helen says now that it destroyed any ambition to learn Spanish. She'd spent half an hour a day for half a year, and face to face with other children, she couldn't understand anything they said, and she had no vocabulary for what she wanted to say to them. She explained how she felt at age seven: "I was convinced that no matter what I did, I'd never learn to speak to anyone, so what was the point?"

In every other subject, I didn't necessarily make learning into a game, but I marketed it successfully. Learning to read was worthwhile, because it quickly lead to reading good stories. Math was satisfying (at least after we ditched Miquon Math). History was entertaining stories. Science was fascinating world studies. My marketing utterly failed with Spanish; instead I convinced them that they *couldn't* learn it.

For our next language study, I did a bit better. We only studied French for four months while sailing in French Polynesia, but Helen and Anna learned considerably more than they had in a similar time with Spanish. I first made up vocabulary lists of words and phrases that they needed with children on the beach, words for furniture so they could play in the dollhouse with French children, and words for boats, dinghies, and so on. We worked in Galore Park's *So You Really Want to Learn French,* although that, too, is aimed at late middle school. Hamish and I made a better job of speaking French to each other and to them than we had in Spanish, but we kept slipping in our attempts to speak French at meal times. Our mealtime conversations tend to have the flavor of a seminar, talking about big issues, history, and the world with the children, and we couldn't do that in French.

Despite the improvements in the way I taught French, I failed to buy a good audio program for us. Plimsleur French had an introductory offer of four CDs, but it wasn't anywhere near enough material, and by the time I realized this, we were out of range of bookstores and internet shopping. Despite the short-comings in their instruction, and the relatively brief exposure, when they met French children, they could organize games and talk together. It was the first time they met with any payback from studying second languages.

Attempt number three (Japanese) was the most successful, but even then, I learned a lot about how to teach it. I found a good introductory audio program (Instant Immersion Japanese) and a moderately good grammar book. I assigned it four days a week. I studied along with Helen and Anna at first, but then life got in the way, and I took a couple of months off. When I returned to the fray, I was shocked to discover that I was actually still ahead of them. I had done far, far fewer repetitions, but what I had done had stayed in my mind. Maybe my mind wasn't as elastic as theirs, but I knew how to make my time pay off, and they didn't.

I realized why most American schools don't begin second language instruction until high school: it's hard work to do it at the elementary or middle school level, unless you can find a true immersion situation. The motivation to study is simply not there, and the drilling and input required from the parent is substantial. At thirteen and fourteen, terrified of getting a C in French, I studied for hours a day and smashed my way through it. Before then, where is that motivation going to come from? It doesn't come from within, and I was wrong to expect it. They probably would have found more motivation to learn to speak to other children if they weren't quite such good friends with each other; only children have a slight advantage here.

When I returned to Japanese with them, I took away their headphones and their private listening to the audio program. I put it on the computer, with the printed transcript in front of us. In the past months, they'd been listening to the audio tracks (about five minutes each) over and over without retention. I pulled them back to Disk 3, track 1 and started to show them how to do it. We listened (and repeated) through once while reading along with the transcript. We stopped. We copied down the vocabulary words. We listened again and repeated. We closed the transcript file. We listened again and repeated. We drew pictures in notebooks to illustrate the locations of "this," "that," (near the listener) and "that" (remote from both). We did drilling from English to Japanese and Japanese to English. We listened again and answered questions. We listened again, trying not to translate into English on our way. The five minute track took over half an hour to get through. This time, they remembered it.

Telling them what to do did not work. I needed to stop my other projects, sit next to them and direct. No primary school teacher would expect students to learn without a teacher at this age, and I think it's easy to be lured by homeschooling promises that your children will do the work themselves, that they'll be self-motivated, that they'll even understand (or be able to figure out) the steps required to learn something like a second language. I feel as though I wasted years of language lessons.

Americans usually start their study of language too late; British schools generally do better, but the main obstacle to my teaching was my ingrained belief that young children learned languages easily. That is simply not the case if you can't put them in a situation where they are surrounded by fluent adults and children for most of their waking hours. If your goal is to have them reach a language level where they can talk to other children at the playground as quickly as possible – and children never slow down or simplify their speech to make things easier – you're going to have to do it yourself, not rely on passive repetition from a computer or audio based program.

Reading Gabriel Wyner's *Fluent Forever: How to Learn Any Language Fast and Never Forget It* this year helped me pull together my discoveries about teaching language, and taught me a few important lessons. I'd realized that we all needed deliberate study of vocabulary and grammar, but I'd never figured out how to combine this with the best of a target language program. Wyner's program is aimed at people who do not have time for true immersion learning, but instead of working with learning translations, as I did in my school studies, and we all did in Japanese, he recommends using pictures instead of translations to learn the new vocabulary:

> Because your flashcards won't have any English on them, you'll learn to see a dog and *immediately* think about the corresponding word in your target language. There's no pesky translation step to get in the way . . . [176]

He recommends drilling with homemade flashcards (especially on the computer, with a program called Anki). I've always been a proponent of flashcards, and indeed, had discovered Anki while learning Japanese, but I hadn't managed to connect the old-school flashcards with the target language ideas of Rosetta Stone. That is one of the many strengths of Wyner's book: he combines the ideas behind target language learning with pictures with the drill and direction of academic programs. He maintains that flashcards must have no English language words on them. Instead of learning that "perro" means "dog," and learning to translate, students should be learning to associate the word "perro" with a picture representation of a dog, ideally their own pet or a dog they know.[177] I wish I had figured this out when I was studying languages in school! All my flashcards were *translations*, which made my learning far slower than it needed to be.

The other key idea in his program is that students should learn the most useful words first. I understood this when we studied French, but forgot about it when I handed over a Spanish grammar book. Wyner has a chapter entitled, "Where to Begin: We Don't Talk Much About Apricots," in which he criticizes typical grammar books for teaching word lists on a similar topic ("apricots" and "bananas," "mother" and "step-sister") more for the convenience of the chapter than because they are the most commonly needed words in that language. He writes:

> Not all words are created equal; we use certain words far more often than others. English has at least a quarter of a million words. But if you only knew the top *hundred* words in English, you'd recognize half of everything you read. We get a *lot* of mileage out of our most frequent words.[178]

In his website, [fluent-forever.com], Wyner offers a list of the 625 most commonly used words to begin with. I found this very helpful – I needed someone to tell me that it was okay not to learn the word for "ruler," "guinea pig," and "accounting" right away.

Designing an Academic Program

Which Language?

Learning a language closer to your own (for example, French speakers learning Spanish) is generally considered easier than learning one that is completely different. According to the US Defense Language Institute's breakdown of their courses, Spanish, French and Portuguese are Category I languages (a 26-week course) while Chinese, Japanese, and Arabic are Category IV languages (a 64-week course). Much of this is of course due to differences in writing, but by comparison German (Category II), which uses the same writing as English, is still harder for English speakers to learn than Spanish, French or Portuguese.[179]

By the end of high school, your child should have basic speaking, reading, and writing skills in a second language, roughly equivalent to three years of high school level language, or perhaps as many as six years of study before high school. In the early years, you have the option of concentrating on spoken language, especially if you are visiting a country that uses the language. This can work well when your children are busy still working out the basics of reading and writing in their native language.

Many homeschooling programs emphatically recommend studying Latin first. For me, the important part of studying languages is communicating with people from other countries, so Latin has never been part of my plan. It does teach a great deal about word roots, and the conjugations prepare native English speakers for coping with conjugations in Spanish, French, and Italian, so there is certainly nothing *wrong* with teaching Latin, but equally, if your goal is communication and travel, then there's equally nothing wrong with beginning with a different language.

Sounds

You'll need some sort of audio program to learn the pronunciations of your target language. I've never made any headway with the pronunciation guides at the beginning of every language book. I have to hear it. I'm lousy at mimicking the sounds of other languages – a friend burst into laughter when she heard me trying to teach Spanish to Helen and Anna, and my college roommates used to find my Chinese drill hysterically funny (especially the Chinese roommate – unfortunately, the only words I remember are the bad words she taught me, instead of the useful words I drilled hour after hour).

In fact, having a thick skin and shrugging off ridicule is probably the most useful attribute in learning a second language. A *growth mindset* (see page 18) will allow you to meet challenges and shrug off failures. I'm only occasionally able to do this: I'm unembarrassed by my mistakes when I speak French with my brother-in-law's girlfriend, but when *he* enters the room, I begin to cringe in embarrassment, because I can't help but compare my horrible French to his fluency.

In Spanish, we used Rosetta Stone to work on the sounds of the language; in French we tried Plimsleur, but I didn't buy enough to give it a fair try. With Japanese, we used Instant

Immersion Japanese, which taught tourist-level vocabulary, and now in Spanish the second time around, we are coming at it from many different directions, including an audio program from a high school textbook, Gabriel Wyner's Pronunciation Trainer, and Skype lessons with a native speaker.

The Pronunciation Trainer from Fluent Forever [www.fluent-forever.com] is a series of Anki flashcards working specifically on the sounds of a language that English speakers find most difficult. For example, in Latin American Spanish, the computer "flash cards" have built-in audio to train you in hearing the difference between *perro* and *pero* and *hierba* and *yerba*. The Language Trainers look like they would be an excellent addition to any beginning or intermediate level language program.

Vocabulary

Practice the words you need to know, using flashcards, without translating them. With our French and Japanese studies, I figured out what we needed to be able to say, and only worked on those words. It's very easy to be caught up in the order of learning as proscribed by the language program or book. When Helen and Anna were using *Galore Park* for Spanish and French, I'd ask them to *learn* every word in each chapter. That was completely unnecessary. Many of the words were only needed to get through the exercises in the chapter. It wouldn't have been "cheating" to learn the five most useful words, use the vocabulary list as a reference for the exercises, and move more quickly onto the next chapter. The faster you can move, the better, especially with elementary and middle school students.

Grammar

You'll need a grammar book to help guide you through the basics. *Galore Park* offers some excellent ones for elementary and middle school. For other languages, we found *Japanese Demystified* very helpful, and we've also used the Wiley self-teaching guides quite effective, including *Practical Spanish Grammar*.

Finding Native Speakers

We met a family with a German father and a Brazilian mother. Their seven-year-old spoke quite serviceable English, and was very willing to speak it to Helen and Anna (they were four and six at the time). In this case, the parents had a good working knowledge of the language, and they taught the language explicitly in their school lessons, and they forced themselves to speak English whenever they were inside the boat. Breakfast, lunch, and dinner were conducted in English. It was interesting to note that the daughter did not pick up the parents' Brazilian and German accented English (perhaps because the parents' accents were different, or perhaps because she had enough exposure to native English speaking children). We tried to follow this technique with Spanish, but Hamish's Spanish was so far beyond mine that it was not very successful. We would start off well, and then lazily slip into English.

This is probably where we are going wrong. In his book, *Fluent in 3 Months,* Benny Lewis notes the importance of immersing yourself in the target language: "You must *speak the language with other human beings.*"[180] Lewis puts his emphasis on fluency, rather than mastery, and maintains that neither a perfect accent nor flawless speech are a requirement of fluency. I remember once encouraging Helen and Anna to speak more Spanish on the playground, and Anna, age about seven, said, "but what if I make a mistake?" I tried to reassure her that it wouldn't matter a bit, but she wouldn't listen.

I have never convinced Helen and Anna to wade in with a language, even though they had plenty of examples of me – in French, in Spanish, and in Japanese – doing just that. When we arrived in Japan, my language skills were about the same as theirs, but after two months of blundering away in Japanese, I could have the basic conversation – Where are you from? What is your job? How old are your children? But what about school? Can I see your boat? Am I on the right train to ...? – with few problems, but Helen and Anna kept their mouths firmly shut.

If you have good internet access, many commercial programs offer Skype lessons with native speakers (we've used Verbal Planet and Homeschool Spanish Academy with great success). These have really improved our Spanish classes, and are ideal when you're studying in a place without many or any native speakers to chat with. Even if you can find native speakers, a gentle teacher who slows down and enunciates may provide an ideal first step before confronting the rapid-paced talk at the playground.

Managing the Classroom

What should your classroom look like? How should the day run? Just as there are a broad range of curricular styles, from unschooling to classical, there's a broad range of classroom styles, which partially correlates with curriculum, but not exclusively so. Of course, an unschooler who regards the whole world as the classroom isn't worried about classroom management, and a classical educator will often have a school-at-home set up with child-sized desks and chairs, and sometimes even a blackboard, but there are classical scholars reading with their feet over their heads in a beanbag chair, and there are child-led homeschoolers with a classroom and a blackboard.

Time management has been a persistent difficulty throughout our homeschool. I was continually looking for ways to shave time off the school day without sacrificing academics. I read about children who complete their elementary school work in two or three hours, but that never happened for us – for both good and bad reasons. The good reason is that our curriculum was open-ended. When was a topic finished? If your students are filling in a worksheet a day in each class, it's easy to be done in a few hours, but if you're talking, thinking, writing, and discovering, it takes longer, but I think your students are almost always learning more. But continually, I was frustrated that school would take us *so long*. Where were these three-hour school days everyone talks about?

In *Teach Like a Champion*, Doug Lemov begins his analysis of excellent teachers in urban schools with a description of a teacher who spends the first day teaching his students how to pass papers around the classroom. If the students pass papers around the room twenty times a day, saving a minute each time can net sixty-three hours of school a year.[181] Homeschool students don't pass papers around the room, but there are many other places where time can be saved in transitions from one subject to another and in discussing the assignments and material.

Here's an example: early on, I tried to teach my children to take responsibility for their own equipment. I gave them pencils, which they labeled with their initials, and I allowed them to go off and sharpen them in the workshop whenever necessary. Do you have any idea how much time an eight-year-old can spend sharpening pencils? Anna would sit down to do spelling with me, one on one. She knew that she was to have her materials gathered and together; I would sit beside her, take out the stack of word cards, and suddenly, she'd discover that she needed to sharpen her pencil. And while she's at it, maybe she needed a drink of water.

Lemov suggests that students not be allowed to sharpen their pencils in class for this very reason. After reading this, I tried to have a stack of pencils sharpened at the beginning of school, but I often failed to have them ready. (Day to day preparation is not my strong point.) The final iteration of the pencil quandary was this: the last item in their list of school assignments was to sharpen three pencils and put them in their boxes for the next morning. This, at last, worked for all of us. It does take time to come up with effective solutions for managing your school, and in all likelihood, after you hit on the perfect solution, it will only be a matter of months before it's obsolete. Within a year of figuring out the pencil sharpening, they both started doing all their work in pen, and it ceased to be an issue at all.

It's a delicate balance, because one of the benefits of homeschooling is students don't need to roll to the clock bell: if they're interested in a topic, why shouldn't they have the opportunity to explore it? But, particularly when they're young and don't have a sense of anticipation of rewards, when should you step in and demand they change topic? Or should you even try? I found that it suited my sanity best to step in – too many days of finishing our school after six or seven hours instead of two or three, meant that they were losing out on time outside, play, exercise, and it was not what I wanted school to look like.

I had to balance my two main goals: that Helen and Anna cover at least the same academic materials that they would in an excellent public school each year and that they played outside, rain or shine, for at least three or four hours a day. If either their free time or their academic progress was cut into, I became frustrated and unhappy with school. Here are some of the ways we organized and compromised to keep it working.

Classroom Behavior

In order for any learning to take place, your children need to be calm. This can be difficult for parents to achieve. In school, no one wants to sound like a cry baby, and a classroom teacher can (sometimes) harness peer pressure to keep order in the classroom. I am sure that Helen and Anna would be better behaved in front of their peers. Anna in particular struggled to remain calm in her early school years. (In retrospect, this was probably because her school work made no sense at all to her because she had learning difficulties, but I hadn't worked that out.)

After reading about the working memory and the long-term memory in *Why Students Don't Like School*, the actual problem with being upset about school work (or for that matter, being upset about anything while trying to do school work) became clear. It's obvious that children can't work when they're fussing, but it helped me to be able to explain to Helen and Anna that they had a limited capacity working brain (we drew a picture of it and stuck it up on the wall). If the working brain was only thinking about the schoolwork, schoolwork was easy; if 75% of the working brain was thinking about how angry it was about the school work, or the impending departure from a favorite cove, or leaving a good friend behind, then schoolwork was going to be much, much harder.

My early years of teaching were peppered by comments like, "pay attention," "focus on your work," "listen up," etc. Doug Lemov explains these phrases are doomed to failure. As adults, we have a behavioral response to "pay attention," but your children may not know it yet. They will do better with concrete instructions that will lead to their paying attention, such as Lemov's example of, "John, put your feet under your desk, put your pencil down, and put your eyes on me."[182] I became much more explicit in telling Helen and Anna exactly what I wanted them to do, whether it was to put their pencils down and look at me, or write down a definition in the back of their math notebooks. I realize that in the early years, I had an assumption that they would understand how to learn something, but in fact, they had absolutely no idea.

I was quite careful to ensure that any required punishment did not punish me. It was a very, very rare thing that I canceled a project or trip, or forbade them a treat that I wanted to partake in. I remember once refusing to allow Anna to go ashore in a tiny village in the Chilean Channels because she hadn't finished her school work, but in the end, I was the one who really regretted not seeing the town.

There are days, however, when Helen and Anna took hours and hours over their work, and it made me crazy because I would rather have been doing something else. In these cases, my taking more of a directional role in school, leaning over their shoulders and holding them accountable for their work made more of a difference than future threats.

I was also careful not to make threats that I wouldn't actually follow through with, because I felt this would make future threats meaningless. If I said, "If you don't finish you won't go ashore," I had to be willing to stick to that 100%.

Sometimes, however, there are days when there's no solution but to stop school. Children will eventually learn their math. One advantage long-term homeschoolers have over short-term homeschoolers is they have a chance to catch up and more leeway to decide what opportunities are too good to miss and when school work needs to be finished, no matter what is missed in consequence. Of course, the most common piece of advice from experienced homeschoolers is "don't sweat the schedule," but when you're starting out, it's almost impossible not to worry about how your children are matching up with those in school. Have you made the right choice? Or are you destroying their future options? Each year, I firmly believed that, well, maybe last year I could have relaxed a bit, but *this year* is critical.

Every family will come to different conclusions about what has to get done when, and how disciplined the school hours need to be. For my part, it was extremely important to me that school be academic yet not take a long time, so in elementary school I found myself more on the discipline side of the scale: we had school during set hours, and they had to do the work. A couple of times in early elementary school, this meant I invoked the standard version of "time out" in our house. We used Stephen Biddulph's idea of standing at the wall, rather than sending the children to their room. In *The Secrets of Happy Children* he recommends this method over banishing them to another room for a "time out" because the child is still with the family, and his behavior is observable and therefore accountable.[183] In later years, while they had frustrations and resentments about work, it was always about the specific work (which often meant that assignment needed to be reassessed), rather than school in general.

By late elementary school, Helen and Anna's increasing independence in school work meant the discipline side disappeared completely. (In fact, I was the one who usually said, "Don't worry about it," and they said, "But I *have* to get it done.") They had deadlines, but most important, they had a curiosity and enthusiasm about learning. They worked at school most mornings and in the late afternoons/early evenings. In middle school, I was usually part of their school mornings, watching lectures, discussing reading assignments, helping with math, but by the end of middle school they did almost all of that independently.

Judging by friends who began homeschooling at different times, however, it seems that the first few years are the hardest, no matter what age you begin. A friend with a very successful and academically-minded thirteen-year-old started homeschooling, but even she had trouble the first year. Despite his strong academic profile (and it had been his choice to homeschool), he wasn't used to having his mother as his teacher, and he tested her at every turn, though he had never pushed his bricks and mortar teachers in this way. If you are planning to homeschool over the long term, this may be a battle worth fighting, even if you don't cover as much in the first few years as you'd hoped. You have time to catch up. However, if you're only leaving schools for a year or two, going with a more child-led approach may be worth it for the pay off in family peace. Many one-year traveling homeschooling families decide to only teach math, for example.

Structure of Individual Classes

Most homeschooling parent teachers are not going to be giving a lecture class, but knowledge about how to structure a class can be helpful in some of the teaching classes they might do, such as working with advanced reading materials or second languages.

David Sousa in *How the Brain Learns* provides a detailed graph of retention over a class period. He divides a typical forty minute class into three sections, Prime Time 1, Down Time, and Prime Time 2, which does not achieve the high level of retention of Prime Time 1. The key time, as he describes it, for imparting new information is roughly between minutes five and fifteen of the class. He maintains that students should only view accurate material during this time, rather than using it to correct homework or for exploratory work. The down slump between minutes fifteen and twenty five can be used to practice materials, and then Prime Time 2 from thirty to forty minutes can be used for closure, or recapping information. (He notes that the longer the class, the higher the percentage of downtime, for example a forty minute class has ten minutes of down time or twenty-five percent; a eighty minute class has thirty minutes of downtime or thirty-eight percent.)[184]

You can use this to your advantage when organizing the school day. For example, say you want to do a difficult history reading. If you join your students for the first twenty minutes, reading together, then leave them for ten or fifteen minutes to write down a summary, and then join them for ten minutes to recap and discuss further, and then give them a break, you will be maximizing their attention. Likewise, in math, you can spend Prime Time 1 teaching and demonstrating the new ideas, Down Time doing practice exercises, and Prime Time 2 correcting and going over those practice exercises. Further practice problems can be assigned as "homework" to reinforce the skill.

Although, as Sousa points out, lecture classes are the least effective way of learning material,[185] they are a very common way of presenting information. As a homeschool teacher, you will likely encounter lecture classes if you buy commercial DVDs (such as the Great Courses) or if you go to online help, such as the Khan Academy lectures, which can provide valuable assistance especially for math and sciences. Video lectures are a great introduction to live lectures, because students can make use of pause, rewind, and even speed controls as they learn to take notes on lecture classes.

The Great Courses lectures are half an hour long, which works well with Sousa's framework of organizing a class, but we found, with frequent pauses for clarification, the lectures routinely took us an hour to get through. We would have perhaps done better to watch for twenty minutes, pause to discuss, draw, or write about the materials we'd just covered, before continuing with the rest of the lecture. When left to her own devices in high school, Helen almost always watches her half-hour physics lectures in two parts, pausing when she feels herself losing focus.

The Khan Academy videos are almost all between seven and fifteen minutes long. As Salman Khan relates in *The One World Schoolhouse: Education Reimagined*, his initial videos were short because that's what YouTube allowed, but even with a relaxation of the YouTube time limits, he has not extended his videos because brain research confirms that ten to fifteen minutes is the most effective amount of time for a lecture.[186] I clearly remember the difficulty of trying to maintain concentration through an hour and a half lecture at Harvard – it couldn't be done without a large mug of coffee and copious note-taking. While my friends preferred the hour and a half classes because they met only twice a week, I much preferred spreading out the work over three one hour lectures, and, when presented with an equal choice between classes, invariably chose the three day a week schedule.

Another option that is becoming popular in some schools is the notion of a "flipped classroom." Instead of the traditional teacher lecture in the school, followed by solo homework exercises at night, the teachers make podcasts of their lectures (or assign a Khan Academy video) as homework and then work through exercises and discussions together as a class. This often works well, because the student can pause or rewind the lecture, and spend the class time getting feedback and having discussions.

In seventh and eighth grade, we flipped math class in a slightly different way. In the morning, when they're fresh, Helen and Anna worked on their "math homework," and then at night, when they were tired but reasonably alert, we went over the answers and had a discussion about the problems. This was a much more effective use of time because they were being creative and problem solving independently at their sharpest time of the day, and using the evening to have the right answer explained if they didn't understand it.

More than One Student

One of the most compelling reasons for not using a boxed curriculum is you can combine subjects for two or more children. Once Anna began school, she joined Helen to have a two-child classroom for science, history, language, and within a couple of years, math. This is a huge time saver, promotes learning through their interaction, yet it can actually add to the teacher's job, because you need to make sure that all the students are having a chance to learn. It's a mini-version of what classroom teachers face every day.

In history and science, we did a lot of reading aloud in the early years. At first, I did all the reading, but gradually Helen and Anna took over from me, which helped them work on reading fluency at the same time as learning the content. Doug Lemov's book, *Teach Like a Champion,* was very helpful in streamlining this approach. He suggests that when one child is reading, the others should be tracking on the page, but that the key to ensuring that it happens is to alternate readers in a random way, sometimes in the middle of a paragraph. He warns, and I certainly found, if you change readers at predictable places, the other students zone out.[187] By simply saying, "Anna" instead of "Thank you, Helen, well read. Okay, Anna, now it's your turn, please read" the transition was fast, efficient, and everyone's focus stayed on the reading.

Hamish built a wooden book stand (two pieces of plywood that slot together, but come apart to lie flat in the school box). Adjusting the book sometimes became a power struggle. In order to track the words as the other reads, they both needed to be able to see it, which meant they have to sit next to each other, with me on the side. Obviously it would be easier to have two copies of the books, but that is not feasible, either in cash or in space aboard. (Once Anna caught up to Helen in math, however, I began purchasing two math books so they didn't have to wait to do their exercises.)

After reading Lemov, I changed the way I ask questions when they were studying a subject together. He writes: "Using this sequence – 'Question. Pause. Name." – ensures that every student hears the question and begins preparing an answer during the pause you've provided."[188] After reading that, I began to ask the question first and then specify which child should answer. If there was a short answer, I asked them to write it down in their notebooks and then I looked over their shoulders to confirm whether it was right or wrong. (This was particularly useful in math and language studies.)

As Helen and Anna progressed through school, discussion became less focused on my questions and more on their thoughts, but taking a bit of time to write down ideas and answers before speaking was still a valuable use of time, even after I stopped directing with questions.

Day to Day Scheduling

In *How the Brain Learns*, David Sousa describes the average circadian rhythms of most people. Adults and children tend to peak and slump about the same time, whereas teenagers are offset by about an hour. This can be useful when scheduling your school day.

Sousa describes that after rising at six a.m., children and adults reach a peak plateau at seven a.m., and work at their best until about noon. Teenagers will start their peak work at eight a.m., and carry on until one p.m. Adults and children have a faster slump down from that peak, reaching bottom at one p.m., and perking up again (although not to morning standards) by two p.m. Teenagers have a slower descent from one p.m. to a low at three p.m., and are ready to concentrate again by four p.m.[189]

In this pattern (which may of course shift slightly due to difference of daylight length and individuals), I find a large echo of the way our school has worked, but I also see where we could have done better: children will be better off quitting at noon and doing an hour of work in the late afternoon; teenagers can work until one and then should quit until about four p.m. I would add that perhaps adults trying to directly teach teenagers should focus their efforts to between eight and noon (or, as we have certainly found works best, between nine and eleven) to work on the teaching classes when both parties are working at their peak efficiency.

Interestingly, this pattern fits exactly to the schedule I had in high school in the 1980s. At Phillips Exeter, where most students were boarding students (I wasn't, but I never left campus before eight p.m.), we had classes until early afternoon, followed by lunch and sports, with a second round of classes in the late afternoon. The late classes were difficult after intense physical activity, but judging by Sousa's claims, it was better than trying to fit those classes in before three. I have certainly noticed that very little constructive work is ever done by anyone in our family between one and three.

Recess?

Back when I was in school, almost every school alloted time for recess; in the younger grades there were two or three outdoor breaks a day, but nowadays many schools are canceling recess entirely, almost certainly to the detriment of the children.[190] When I started teaching Helen and Anna on board, I assumed they would want to go outside and run around for a bit and then come back and finish up, but they hated doing that. Right from the start, they preferred finishing their work and then going outside, and they always considered it a punishment to be brought back inside to finish the rest of the day's work. In the first year of teaching both of them at age six and five, they had absolutely no notion of the future, even in terms of an hour hence. Saying, "work at this now and then you can play outside" or whatever carrot I had to offer made no difference.

For the past several years, Anna has frequently taken a break from school and paced around the deck for five or ten minutes to burn off some energy, but they've always said no to the possibility of going off playing for an hour and then returning to school. Your kids may be different, of course, but there's certainly no requirement for recess if school only takes three or four hours. By high school, when schoolwork took considerably longer periods, Helen and Anna both split their work up into mornings and late afternoon/evenings.

Scheduling Classes

In elementary and middle school, I tried to be available to help Helen and Anna while they are doing school, and if I were going to be fully occupied and unable to help for some reason, I made sure the assignments were suitably simple so they can do them on their own.

In middle school, however, I found it useful to schedule some classes for a specific time of day. Before that, I would simply try to keep an eye on things, and tell them to come together for history or math when it seemed convenient, but this meant that joint lessons were often pushed to the end of the day, and everyone would be grumpy at being pulled away from something else.

We solved that by putting the joint classes on the schedule at a specific time. So, for example, if there was a math lesson needed for them to understand the day's math, I wrote 8:00 Math lecture w/ Kate. If it was simply more review of math material, there was no math time on the schedule. On days when there was no need for a math lesson, it was a good time to schedule a history lesson, so I would write: 8:00 History w/ Kate, and we spent an hour going through the reading and making a formal outline or whatever.

By middle school, Helen and Anna did most of their history reading independently, but when we didn't have math, I often did history with them, to make sure they were comprehending the reading and to reinforce skills.

Because Helen and Anna did so much of their work together, the scheduling really only came into play for things they did together, and I could usually balance their needs the rest of the time. However, if your students are doing more separate work, it can be useful to schedule classes for them to ensure that you're available to help them at that time period, and that your other children know they should be working on review work during that time, because they aren't going to be able to get your attention.

Many of the books I've read about homeschooling suggest that all the classes are scheduled, which does help children gain a sense of time, but quite often work goes faster or slower than an hour per class, and scheduling school "to the bell" teaches students that *their* interest in their work doesn't matter. As New York Teacher of the Year turned educational critic John Gatto declares: "The lesson of bells is that no work is worth finishing, so why care too deeply about anything?"[191] I tried to schedule a few things, and then give them the responsibility for working the rest of their assignments into the rest of the morning. This gave them practice at taking control of their own work (in the way homework would at a regular school), cut down on the number of interruptions, and streamlined the process of getting ready for joint classes. Without a set time, it was easy for Helen and Anna to take fifteen minutes "getting ready" for a class.

A day's schedule for Helen might look like:

- 8:00 Japanese
- 9:00 Math
- [10:00 Spelling (Anna)]
- Diary
- Dishes
- Math workbook
- Japanese flashcards
- Piano
- History reading & summary
- Last thing: sort out school boxes, sharpen 3 pencils and put into box, put box away

(Pleasure reading at this stage was entirely independent, so it wasn't on the school schedule.)

In the tropics, school typically started at 6:30 or 7:00 (in the winter in Alaska, it was 9:00 or 9:30), which gave Helen up to an hour and a half to warm up before the scheduled classes – then she preferred to do piano as her first subject. However, even if she hadn't finished piano, she knew she needed to stop at 8:00 for Japanese. Japanese took about forty minutes, which left her twenty minutes before the math lecture. She could chose whether to take a ten-minute break, do her diary, or study her history flashcards. She also knew that she was to separate math workbook from math lecture, Japanese flashcards from Japanese, and so on. This helped teach her how to make the best use of her time, without learning to do so on my time.

Helen and Anna have very different strategies for getting through the school day, and it changes year to year. A few years ago, Anna started off first thing, and numbered the day's assignments in order. Then she began charging through them. She became very annoyed at the thought of having to pause for breakfast. Helen preferred a slow warm up, a leisurely session at the piano, and took her time over each subject. Anna was highly efficient, with minimal transitions between subjects, and a 10-minute exercise break whenever she needed one. Helen took far longer over her school work, and could be found hidden away with a novel when she was supposed to be making a transition, but on the other hand, she did her work tidily and thoroughly. I have utterly failed at teaching them to take the best of each other's study habits and leave the worst behind.

These days it's almost the opposite. Helen charges up at five a.m. and plunges straight into her math, and Anna is the one to sleep in. Helen plays the piano now before supper. Now Helen is the one to make quick transitions, and Anna is the one to be found sneaking a novel when a chemistry deadline looms. This is one of the great things about homeschooling – as long as the baseline work is being done well, it doesn't matter what time of day it happens, although I do insist that they get out of the house in the afternoon, when their concentration is at its lowest and the day is usually at its best.

Sleep

> "I really wish I'd listened to what my mother told me when I was young."
> "Why, what did she tell you?"
> "I don't know, I didn't listen."
>
> – Douglas Adams[192]

My mother knew all along what researchers are just discovering about children's sleep. All through elementary and middle school, I had a ridiculously early bedtime. My peers were up watching the *Six Million Dollar Man* or whatever the show of the year was, and I was in bed, stewing about not being allowed to stay up as late as my friends. I was also one of the top students in the class.

In *NurtureShock*,[193] Po Bronson and Ashley Merryman discuss recent scientific findings about children in ten chapters; chapter two, "The Lost Hour," describes how children now sleep an hour less per day than they did a generation ago and examines the profound effects it has on their academic achievement.[194] It turns out that my mother was right, after all. How annoying is that?

"Because children's brains are a work in progress until the age of 21, and because much of that work is done while a child is asleep, this lost hour [of sleep] appears to have an exponential impact on children that it simply doesn't have on adults," write Bronson and Merryman. They summarize several experiments that point to lack of sleep causing serious academic performance declines, as well as being potentially implicated in other rising problems such as obesity, ADHD, and perhaps even teenage moodiness.[195]

In one experiment, fourth and sixth graders were sent home with a sleep recording wrist sensor and instructions to go to bed either half an hour earlier or half an hour later than normal. They found:

> The performance gap caused by an hour's difference in sleep was bigger than the gap between a normal fourth-grader and a normal sixth-grader. Which is another way of saying a slightly-sleepy sixth grader will perform in class like a mere fourth-grader. [196]

Children sleep differently from adults and use that sleeping time to process the day's learning, to shift information from the working brain into long-term memory. Without enough sleep, children are unable to retain the information they learned during the day. Bronson and Merryman write, "this is why a good night's sleep is so important for long-term learning of vocabulary words, time tables, historical dates, and all other factual minutiae."[197] Sleep isn't the whole story in learning – as Daniel Willingham describes, students also must think about the material in a particular way,[198] while it is still in their short-term working memories. Reading about the effect of missing sleep has led to a considerable revision of sleep schedules on board *Seal*.

I have a suspicion that this may be at the root of the academic difference between Helen and Anna. In elementary school, Anna went to bed when she was tired. (This is a child who never took a nap when she was a baby or toddler.) Helen, by contrast, didn't want to miss anything, and would stay up, even if she was exhausted. In earlier years, this worked fine, as they would sleep late to get the sleep they needed. Having them sleep late worked particularly well when we were chartering, as the charter guests could rise and caffeinate before the children appeared. Our base in South America meant that dinners were served extremely late when we were in port.

In the tropics, however, there was a great benefit to rising early – five o'clock seemed to work best – in order to start school before the heat of the day started to affect us.

Helen studying math during the heat of the day after a late night was a classic example of what Bronson and Merryman describe: "A tired brain perseverates – it gets stuck on a wrong answer and can't come up with a more creative solution, repeatedly returning to the same answer it already knows is erroneous."[199] Could all her troubles finishing school on time be because she went to bed an hour or two later than her sister? (Within a few years, Helen was the one going to bed early, and Anna had become the night owl. The one sure thing about homeschooling is that as soon as you think you have a handle on the status quo, it changes.)

The National Sleep Foundation and the American Academy of Pediatrics recommends **ten to eleven hours** of sleep every night up to the age of twelve, eight and a half to nine and a half hours from the ages of thirteen to nineteen, and eight hours of sleep a night after that.[200] Even Anna isn't getting that much sleep – in the tropics, at age ten, she typically slept from about eight to five, or nine hours, which I believed was more than enough. And I certainly never considered that lack of sleep would have a quantifiable effect on their academic abilities – sure, parents know that lack of sleep can make a child grumpy, but I didn't know it could effect their very abilities.

Bronson and Merryman summarize several studies of high school students: "Teens who received A's averaged about fifteen more minutes sleep than the B students, who in turn averaged fifteen more minutes than the C's. . . . Every fifteen minutes counts."[201] Could that be all there is to it? It is certainly worth trying to schedule more sleep in your homeschool.

Daniel Willingham's analysis of the data suggests that sleep is not as important as all this,[202] and that most of the association is merely correlational – does the lack of sleep **cause** the problems itself, or is it merely a symptom? Or in other words, did I do well in school because my mother made me go to bed early, or because, being the type of mother who put up with the howls of forcing me to bed early, she was also the sort of mother who pushed me academically, and made sure she knew exactly what grade I received on every test, and asked how I could do better?

It reminds me a bit of a friend who started driving with the headlights on in the daytime after reading that people who did so were less likely to have accidents. He admitted that of course, it may be simply that the people who drive with their headlights on in the day are also the same people who are less likely to have accidents in the first place, but why not put yourself in the favorable pool, especially when it has such a low cost? I feel the same about trying to get Helen and Anna a bit more sleep. The studies which show students do better with more sleep may not be cause and effect, but the costs of that hour extra of sleep are not great, and are potentially extremely beneficial.

Conveying Assignments and Keeping Records

Every family I've spoken with conveys assignments in a slightly different way. Through elementary and middle school, we tried out quite a few methods, and the system has changed with the age of the children and the complexity of the assignments. In the early years, I simply told them what to do next. After that, I switched to a seven day schedule, where the workload was divided up into various days, but I told them what their individual assignments were on each day. Next came a white board, where I wrote the day's assignments (and the date, which helped them learn the concept, which can be hard for homeschoolers when the days of the week are fairly irrelevant).

The difficulty with the white board was two-fold. First, traveling around in remote parts of the world, it's hard to have enough white board markers. In Uruguay, we were able to purchase refillable ones, but eventually, we ran out of the pot of refill ink and couldn't replace it. The second problem with the white board was I then had to keep records of what we'd done. I kept a list in a notebook of each day's work, and that worked fairly well, but sometimes I'd get out of the habit and forget for weeks at a time. We had to do evaluations with the state of New Hampshire at that stage (they have since waived submitting homeschool evaluations to the local school board), and I wrote up an annual summary of what each child had accomplished over the year, but fortunately no one ever asked to see my daily logs.

While we were traveling through the Pacific, it was very hard to keep to a day-related schedule, because we'd miss four Mondays in a row, for example, as we moved the boat between island groups. That year, I made up four assignment cards for each girl on colored index cards, and merely announced at the beginning of the day which color schedule they were to do. That worked very well for making sure we didn't miss out on any subjects, but it still left me with a record-keeping problem.

Between fourth and seventh grades, we adopted "the Anton." (We are a family fond of silly puns and abbreviations. It is the check-off book, hence Anton Chekhov.) I certainly could have introduced it in late elementary school if I'd thought of it. I made a rough seven-day schedule to distribute subjects through the week, but I wasn't strict about which day of the week matched what schedule (in case we missed a couple of Mondays in a row). Referring to the master schedule, I would write the day's assignments for the girls. I define the assignments specifically. In the early years, I let them "do the next lesson" in math, for example, and I know there were many days when I was busy with other things that nothing actually happened. They are more accountable with specific page numbers and exercises.

I tried to write up the Anton the night before, and then, if the girls woke up early, they could start school without me. We spent several weeks in a bay with a family with four children; Helen and Anna were up every morning before the sun and had their schoolwork done by nine-thirty so they could be ashore at ten with the other kids.

I put tick boxes on each subject (and many of them were the same assignment for both girls). The Anton worked extremely well for them to have independence about the order of assignments, yet be accountable for doing it, and all my record keeping was done in one move.

When they were in sixth and seventh grade, we moved to a calender app on a family tablet. The Anton worked extremely well for day by day assignments, but it didn't work so well for long term assignments such as paper or reading deadlines. The calendar app worked better than a wall calendar because there is plenty of room for detail, and they could see ahead to general family schedules and the school deadlines.

By the time Anna was in seventh and Helen was in eighth, however, I found that the calender app didn't have enough room for assignments, so I began typing up monthly schedules, with a split page of a calendar on top with paper deadlines and math test dates, followed by a reading and writing list on the bottom that they needed to do in the month. By this point, they were in charge of figuring out when to achieve all that reading and writing, and how to mix daily assignments with long term assignments.

I'm relieved that the long term assignments finally work. In late elementary and middle school, I was always puzzled how little success I had with having them plan long term assignments, and I was sure that I was able to do so at a far younger age. In retrospect, however, I think my parents made sure they knew when my deadlines were, and they were able to push me to work on the various projects, even if the teachers didn't.

School Year Schedule

Most American states require 180 to 190 school days a year, usually taking place from September to June. In England, it's 195. There are a few three day weekends, and several weeks off, and of course, weekends off. Homeschooling, this schedule doesn't make sense. Although we have met many families who persist with the Monday to Friday schedule, we had school seven days a week much of the time during elementary and middle school.

In the early years, having school seven days a week is a huge boon for the teacher. I don't know how elementary school teachers handle Mondays, because whenever we took a day or two off in those early years, it would take another two days to get back in the groove.

The other advantage of having school seven days a week is one has great liberty to cancel school. For about half the year, we take paying guests on board the boat, and I'm much too busy for school. I declare this summer vacation, and we have to focus a bit more to get a year's work done in the time remaining. For two years, however, we didn't charter as we crossed the Pacific, and the school year took an entire year. Once, I counted it up and was surprised to discover that in the previous 144 days, we had done

78 days of school. It seemed like far more, but even at that rate, we easily have accomplished the standard "school year" in a year.

School works best when I consider it my job and devote myself completely to it. I can write emails or read a book, but anything more exacting – fixing things on the boat, organizing business projects, or writing articles – turns their questions into an interruption, and it simply doesn't work. By the time they were twelve and ten, I could leave them fairly unsupervised for several days in a row, and school continued to happen, but that wouldn't last for more than a few days. We all three are tired after a day at school.

Evaluations

For several years, we did annual evaluations with a certified teacher. It meant we had to be in New Hampshire at some point during the year for the evaluation, but we were visiting grandparents there anyway. The evaluations were a requirement for homeschooling for the state of New Hampshire, and I figured it could be helpful for us to be officially registered somewhere as homeschoolers. In the early years, the evaluator was a useful tool in setting the scene for school. Why do they have to do neat presentation of their work? Why can't they eat the corners of their math book pages? Why do we have to have school today? After several years of homeschooling, that becomes less important. The evaluator also helps encourage the parent, by letting you know whether or not you're on track to meet the local standards.

(Sometimes, talking with classroom teachers isn't a help, however, since they don't spend day after day with your child. I asked an elementary school teacher to evaluate Anna's writing, and he felt it was fine and would take care of itself – he had seen children her age working at a far lower level. As her parent and teacher I could see that there was a significant lag in comparison with the quality of the rest of her work, but the encouragement from a professional meant about a six-month delay in my figuring out she had genuine learning difficulties.)

Every year, even when we haven't had the evaluations, I have declared the "Year's End," done end-of-year testing and written up a comprehensive summary of what each child has done over the school year. I don't think anyone is going to ask to see this for elementary school and probably not even for middle school, but it helps me to have a record of it, especially as I am fairly slack about day to day record keeping.

Many land-based homeschoolers have their children do the annual standardized testing at local schools, which seems like a great idea, especially as it habituates the children to the standardized testing that they will face in their college applications, but meeting that schedule can be difficult. Old editions of the New York State Regents Exam are available online, so another option is to have your children take that exam at the end of each school year, so you can see how they are doing. For those needing or wishing for professionally scored exams in the US, Seton Testing [www.setontesting.com] offers many of the common standardized tests for home administration.

Who's the Teacher?

In nearly every homeschooling family we have met in real life the mother is the teacher, but that doesn't have to be the case – we do know one family where the father is the primary teacher, and another where the parents alternated every six weeks. Online, I've met numerous single-parent mothers who homeschool, although never in real life. I've worked on board a yacht as a tutor, and we've met another boat with a tutor.

Even if one parent is the dedicated teacher, the support of the other parent (and family members) makes a huge difference. We've met a fair number of parents (generally not the teaching parent!) who resent the schooling and complain that it is a waste of time. If one parent sees schooling as an imposition, perhaps you can strike a bargain not to negotiate school time in front of the children.

One of you is probably going to be better at explaining things, one of you is probably going to have more patience and more rigidness to enforce the school hours. But that doesn't mean you can't sometimes farm things off on the other parent, especially when you're nearing the end of your patience. I do 99% of the formal schooling and Hamish does most of the day to day maintenance and we split much of the cooking, probably fairly evenly if one looks at the entire year.

Although I do most of the formal schooling, Hamish is very much involved in teaching Helen and Anna academic subjects outside of school hours. I said earlier that our meals tend to sound like seminars, and Hamish is very good at leading them into a discussion of some element that we've covered recently, or something he's read about. I make a point to show him Helen and Anna's work (in front of Helen and Anna) when they've done a particularly thorough job. I didn't give letter grades for work until high school, but in the earlier years, if I showed it to Hamish, it was the equivalent of an "A," and I think it has more impact at that stage than a mere letter on the top of their paper.

What is School?

If you're starting out with older children, they already have the concept and the behavior of school down, and they will probably be simply delighted that it now takes three hours instead of six (plus the commute). With children who've never been to school however, it can be difficult to define the time as "school," since there is no sharp division between home and school.

During the first year of school, when Helen only studied reading from *Teach Your Child to Read,* and worked through *Get Set for Kindergarten* from Handwriting Without Tears, I didn't do very much to set the scene, although we did use the Handwriting Without Tears CD of songs about such things as starting letters at the top (Anna starts her letters at the bottom, of course), and a catchy one about the Ant, the Bug and the Bee, although I can't remember the point of it now. Putting the music on was a signal that it was school time. At this stage, school took about forty minutes a day, and was almost all directly supervised, so it went fairly smoothly. We took time off for ocean passages and charter work, so the 100 days of reading lessons lasted about six months.

By the next year, however, school was a bit more demanding, and I needed a way to separate it from the rest of our lives, which took place in the same space. If you have a larger home, it may be worthwhile making a dedicated space for school in your house, ideally with desks or adjustable tables suited to your students' heights. In the Falkland Islands, students living in "Camp" (anyone not in town) are homeschooled with government assistance until age ten. The school program is so thorough that they even loan age-appropriate furniture to the families, so that the children are working with good posture.

Our table is too high for the children to use as a writing or typing desk. I have tried to get around this in various ways. Helen and Anna have desks in their room which are more or less the right height, but they prefer working in the kitchen. Posture does help penmanship and typing, and it is probably most important when working at a computer to avoid repetitive strain injuries. My dream boat has a school room / office in it, with a typing-height table for working, but even if we had that, I suspect they'd be up in the saloon looking out the windows.

I have tried to delineate school in various ways. At first, we started every school day with the songs, then we moved to realistic drawing, where I would pick something from the galley (a mug, a glass of water, a sponge, etc.) and we would all three sit around the table and sketch it in pencil. That worked very well for a while, but eventually it became a delaying tactic, and Helen and Anna could spend most of the morning on their drawings. By this time, they spent much of their free time drawing (I buy a ream of printer paper for every voyage), so after the next summer break, I quietly removed the drawing part of the lessons.

The next experiment was uniforms. This sounds a bit crazy, but it worked surprisingly well. For starters, it got them out of their pajamas in the morning and kept their grubby outdoor clothes off the furniture. Changing their clothes was a symbol that school had begun, and shedding them was the sign it had ended. At this time, we were based in South America, and all the kids they saw going to school were wearing uniforms, which certainly played a part. Argentine children wear what looks like a doctor's lab coat over their clothes – that is a very simple way to mark school time. By the next school year, the uniforms were no longer necessary; Helen and Anna had been indoctrinated into the idea that they had school every morning, and there was no longer a need to make such a bold statement.

We have friends who have continued to make a sharp delineation between school time and the rest of the time. They are extremely dedicated homeschool teachers, and spend about twenty minutes a day organizing their lesson plans, and run a far more school-like school than I do, with a blackboard and beginning the school day with stretching, singing and working on memorizing a poem.

Standards and Objectives

M ost national or state school programs have a published set of standards that professional teachers need to make sure they are meeting. Looking through the standards of your local district can be very helpful (and likely reassuring), but it's not necessary to introduce the standards explicitly in to your classroom. Some bricks and mortar schools go so far as to have the objective for the day written on the board in each class, so the students, and more importantly, academic observers, can see what the teacher is trying to achieve for a particular day.

This can be extremely helpful in streamlining the efforts of a cadre of thousands or millions of teachers, but for the homeschooling parent, it is probably easiest to skim through the standards, reassure yourself that you're on the right track, and teach content instead. Let the textbook authors wade through the standards (and if you end up using an older textbook with slightly outdated standards, it is probably not going to matter too terribly much). If you're teaching out of the right "grade level" math book, for example, you can be pretty confident that your students are working at the appropriate pace. The standards do change through the years, and different countries and districts teach subjects in different orders (even in mathematics), so it is probably helpful to stick with one program or nationally aligned curriculum throughout primary mathematics.

I've never tried to align our school specifically to a set of standards. Instead, we have focused on content. In history, for example, I want them to learn the history of the period under study, and that is the stated "goal" of the schooling. The techniques of historical analysis come slowly over years of practice, and they will learn those techniques as a byproduct of their study of history. I may have it as a background goal, for example, that they learn "outlining," but such techniques are never explicit. The techniques of learning are a continuum that develops over every year of education through the study of content. When writing up the annual evaluations, I blathered on about "developing skills in ... " and so on, but it didn't play a role in our day to day school.

I have never had to face the question, "what is the point of learning this?" If your school is haunted by that question, explicit referral to standards could be beneficial. However, it is probably more effective to try to establish a culture of knowledge in the family, so that the "what's the point?" question has no way in.

The other objection I have to using explicit standards when homeschooling is that they can increase the pressure for "moving on" to new topics before the primary goals have been reached. California, for example, has the stated goal that "The California State Board of Education acknowledges that the goal for 8th grade students is Algebra I. However, they also recognize that not all 8th grade students have the necessary prerequisite skills for Algebra I. Consequently, the State Board of Education adopted two sets of standards for 8th grade."

Not so long ago, algebra was strictly the provenance of high school, and only a few middle schools offered it to their very best students. For homeschoolers, a thorough understanding of a concept is far more valuable than the procession through the sequence. If your children wind up a year or so behind at the end of their schooling, yet have superb understanding, they will be better off in the long run. School can always be delayed a year if necessary, and if you continue homeschooling, you can teach each subject at the level appropriate to the child. If you compare Anna as a fifth grader to the California standards, she was working on seventh grade math, history, science, and reading, but at a fourth grade level in writing and spelling, and she still hadn't mastered cursive writing (third grade). In a regular school, the spelling and writing would hamper her progression in the other subjects, particularly history, but there's no need for that in homeschooling. A year later, her composition level jumped a grade or two, without pausing at the intermediate stages.

E.D. Hirsch, an education researcher / philosopher has founded the Core Knowledge Foundation, and has recently released their 285-page Core Knowledge Sequence for free download, a series of standards for Kindergarten through Eighth Grade. The Standards are in use in schools in various parts of the US, and the central tenet is that students – particularly disadvantaged ones – need exposure to a specific core of content in order to progress in school. Specific goals for content and skills are clearly laid out, year by year.[203]

(Lest you think this endorsement of the Core Knowledge Sequence means I'm advocating *What Your [Whatever] Grader Needs to Know,* which purports to seed "cultural literacy," I have to tell you they make my skin crawl. They contain digests of wonderful stories, crammed together. No kid is going to remember the stories in this way. It's like a SparkNotes to Education, and like SparkNotes, it can only get you through the exam, not into a lifetime of knowledge.)

I agree wholeheartedly with much of the sequence, and it is very similar to what I've taught Helen and Anna. I do object that "evolution" isn't specifically mentioned until the seventh grade; as I've said earlier this should be introduced right away – it's the only way in which biological sciences make sense.

The history program is far more scattered than I would like. If I were outlining a program from scratch again, I would rely heavily on the Core Knowledge Sequence for most subjects, but the subject order I outlined in the History chapter (page 225) for chronological history.

As in the California sequence, the Core Knowledge Sequence has moved algebra firmly back to the eighth grade; again, as discussed above, that seems like a broad leap if the underlying elementary school mathematics teaching doesn't change profoundly. If you use a thorough, concept-driven curriculum such as Singapore or Mammoth, your children should be ready for algebra in the eighth grade, but not at the expense of rushing your children into it before they have the elementary math mastered.

The language used in many of the standards is very vague; the same words could apply to a first grader or a fourth grader. If you are planning to homeschool all the way through elementary school, it may be worth looking at the goals for the end of third grade, and taking the long view. Children proceed in stair-like jumps, rather than a ladder-like smooth slope. Instead of worrying about each milestone for kindergarten, first, and second grades, see where they are at age nine, when skills tend to smooth out. There's nothing wrong with you or your children if those age nine skills happen at eight or ten. You're homeschooling.

Links:

- US Common Core:
  [www.corestandards.org/read-the-standards/]

- UK National Curriculum:
  [www.gov.uk/government/collections/national-curriculum]

- California Standards:
  [www.cde.ca.gov/be/st/ss/index.asp]

- US Core Knowledge Foundation:
  [www.coreknowledge.org/]

Budget & Ordering Supplies

Homeschooling is probably going to cost you more than a state/public education and considerably less than a private education. In remote regions or while traveling in countries without libraries in your language, it will not be possible to do it as inexpensively as a homeschooler with access to a good local library. Making your own curriculum is going to be far cheaper than a boxed system, especially if you have more than one child.

Families with access to a laptop and a library can significantly cut down on these costs. The budgets presented here are for families living without library access, but unwilling to sacrifice academic opportunities.

Even without a library, there are ways to cut costs. Buying second hand books is a good start. (Try to avoid ones that have been highlighted. It's better if they aren't underlined, but highlighting is far worse and can make the book almost unreadable. Don't buy used books online if they don't provide details on the condition.) Another way to save money with textbooks is to buy the previous edition. If Amazon offers the new chemistry book, edition eight for $140, you can probably find a new copy of edition seven for $35 or so. I wouldn't recommend this approach for astronomy, however, as our understanding is changing extremely rapidly. Atlases are a big expense, but again, the second to latest edition can offer big savings.

The other question to ask before buying a second hand textbook, particularly if it is a textbook aimed at schools rather than homeschoolers, is do I need solution manuals? Generally, I recommend looking at commercial textbooks aimed at schools rather than homeschooling packages, particularly for the sciences and history. In my case, I'm not concerned with the answers for history textbooks – I'm comfortable evaluating my students' work. In the case of the sciences, however, I want that help. To teach physics, for example, I want to have the answers to make sure I'm on the right track. I recently purchased a second hand copy of Conceptual Physics 10/E from Amazon for $50. This seemed like a great bargain until I realized I could not access a solution manual. The publisher, Pearson, offers online teacher's manuals for free to homeschoolers, but only if you are a registered homeschooler and you have bought the textbook directly through Pearson. In this case, the 11/E of Conceptual Physics direct from Pearson purchasing costs $127 (plus free shipping); or more than double the cost of a clean copy of the 10/E. But, if you look at homeschooling packages, such as Saxon Homeschooling Physics, you pay extra for the teaching manuals, and so $127 for the whole package suddenly doesn't seem so outrageous. I'm uninterested in teacher manuals and solutions for history and English, so I can investigate second-hand options; I want them for foreign languages, science, and mathematics, so I'm more likely to pay full price for those in exchange for the perks. (All prices from 2014.)

Kindles (or other ebooks) and a laptop can be very useful for your older students, but they can be previous generation versions. Friends and relatives might be upgrading, and it's amazing how old a computer you can use if children aren't gaming. Kindle offers a "sponsored" version for slightly over half price. When you have internet access, it displays ads when the device is turned off, but once you're out in the middle of nowhere, it reverts to standard Kindle behavior, since it can't download the new ads. (In any event, the ads are extremely non-intrusive.)

We like the Great Courses videos for older students (late middle school, high school, and for the parents), but similar material can also be found for free online. In addition, the Great Courses programs all go on sale once a year, so if you plan ahead and subscribe to their mailing lists, you can save up to 75% on the list price. If you will be traveling, perhaps a friend with a stable mailing address could do this for you.

I also try to buy textbooks and lab equipment early. I purchased most textbooks long before the girls were ready to read them alone, so that we could use them through two cycles of study.

You will need to put aside an amount of money – $1500 a year for the first child and $500 for the second child is a generous allowance – to get the books you need, and the money needs to be available all at once so that you can pre-order books all together when you are in a convenient place to receive them if you are traveling or living internationally. We have met families trying to do it on almost no budget – getting books from other yachts, picking up the odd book locally, etc., but that can make a cohesive education difficult. Once you find a program you like, particularly in mathematics, it is best if you continue with that series over many years. The budget will need to increase with each passing year.

For comparison, in 2016, the Calvert School without teaching support cost $1460 US for grades 1-5 and $1700 US for grades 6-8. There are discounts available to additional siblings and other savings offered through the year if you buy early. This does not include any of the computers, ebook readers or other materials listed in the price list below, nor does it include extra reading materials which you will need if you don't have library access.

School in a Box – Out of the Box

Many beginning homeschoolers are filled with worries about how to do it, how to sit down on Monday morning at the kitchen table and begin school. Many parents want to buy a box labeled "Kindergarten" and "First Grade" and have it all done for them. There are companies where you can do just that, but in my experience, children seldom work on grade level in anything. If you're letting them work at their correct pace, they will naturally move ahead quickly in some subjects and lag behind in others.

For those parents looking for a box, here's an example of a box without a box.[204] Many of the suggested programs are scripted, particularly in the early years, which means the curriculum will tell you exactly what to say and how to teach the program. Because each subject comes from a different company, however, your child can charge ahead in math, move more slowly in writing, or race ahead in reading and go more slowly in math.

This example program also eases the child slowly into school, adding subjects as the years go by.

A Starter Kit (Age 4-6)

- 100 read aloud books ($500)*
- Wildlife identification guides (birds, mammals, insects, etc.) ($50-$100)*
- A children's science encyclopedia ($25)*
- Math manipulatives
  - Cuisenaire Rods ($16 new)
  - Poker chips ($8 new)
  - Base 10 Blocks ($18 new)
- Paints and drawing materials*
- And only when your child is ready and interested ... a phonics-based reading program such as Teach Your Child to Read in 100 Easy Lessons ($14) or All About Reading ($120 / each of 4 levels)

After 6 months – 1 Year Add

- 25-50 easy books (2nd – 3rd grade level) ($250)*
- A math program such as Singapore ($75-$100) or Mammoth ($37) (mastery-based, not enough review for some; usually needs teaching) or Saxon ($135) (spiral, drill-heavy; scripted in the early years, self-teaching later on)
- A handwriting program such as Handwriting Without Tears ($9.50)
- Plenty of paper with lines in the same style as your handwriting program, in case the child wants to write ($12 for 500 sheets of Handwriting Without Tears paper)

---

* Starred items are not included in packaged curricula, and so shouldn't be included in cost comparisons.

After 6 months – 2 Years Add

- An experiment-based or natural history based science program such as Pandia Press R.E.A.L. Science Odyssey's Life, followed by Earth and Space Science, Physics, and Chemistry ($70 each)
- Experimental tools such as the Young Scientists' Club or the Home School Science Tools' kit for the R.E.A.L. Science Odyssey books ($50-$80 / year)
- The Magic School Bus series of cartoon books ($25-$50)*
- 25-50 children's books (3rd-5th grade reading level) ($250)*
- Copy work for children who haven't begun writing on their own
- A program of writing prompts or descriptive letters for children who aren't writing on their own, or are not writing summaries several times a week about science or history
- A history program, such as Story of the World or picture books, easy readers, and read-alouds as described in the History chapter ($10-$15 each for Story of the World)
- Re-evaluate math program – is it still working for you? Singapore students may need to add a daily math review, Saxon students may need less drill, enthusiastic math students may appreciate a move to Beast Academy. Don't stop using manipulatives.
- A musical instrument?

After 1 – 3 Years Add

- A second language program if one isn't being learned from a parent. (Duolingo is very popular.)
- A phonics-based spelling program for students who aren't spelling accurately after a couple of years of a strong reading and writing experience, such as All About Spelling. ($40/level)
- Math facts / mental math emphasis
- 25-50 more children's books (3rd–5th grade level) ($250)*

After 3 – 4 Years Add

- A typing program, such as English Type ($45)[*]
- A writing program that builds on the summary work in history and the sciences, and includes imaginative writing and writing based on outside research
- A grammar program if a strong reading and writing experience has not provided adequate skill

Table 18: Sample Costs Per Year, Elementary School

	Homeschool Teacher List	Calvert	Oak Meadow	Extra books & materials budget[+]
K	$160	$1,150	$300-$450	$500
Grade 1	$200	$1,460	$350-$500	$300
Grade 2	$200-$300	$1,460	$440-$590	$300
Grade 3	$250-$350	$1,460	$430-$580	$300
Grade 4	$250-$350	$1,460	$490	$300

---

[*]   Starred items are not included in packaged curricula, and so shouldn't be included in cost comparisons.

[+]   This extra book and materials budget is needed for all the above programs, but you will need considerably less if you have access to a library

Sample Sixth Grade

Core

- Singapore Math Texts $20 (save with secondhand)[*]
- Singapore Math Workbooks (new) $18
- Singapore Math answer keys (years 4-6), $7
- Daily Math Review $8
- Duiker & Spielvogel history text (secondhand) $65 (will use for all four years of middle school history and again in high school)
- Miller & Levine, Biology or Reece, Campbell's Biology (secondhand) $20-$50
  or Pandia Press R.E.A.L Sciencey Odyssey Biology Level 2 ($105 - $175)
- Art supplies and notebooks $100
- All About Spelling (1 levels) (new) $40
- Strunk & White, Elements of Style, $10

No Library Access

- Detailed history of your own country: approximately $40
- Dorling Kindersley history and science books: (secondhand) $50-$200
- Literature: books & electronic books: $400
- Foreign language books & audio: $60
- Kindle ebook reader (sponsored version): $70

Other Items We Used

- [Dissection tools] $130

---

[*] Be extremely careful with matching math program workbook editions if you decide to buy the textbooks second hand. Singapore has three editions: US, California Standards, and Common Core, plus different revisions of each one which are incompatible. The different editions structure learning in the same way, but introduce topics in different orders.

- [Microscope] $400
- Great Courses, Major Transitions in Evolution, on sale, DVD course $100
- Galore Park So You Really Want to Learn English and answer key: $40
- Test Prep 6 for standardized testing $7
- Beginning Piano DVD course: $100
- Casio keyboard: (new) $125 (61 keys) or $500 (88 keys)
- Laptop computer: $250

The core list costs under $400 for the year, plus another $600 for those without library access. Everything but the math workbooks, test prep, and art supplies are reusable for a younger student. Multi-year electronics add about $350, high school science equipment can easily be another $500, but that will see you through many years of homeschooling. Full high school lab sciences is probably the biggest expense most homeschoolers will face, so we try to buy early to have the most use out of the tools. One child taught herself piano for a $200 investment, but the $500 keyboard is much better, and she later found that a real teacher was a huge improvement on a DVD.

Traveling Families

Life on board a sailboat or on the road can be far more social than you might expect, even when you're cruising in remote regions. We find, almost without exception, that everyone we meet is someone we want to know better. The parent teacher on board a boat has to work hard to keep interruptions at bay if school is to be accomplished in the minimum amount of time. Homeschoolers in a house can find a quiet room or go to the library if the plumber has to pay a visit, but on board, there is no such freedom.

Almost all boat kids have school in the morning, so that's fairly easy – the other kids won't be free until the afternoon, either. We've had more trouble with Hamish's and my friends stopping by, or other cruisers coming to introduce themselves. It is hard to turn someone away, but if they come aboard and I put the kettle on, that's effectively the end of school for the morning.

One winter, we spent several months tied up to the dock in Ushuaia, Argentina, and I had to put a sign in the window saying, "School time – please come back later." That worked very well, because most people stopped there and didn't knock. Even a conversation in the cockpit winds up distracting the children, as they are bound to be more interested in what you're saying than in long division.

It's even harder to control the boat-supplied interruptions. We often joke that cruising on board a sailboat is the art of "pump repair in exotic places," and there's always something that needs mending. Hamish does far more than his share of maintenance while I teach school, but when he needs a hand, or the job is in the main living space, or it is slightly more interesting than their schoolwork, it can be hard to keep Helen and Anna focused.

According to Helen, it was even worse when Hamish and I talked about what we were going to do in the afternoon or later in the week. We try not to talk in the in the same room when they're studying, but we often do.

When you're traveling, one way to solve this dilemma is to slow down. We find that we stay places longer than boats without children, and visit fewer places along the way. We take a week to do two day's worth of sight-seeing. Often, Hamish will dinghy in to town and do the shopping while the girls and I do school, but I don't want them to miss all the open air markets, so I make sure that once in a while we cancel school in favor of going to the market.

We've met quite a few American boats with children following the Calvert system. We haven't met any who are using the Calvert accreditation program; instead the parents simply buy the box, and do the evaluating part themselves. I think this may be a reflection of the current rising trend in homeschooling in general; twenty years ago homeschooling was still very unusual, and the accreditation was an important part of what Calvert had to offer.

The children on Calvert seem to have school all day long, Monday to Friday, often until four p.m., which is far longer than they would be in regular school, even counting the bus, standing in line, going to lunch, and taking recess. Ideally, I plan our school on *Seal* to last from from eight a.m. to twelve noon; usually it takes until one or two in the afternoon. Of course, it has run until four o'clock, particularly if there is nothing interesting for the children to do on shore.

Our shorter days are a reflection of two things – one, we have seven days of school a week, so our week is forty percent longer. Two, I only assign the work that won't be done without my assigning it. Reading happens at some other part of the day. I aim for roughly thirty hours of independent reading a month, and it doesn't matter to me if that's made up of five hours on six days or one hour on thirty days. Much of school was opportunistic: when Wendy Beckett's *The Story of Painting*, arrived in a sea freight shipment to the Falkland Islands eight years ago, Anna and I sat and poured over it for much of the afternoon. I later overheard her boast to a local friend, "I didn't have school today," and I thought to myself, "that's what you think."

For many families, however, following a fixed program such as Calvert is the only way they're comfortable leaving schools behind, and it can work particularly well for children accustomed to working at "grade level" at bricks and mortar schools before they left. The teacher support programs of Calvert and Oak Meadow may be just what you need to have the confidence to take on schooling along with all the other life changes in going on the road, especially if you are only leaving for a short time.

In addition, many families buy the box without the teaching support, and then use it as a baseline program for the "teach when you must" subjects, and allow students to unschool where they can in other subjects.

School at Sea?

In every article I've read about people setting off sailing with their families, they invariably say the children will do the bulk of their schoolwork on passages. When you meet families who have been out for a few years, they all seem to say they never have school on passages. (Lots of older men, on their second wives, have told me their now grown-up children did all their school work on passage, but either that was a tougher generation, or they've just forgotten what it was like.)

I certainly couldn't run school and manage a watch. On one twenty-six day passage when the girls were nine and ten, we had a bit of school after a week at sea, but it was less than a quarter of what we normally did at anchor. When I taught school to teenagers on a yacht across the Pacific, they were able to stand a two-hour watch on their own long before they could do school unsupervised.

Ordering Supplies

If you are living or traveling remotely, the best way to do the ordering is to organize a friend or relative to be your freight consolidator, particularly if you can find someone in the United States, where there is a much larger secondhand market than other English-speaking countries. Then, about three or four months from the end of the school year, or before you are at a reliable address for shipping, commit to spending a couple of days on the internet doing your ordering. Ship everything to your long-suffering friend who, in a month's time when everything arrives, can wrap it up and ship it to you care of a marina or post office or a third cousin once removed in whatever country you plan to be in at that time. This is why it's important to have at least half a year beyond what you expect to use on board, in case there are problems with shipping or finding a country where you will be long enough to receive it. (You should be planning to be in the area for several months if you are using boat mail, which can take anywhere from three days (because they shipped it air anyway) to three months.) More expensive, but faster and usually more reliable, except in parts of South America, are courier services such as UPS, FedEx, or DHL.

This is obviously less serious when you're traveling in countries which share your teaching language, but when you're outside that band, pre-planning your book purchases is the key to running a successful program. Consolidating the shipment to a once-a-year package and doing it early enough that you can ship boat mail will make shipping costs fairly negligible.

This may seem like the deal-breaker for writing your own curriculum, but actually, especially if you have a friend acting as your freight agent, it can work better than the packaged curricula. We know of boat children who had to go two or three months without their schoolwork, because they missed the box, changed plans, or the company or national school program didn't appreciate the shipping urgency. Sure, the two or three months were a holiday, but then the children (and the teacher) had to cram a school year into two-thirds of the usual time.

If you buy a boxed program or a year's worth of supplies at one time, it is almost certainly worth buying the next year or two of Math Mammoth Light Blue curriculum to have on hand. It's the least expensive, high quality program out there (and occasionally there are sales on the entire grades 1-7 package). I tried to teach algebra without a book to my fifteen-year-old student while we were crossing the Pacific. Never again! I always made sure I had at least one full year in advance stowed under a bunk so Helen and Anna would never run out.

For International Readers

For simplification, I have used the terms most commonly used in most (but not all) of the US. I have also used the US grade system to refer to school years. The British system is one year ahead of the American system, so a US child would be grade 2, while a British child with the same birthday would be in year 3. However, in terms of academic requirements, the British system is generally a year ahead of the American one as well, so when shopping for books, or trying to figure out requirements across cultures, it generally works very well to simply consider the two systems equivalent – a US second grader would use books designed for UK Year 2, and vice versa.

US/UK terminology and a broad range of equivalent grades and school years for many English-speaking countries follows on the next pages.

Table 19: International School Year Equivalents

Start Age*	USA & Canada	England & Wales	Scotland
4		Reception	Nursery
5	Kindergarten	Key Stage 1/Year 1	Primary 1
6	Grade 1	Key Stage 1/Year 2	Primary 2
7	Grade 2	Key Stage 2 / Year 3	Primary 3
8	Grade 3	Key Stage 2/ Year 4	Primary 4
9	Grade 4	Key Stage 2/ Year 5	Primary 5
10	Grade 5	Key Stage 2/Year 6	Primary 6
11	Grade 6	Key Stage 3/Year 7	Primary 7
12	Grade 7	Key Stage 3/Year 8	S1 (First Year)
13	Grade 8	Key Stage 3/Year 9	S2 (Second Year)
14	Grade 9	Key Stage 4/Year 10	S3 (Third Year)
15	Grade 10	Key Stage 4/Year 11	S4 (Fourth Year)
16	Grade 11	AS Level (6th Form)	S5 (Fifth Year)
17	Grade 12	A Level (6th Form)	S6 (Sixth Year)

---

*   In the US, August birthday children are sometimes held back at the parents' request until the following year. Beginning in 2015, schools in the UK may offer this option as standard for summer-born children.

Northern Ireland	Ireland	New Zealand	Australia	Start Age
Primary 1	Junior Infants*			4
Primary 2	Senior Infants	Year 1	Foundation	5
Primary 3	First Class	Year 2	Grade 1	6
Primary 4	Second Class	Year 3	Grade 2	7
Primary 5	Third Class	Year 4	Grade 3	8
Primary 6	Fourth Class	Year 5	Grade 4	9
Primary 7	Fifth Class	Year 6	Grade 5	10
Year 8	Sixth Class	Year 7	Grade 6	11
Year 9	First Year	Year 8	Grade 7	12
Year 10	Second Year	Year 9	Grade 8	13
Year 11	Third Year	Year 10	Grade 9	14
Year 12	(Transition)	Year 11	Grade 10	15
Year 13	Fifth Year	Year 12	Grade 11	16
Year 14	Sixth Year	Year 13	Grade 12	17

---

*   Irish students can begin at age 4 or 5 in many places, and the sometimes optional Transition Year also can shift students ahead or behind this schedule.

UK Terms

Primary – Age 4 or 5 to 11 or 13
Prep – private primary school
Secondary – Age 11 or 13 to 18
Public – private secondary school
State – free, government-run, tax-payer funded education
Independent – any school that charges fees

US Terms

Prep – private high school
Public – free, government-run, tax-payer funded education
Private – any school that charges fees

In this book, I use "elementary school" to mean US grades 1-4 (ages 6-10) and "middle school" to mean US grades 5-8 (ages 10-14). Many US school districts make the division in different places, some extending elementary school to fifth or sixth grade. Often this depends on building space rather than educational philosophy.

Detailed Table of Contents

List of Tables

Notes & Sources

In lieu of a bibliography, each source has a full listing at the first mention on each page of the notes; subsequent mentions use abbreviated formats.

1 David & Micki Colfax, *Homeschooling For Excellence: How to Take Charge of Your Child's Education – And Why You Absolutely Must* (New York: Warner Books, 1988).

2 Thomas Newkirk, *Holding on to Good Ideas in a Time of Bad Ones: Six Literacy Principles Worth Fighting For* (Portsmouth, NH: Heinemann, 2009), Kindle Location 2677.

3 A. Noel, P. Stark, and J. Redford, *Parent and Family Involvement in Education, From the National Household Education Surveys Program of 2012* (NCES 2013-028) (Washington, DC: National Center for Education Statistics, Institute of Education Sciences, US Department of Education, 2012), accessed March 2, 2015, http://nces.ed.gov/pubsearch. US population statistics from "United States QuickFacts," *United States Census Bureau,* accessed March 2, 2015, http://quickfacts.census.gov/qfd/states/00000.html.

4 Mathew Hennessey, "Why More Urban Parents Are Choosing Homeschooling," *Time Magazine* (August 17, 2015), accessed September 3, 2015, http://time.com/4000391/city-homeschooling-education-trend/ and Bridget Samburg, "Our Kids Don't Belong in School," *Boston Magazine* (August 25, 2015), accessed September 3, 2015, http://www.boston magazine.com/news/article/2015/08/25/homeschooling-in-boston/.

5 Laura Brodie, "One Good Year: A Look at Short-Term Homeschooling," *Brain, Child Magazine* (August 27, 2014), accessed March 9, 2015, http://www.brainchildmag.com/2014/08/one-good-year-a-look-at-short-term-homeschooling/.

6 E. D. Hirsch Jr., *Cultural Literacy: What Every American Needs to Know* (Boston: Houghton Mifflin, 1987).

7 Discussed in Carol Dweck, *Mindset: The New Psychology of Success* (New York: Ballantine Books, 2008), Daniel T. Willingham, *Why Don't Students Like School? A Cognitive Scientist Answers Questions About How the Mind Works and What it Means for the Classroom* (San Francisco: Jossey-Bass/John Wiley & Sons, 2009), and summarized in Po Bronson and Ashley Merryman, *NurtureShock: New Thinking About Children*, 2nd ed. (New York: Twelve, 2011).

8 K. Anders Ericsson, Ralf Th. Krampe, and Clemens Tesch-Romer, "The Role of Deliberate Practice in the Acquisition of Expert Performance," *Psychological Review*, 100, no. 3, (1993): 363-406, discussed in Willingham, *Why Don't Students Like School?*, 106.

9 Willingham, *Why Don't Students Like School?*, 131.

10 *Ibid.*

11 Praise is further discussed in Bronson and Merryman, "The Inverse Power of Praise," *NurtureShock.*

12 Doug Lemov, *Teach Like a Champion: 49 Techniques that Put Students on the Path to College* (San Francisco, CA: Jossey-Bass, 2010), Kindle location 4182.

13 Carol Dweck, *Mindset: The New Psychology of Success* (New York: Ballantine Books, 2008), Kindle location 1205. Also discussed in Po Bronson and Ashley Merryman, *NurtureShock: New Thinking About Children*, 2nd ed. (New York: Twelve, 2011), 14.

14 *Ibid.*, Kindle location 934.

15 *Ibid.*, Kindle location 676.

16 Salman Khan, *The One World Schoolhouse: Education Reimagined* (New York: Twelve, 2012), 20.

17 E.D. Hirsch, Jr., "Building Knowledge: The Case for Bringing Content into the Language Arts Block and for a Knowledge-Rich Curriculum Core for all Children," *American Educator* (Spring 2006), accessed January 14, 2013 http://www.aft.org/newspubs/periodicals/ae/spring2006/hirsch.cfm.

18 Howard Gardner, *The Unschooled Mind: How Children Think & How Schools Should Teach* (New York: Basic Books (Harper Collins), 1991), *passim.*

19 George D. Nelson, "Science Literacy for All in the 21st Century," *Project 2061,* accessed 19 November 2015, http://www.project2061.org/publications/articles/articles/ascd.htm, reprinted from *Educational Leadership* 57, no. 2 (October 1999).

20 Daniel T. Willingham, *Why Don't Students Like School? A Cognitive Scientist Answers Questions About How the Mind Works and What it Means for the Classroom* (San Francisco: Jossey-Bass/John Wiley & Sons, 2009), 89.

21 Gary Stix, "How to Build a Better Learner: Brain Studies Suggest New Ways to Improve Reading, Writing and Arithmetic and Even Social Skills," *Scientific American* (August 2011): 56.

22 Willingham, *Why Don't Students Like School?*, 125.

23 Valerie Strauss, "Howard Gardner: 'Multiple intelligences' are not 'learning styles,'" *The Washington Post* (October 16, 2013), accessed November 19, 2015 https://www.washingtonpost.com/news/answer-sheet/wp/2013/10/16/howard-gardner-multiple-intelligences-are-not-learning-styles/.

24 Howard Gardner, "In a Nutshell," *MultipleIntelligencesOasis.org* (2013): 28, accessed November 19, 2015, http://multipleintelligencesoasis.org/wp-content/uploads/2013/06/in-a-nutshell-minh.pdf.

25 Howard Gardner, *The Unschooled Mind*, 207.

26 Dweck, *Mindset,* Kindle location 135.

27 Stix, "How to Build a Better Learner," 55.

28 Stephen A. Stahl, "Different Strokes for Different Folks? A Critique of Learning Styles," *American Educator* (Fall 1999): 3.

29 Phil Revell, "Each to their own: The government espouses the theory of learning styles with scant regard to the evidence," *The Guardian* (May 31, 2005), accessed January 9, 2013, http://www.theguardian.com/education/2005/may/31/schools.uk3.

30 Marina Koestler Ruben, *How to Tutor Your Own Child: Boost Grades and*

Inspire a Lifelong Love of Learning – Without Paying for a Professional Tutor (Berkeley, California: Ten Speed Press (Random House), 2011), Kindle location 1020.

31 Doug Lemov, *Teach Like a Champion: 49 Techniques that Put Students on the Path to College* (San Francisco, CA: Jossey-Bass, 2010), Kindle location 5484.

32 Harold Pashler, Patrice M. Bain, Brian A. Bottge, Arthur Graesser, Kenneth Koedinger, Mark McDaniel, and Janet Metcalfe, *Organizing Instruction and Study to Improve Student Learning* (NCER 2007-2004), (Washington, DC: National Center for Education Research, Institute of Education Sciences, US Department of Education, 2007), 30, http://ies.ed.gov/ncee/wwc/practiceguide.aspx?sid=1.

33 William H. Armstrong, *Study is Hard Work,* 2nd ed. (Boston: David R. Godine, Publisher, 1995), 20.

34 Nadine Slavinski, "6 Tips for Home-schooling Sailors." *Women and Cruising* (December 4, 2010), accessed January 9, 2012, http://www.womenandcruising.com/blog/2010/12/6-tips-for-home-schooling-sailors/.

35 Marie Rippel, *All About Spelling: The Program that Takes the Struggle Out of Spelling, Level 7* (Eagle River, WI: All About Learning Press, 2012), 12-13; Gabriel Wyner, *Fluent Forever: How to Learn Any Language Fast and Never Forget It* (New York: Harmony Books (Random House LLC), 2014), *passim*; Pashler, *et. al., Organizing Instruction.*

36 Original graphic; schedule based on Gabriel Wyner, *Fluent Forever: How to Learn Any Language Fast and Never Forget It* (New York: Harmony Books (Random House LLC), 2014), Kindle location 4397.

37 *Ibid.,* Kindle location 834.

38 Pashler, *et. al., Organizing Instruction,* 21.

39 Po Bronson and Ashley Merryman, *NurtureShock: New Thinking About Children,* 2nd ed. (New York: Twelve, 2011), ch. 8.

40 "Official entrance age to primary education (years)," The World Bank Data , accessed April 2, 2016, http://data.worldbank.org/indicator/SE.PRM.AGES.

41 Caroline Sharp, "School Starting Age: European Policy and Recent Research," Paper presented at the LGA Seminar 'When Should Our Children Start School?' (LGA Conference Centre, Smith Square, London, 1 November 2002), accessed February 10, 2015, www.nfer.ac.uk/nfer/publications/44410/44410.pdf.

42 Nick Gibb MP and the Department of Education, "Summer-born children 'to get the right to start school later,'" UK Govt Press Release (September 8, 2015), accessed December 12, 2015, https://www.gov.uk/government/news/summer-born-children-to-get-the-right-to-start-school-later.

43 Keith Rayner, Barbara F. Foorman, Charles A. Perfetti, David Pesetsky, and Mark S. Seidenberg, "How Should Reading be Taught?" *Scientific American* (March 2002): 86.

44 Dorothy H. Cohen, *The Learning Child* (New York: Shocken Books, 1972), 83-84.

45 National Governors Association Center for Best Practices, Council of Chief State School Officers, *Common Core State Standards for English Language Arts & Literacy in History/Social Studies, Science, and Technical Subjects* (Washington, DC: National Governors Association Center for Best Practices, Council of Chief State School Officers, 2010), 11-17.

46 Laura Brodie, "One Good Year: A Look at Short-Term Homeschooling," *Brain, Child Magazine* (August 27, 2014), accessed March 9, 2015, www.brainchildmag.com/2014/08/one-good-year-a-look-at-short-term-homeschooling/comment-page-1/.

47 Richard Feynman, *"Surely You're Joking, Mr. Feynman" (Adventures of a Curious Character)* (Vintage Digital, 2014), 71.

48 Singapore Grading System, accessed November 20, 2015, http://www.singaporeeducation.info/Education-System/Grading-System.html.

49 Donald P. Hayes, "A Spectrum of Natural Texts: Measurements of their Lexical Demand Levels," Ms., (Cornell University: Department of Sociology, 2006), accessed 30 January 2015, www.soc.cornell.edu/hayes-lexical-analysis/schoolbooks/Papers/ASpectrumOfNaturalTexts.pdf.

50 Bobby Lynn Maslen, *Mat* (Np: Bob Books Publications, 2013).

51 Sarah Beck, Associate Professor of English Education in the Department of Teaching and Learning at NYU Steinhardt, manuscript comments (March 2015).

52 Angeline Stoll Lillard, *Montessori: The Science Behind the Genius* (Oxford: Oxford UP, 2005), 28.

53 Some time after writing this, I was amused to receive an email update from Marie Rippel of *All About Spelling* entitled "FAQ: What is a schwa, and why does it matter?" and was relieved to see that her blog entry on teaching the schwa covers the entire subject without mentioning the name to the children.

54 Keith Rayner, Barbara F. Foorman, Charles A. Perfetti, David Pesetsky, and Mark S. Seidenberg, "How Should Reading be Taught?" *Scientific American* (March 2002): 91.

55 *Ibid.*, 88.

56 Regie Routman, *Literacy at the Crossroads: Crucial Talk About Reading, Writing, and Other Teaching Dilemnas* (Portsmouth, NH: Heinemann, 1996), 12-13.

57 *Ibid.*, 9-10.

58 Bonnie B. Armbruster, Fran Lehr, Jean Osborne, *Put Reading First: The Research Building Blocks of Reading Instruction*, 2nd ed. (Jessup, MD: National Institute for Literacy, 2003), 25.

59 Failings of the National Reading Panel discussed in Thomas Newkirk, *Holding on to Good Ideas in a Time of Bad Ones: Six Literacy Principles Worth Fighting For* (Portsmouth, NH: Heinemann, 2009), Kindle location

376 and Kelly Gallagher, *Readicide: How Schools Are Killing Reading and What You Can Do About It* (Portland, ME: Stenhouse Publishers, 2009), Kindle location 805-890.

60 "Facts: On the Nature of Whole Language Instruction," *Heinemann Fact Sheets* (August 2003), accessed January 23, 2013, www.heinemann.com/shared/onlineresources/08894/08894f6.html.

61 Nicholas Lemann, "The Reading Wars," *The Atlantic* (November 1997), accessed May 19, 2014, www.theatlantic.com/past/docs/issues/97nov/read.htm.

62 "Effective Reading Instruction for Students with Dyslexia," *International Dyslexia Association* (2015), accessed December 13, 2015, eida.org/effective-reading-instruction/ and "Homeschooling Fact Sheet," *International Dyslexia Association* (2015), accessed December 13, 2015, eida.org/homeschooling-fact-sheet/.

63 Anne-Marie Chang, Daniel Aeschbach, Jeanne F. Duffy, and Charles A. Czeislera, "Evening use of light-emitting eReaders negatively affects sleep, circadian timing, and next-morning alertness," *PNAS* 112, no. 4, Proceedings of the National Academy of Sciences of the United States of America (January 27, 2015), accessed December 13, 2015, www.pnas.org/content/112/4/1232.full.pdf.

64 Thomas Newkirk, *Holding on to Good Ideas in a Time of Bad Ones: Six Literacy Principles Worth Fighting For* (Portsmouth, NH: Heinemann, 2009), Kindle location 1910.

65 Nancie Atwell, *The Reading Zone: How to Help Kids Become Skilled, Passionate, Habitual Critical Readers* (New York: Scholastic Inc., 2007), Kindle location 2253.

66 Jeanette Veatch, *How to Teach Reading With Children's Books*, as cited in Atwell, *The Reading Zone,* Kindle location 616.

67 Rosemary Fink, "Successful dyslexics: A constructivist study of passionate interest reading," *Journal of Adolescent & Adult Literacy* 39, no. 4 (December 1995): 268.

68 *Ibid.,* 272.

69 *Ibid.,* 277.

70 *Ibid.,* 274-5.

71 Excerpted from "Dyslexia Basics." *International Dyslexia Association* (2015), accessed December 13, 2015, eida.org/dyslexia-basics/.

72 "Effective Reading Instruction for Students with Dyslexia," *International Dyslexia Association* (2015), accessed December 13, 2015 eida.org/effective-reading-instruction/.

73 Chang, *et. al.,* "Evening use of light-emitting eReaders . . . "

74 Atwell, *The Reading Zone*, Kindle location 710.

75 Shelley Harwayne, Forward, in Atwell, *The Reading Zone,* Kindle location 99.

76 Atwell, *The Reading Zone,* Kindle location 158.

77 Nancie Atwell, *The Reading Zone: How to Help Kids Become Skilled, Passionate, Habitual Critical Readers* (New York: Scholastic Inc., 2007), Kindle location 578.

78 *Ibid.*, Kindle location 254.

79 *Ibid.*, Kindle location 1997.

80 Kelly Gallagher, *Readicide: How Schools Are Killing Reading and What You Can Do About It* (Portland, ME: Stenhouse Publishers, 2009), Kindle location 1238.

81 For a discussion of declining reading through school career, see Thomas Newkirk, "When Reading Becomes Work: How Textbooks Ruin Reading." *Independent School Magazine* (Winter 2008) accessed April 10, 2014, www.nais.org/Magazines-Newsletters/ISMagazine/Pages/When-Reading-Becomes-Work.aspx. For the relationship between school textbook reading levels and SAT scores, see Donald P. Hayes, Loreen T. Wolfer, Michael F. Wolfe, "Schoolbook Simplification and Its Relation to the Decline in SAT-Verbal Scores," Preprint. Appeared in *American Educational Research Journal* 33, no. 2 (Summer 1996): 489-508, accessed January 31, 2015, www.soc.cornell.edu/hayes-lexical-analysis/schoolbooks/Papers/ASpectrumOfNaturalTexts.html.

82 National Governors Association Center for Best Practices, "Appendix B: Text Exemplars and Sample Performance Tasks," *Council of Chief State School Officers Common Core State Standards English Language Arts & Literacy in History/Social Studies, Science, and Technical Subjects* (Washington D.C.: National Governors Association Center for Best Practices, Council of Chief State School Officers, 2010), *passim.*

83 Carol Jago, *With Rigor For All: Meeting Common Core Standards for Reading Literature* (Portsmouth, NH: Heinemann, 2011) and Carol Jago, Renee H. Shea, Lawrence Scanlon, and Robin Dissin Aufeses, *Literature & Composition* (Boston: Bedford/St. Martin's, 2011).

84 Gallagher, *Readicide.*

85 *Ibid.*, Kindle location 1835.

86 Penny Kittle, *Book Love: Developing Depth, Stamina, and Passion in Adolescent Readers* (Portsmouth, NH: Heinemann, 2013), 20.

87 Atwell, *The Reading Zone*, Kindle location 2197.

88 William H. Armstrong, *Study is Hard Work,* 2nd ed. (Boston: David R. Godine, Publisher, 1995), 48.

89 Carol Jago, *With Rigor For All,* 43 discussing the research of W.E. Nagy, R.C. Anderson, and P.A. Herman, "Learning Word Meanings from Context During Normal Reading," *American Educational Research Journal* 23:237-70.

90 Discussed further in Isabel L. Beck, Margaret G. McKeown, and Linda Kucan, "Taking the Delight in Words Using Oral Language to Build Young Children's Vocabularies," *American Educator* (Spring 2003), accessed January 14, 2013, www.aft.org/newspubs/periodicals

/ae/spring2003/beck.cfm.

91 David A. Sousa, *How the Brain Learns: A Classroom Teacher's Guide* (Thousand Oaks, CA: Corwin Press, Inc., 2001), 182.

92 M.L. Kamil, G.D. Borman, J. Dole, C.C. Kral, T. Salinger, and J. Torgesen, *Improving Adolescent Literacy: Effective Classroom and Intervention Practices: A Practice Guide* (Washington, DC: National Center for Education Evaluation and Regional Assistance, US Department of Education, 2008), 12, accessed January 23, 2013, ies.ed.gov/ncee/wwc.

93 *Ibid.*, 13.

94 Marjorie Garber, *Shakespeare After All* (New York: Anchor Books, 2005), Kindle location 129.

95 Thomas Newkirk, "When Reading Becomes Work: How Textbooks Ruin Reading," *Independent School Magazine* (Winter 2008), accessed April 10, 2014, www.nais.org/Magazines-Newsletters/ISMagazine/Pages/When-Reading-Becomes-Work.aspx.

96 Carol Jago, *With Rigor For All: Meeting Common Core Standards for Reading Literature* (Portsmouth, NH: Heinemann, 2011), 74.

97 Doug Lemov, *Teach Like a Champion: 49 Techniques that Put Students on the Path to College* (San Francisco, CA: Jossey-Bass, 2010), Kindle location 4843.

98 While I've followed many of Bauer and Wise's recommendations for the study of history, I prefer Duiker and Spielvogel's *Essential World History* to their choice for middle school history (*The Kingfisher History Encyclopedia*). The Kingfisher Encyclopedia is extremely dense, and doesn't make for very enjoyable reading; Duiker and Spielvogel, sometimes used in American AP World History classes (roughly the equivalent of the British A Level), is more pleasant to read. *Cf.* Susan Wise Bauer and Jessie Wise, *The Well-Trained Mind: A Guide to Classical Education at Home,* 2nd ed. (New York: W. W. Norton & Co., 2004).

99 Thomas Newkirk, *Holding on to Good Ideas in a Time of Bad Ones: Six Literacy Principles Worth Fighting For* (Portsmouth, NH: Heinemann, 2009), Kindle Location 217.

100 Sousa, *How the Brain Learns*, 85.

101 Discussed further in Sousa, *How the Brain Learns,* 118.

102 William H. Armstrong, *Study is Hard Work,* 2nd ed. (Boston: David R. Godine, Publisher, 1995).

103 Susan Gilroy, "Interrogating Texts: 6 Reading Habits to Develop in Your First Year at Harvard," *Harvard Library Research Guides* (Cambridge: President and Fellows of Harvard College, 2013).

104 Armstrong, 79.

105 Kate L. Turabian, *Student's Guide to Writing College Papers,* 4th ed., Revised Gregory G. Colomb, Joseph M. Williams (Chicago: University of Chicago Press, 2010), 24.

106 Peter Elbow, *Writing With Power: Techniques for Mastering the Writing*

Process, 2ⁿᵈ ed. (New York: Oxford UP, 1998), Kindle location 123.

107 Peter Elbow, *Writing With Power: Techniques for Mastering the Writing Process,* 2ⁿᵈ ed. (New York: Oxford UP, 1998), Kindle location 214.

108 National Governors Association Center for Best Practices, *Council of Chief State School Officers Common Core State Standards English Language Arts & Literacy in History/Social Studies, Science, and Technical Subjects* (Washington D.C.: National Governors Association Center for Best Practices, Council of Chief State School Officers, 2010), 19-20 & 42.

109 Thomas Newkirk, *Holding on to Good Ideas in a Time of Bad Ones: Six Literacy Principles Worth Fighting For* (Portsmouth, NH: Heinemann, 2009), Kindle location 1351.

110 *Ibid.,* Kindle location 2383.

111 Donald Graves, *Writing: Teachers & Children at Work* (Portsmouth, NH: Heinemann Educational Books, 1983), 90.

112 *Ibid.,* 43.

113 Thomas Newkirk, *More Than Stories: The Range of Children's Writing* (Portsmouth, NH: Heinemann, 1989), 36-37.

114 Don Murry, "The Day Book," *The Essential Don Murray: Lessons from America's Greatest Writing Teacher,* ed. Thomas Newkirk and Lisa C. Miller (Portsmouth, NH: Boynton/Cook Publishers (Heinemann), 2009), 40.

115 Peter Elbow, *Writing With Power,* for example.

116 Kate L. Turabian, *Student's Guide to Writing College Papers,* 4ᵗʰ Ed. Revised by Gregory G. Colomb, Joseph M. Williams, and the Univ. of Chicago Press Editorial Staff (Chicago: Univ. of Chicago Press, 2010).

117 "Family Dinner Box of Questions: Cards to Create Great Conversations." Family Dinner Large Box # 5706 (Westport, CT: Melissa and Doug LLC). www.melissaanddoug.com.

118 Sue Wheeler's Time Expansion exercise. Discussed in Newkirk, *Holding on to Good Ideas,* Kindle Location 1359.

119 There are many examples of this sort of assignment out there, including almost every English textbook, or teaching articles such as Diana Mitchell, "Fifty Alternatives to the Book Report," *English Journal,* National Council of Teachers of English (January 1998): 92-95.

120 Nancie Atwell, *The Reading Zone: How to Help Kids Become Skilled, Passionate, Habitual Critical Readers* (New York: Scholastic Inc., 2007), Kindle location 1279.

121 R.V. Cassill, "Writing about Fiction," *The Norton Anthology of Short Fiction,* Shorter 4ᵗʰ ed. (New York: W. W. Norton & Co., 1990), 873.

122 Kelly Gallagher, *Write Like This: Teaching Real-World Writing Through Modeling & Mentor Texts* (Portland, ME: Stenhouse Publishers, 2011), Kindle location 361.

123 Kylene Beers and Robert E. Probst, *Notice & Note: Strategies for Close Reading* (Portsmouth, NH: Heinemann, 2013), *passim.*

124 Will Fitzhugh, "Meaningful Work: How the History Research Paper

Prepares Students for College and Life," *American Educator* (Winter 2011-2012): 40.

125 Will Fitzhugh, "Meaningful Work: How the History Research Paper Prepares Students for College and Life," *American Educator* (Winter 2011-2012): 33.

126 Don Murray, "The Listening Eye," *The Essential Don Murray: Lessons from America's Greatest Writing Teacher,* ed. Thomas Newkirk and Lisa C. Miller (Portsmouth, NH: Boynton/Cook Publishers (Heinemann), 2009),151.

127 Murray, "Internal Revision," *The Essential Don Murray,* 124.

128 William R. Klemm, "Why Writing by Hand Could Make You Smarter," *Psychology Today* (March 14, 2013), accessed April 3, 2016, www.psychologytoday.com/blog/memory-medic/201303/why-writing-hand-could-make-you-smarter.

129 National Governors Association Center for Best Practices, *Council of Chief State School Officers Common Core State Standards English Language Arts & Literacy in History/Social Studies, Science, and Technical Subjects* (Washington, DC: National Governors Association Center for Best Practices, Council of Chief State School Officers, 2010), 19.

130 James Thayer, "How Many Words a Day?" *Author Magazine* (April 2009), accessed January 10, 2010, www.authormagazine.org/articles/thayer_james_2009_04_09.htm.

131 Jo Boaler, *How to Learn Math: For Teachers and Parents* (Stanford OpenEdx, Summer 2013), *passim,* www.youcubed.org/how-to-learn-math-for-teachers-and-parents/

132 Richard E. Clark, Paul A. Kirschner, and John Sweller, "Putting Students on the Path to Learning: The Case for Fully Guided Instruction," *American Educator,* (Spring 2012): 8.

133 "First Grade Homeschool Curriculum," *Calvert School* (website), accessed December 7, 2012, homeschool.calvertschool.org/why-calvert/homeschool-curriculum/f. This statement was published when Calvert was in the process of changing over entirely to Singapore Math; as of 2016, they offered a choice of curricula, accessed April 3, 2016, www.calverteducation.com/curriculum/lower-school.

134 Martha Miller, "Homeschool algebra 1 curriculum - recommendations for home schooling high school math," *Math Mammoth* (website), accessed November 1, 2012, www.mathmammoth.com/complete/algebra_1.php.

135 For the middle school sequence, Art Reed, "Which Book Should Be Used After Math 76? Math 87 or Algebra ½?" *Homeschool With Saxon* (website) (October 2015), accessed May 28, 2016, www.homeschoolwithsaxon.com /newsletterpage-2015.php#0115. A very brief discussion of the Saxon Integrated (original) and Saxon Traditional (new) programs can be found on the Hougton Mifflin Harcourt site, accessed 28 May, 2016, http://www.hmhco.com/shop/education-curriculum/math/homeschool/saxon-math-homeschool#resources-faq.

136 Daniel T. Willingham, *Why Don't Students Like School? A Cognitive Scientist Answers Questions About How the Mind Works and What it Means for the Classroom* (San Francisco: Jossey-Bass/John Wiley & Sons, 2009), 88-89.

137 Doug Lemov, *Teach Like a Champion: 49 Techniques that Put Students on the Path to College* (San Francisco, CA: Jossey-Bass, 2010), Kindle location 1525.

138 *Ibid.*, Kindle location 2118.

139 *Ibid.*, Kindle location 1534.

140 Raina Fishbane, as quoted in Marina Koestler Ruben, *How to Tutor Your Own Child: Boost Grades and Inspire a Lifelong Love of Learning – Without Paying for a Professional Tutor* (Berkeley, California: Ten Speed Press (Random House), 2011), Kindle Location 248.

141 Liping Ma, *Knowing and Teaching Elementary Mathematics: Teachers' Understanding of Fundamental Mathematics in China and the United States,* The Studies in Mathematical Thinking and Learning Series (Mahwah, New Jersey: Lawrence Erlbaum Associates, Publishers, 1990), Kindle location 1079-1139.

142 *Ibid.,* Kindle location 369.

143 *Ibid.,* Kindle location 1276.

144 Thomas H. Sidebotham, *The A to Z of Mathematics: A Basic Guide* (New York: John Wiley & Sons, 2002).

145 Gregory Cochrane and Henry Harpending, *The 10,000 Year Explosion: How Civilization Accelerated Human Evolution* (New York, NY: Basic Books, 2009).

146 Willingham, *Why Don't Students Like School?*, 51-53.

147 Daniel T. Willingham, "Ask the Cognitive Scientist: The Privileged Status of Story," *American Educator* (Summer 2004), accessed January 13, 2013, www.aft.org/newspubs/periodicals/ae/summer2004/willingham.cfm

148 "National Curriculum in England: History Programmes of Study" (September 11, 2013), Department for Education, accessed May 22, 2016, https://www.gov.uk/government/publications/national-curriculum-in-england-history-programmes-of-study/national-curriculum-in-england-history-programmes-of-study.

149 California Department of Education, *History–Social Science Content Standards for California Public Schools, Kindergarten Through Grade Twelve* (Sacramento, CA: California Department of Education, 2000).

150 Susan Wise Bauer and Jessie Wise, *The Well-Trained Mind: A Guide to Classical Education at Home,* 2nd ed. (New York: W. W. Norton & Co., 2004).

151 Sheldon M. Stern and Jeremy A. Stern, *The State of State U.S. History Standards 2011* (Washington, DC: Thomas B. Fordham Institute, February 2011), 2, accessed May 4, 2013, www.edexcellence.net.

152 Sheldon M. Stern and Jeremy A. Stern, *The State of State U.S. History Standards 2011* (Washington, DC: Thomas B. Fordham Institute, February 2011), 8-9, accessed May 4, 2013, www.edexcellence.net.

153 California Department of Education, *History–Social Science Content Standards for California Public Schools, Kindergarten Through Grade Twelve* (Sacramento, CA: California Department of Education, 2000), 3-4.

154 Rebecca Rupp, *Home Learning Year by Year: How to Design a Homeschool Curriculum from Preschool Through High School* (New York: Three Rivers Press, 2000), 79-80.

155 Samuel S. Wineburg, "On the Reading of Historical Texts: Notes on the Breach between School and Academy," *American Educational Research Journal* 28, no. 3, (Autumn 1991): 495-519, www.jstor.org/stable/1163146.

156 Harold Pashler, Patrice M. Bain, Brian A. Bottge, Arthur Graesser, Kenneth Koedinger, Mark McDaniel, and Janet Metcalfe, *Organizing Instruction and Study to Improve Student Learning* (NCER 2007-2004), (Washington, DC: National Center for Education Research, Institute of Education Sciences, US Department of Education, 2007), 7, ies.ed.gov/ncee/wwc/practiceguide.aspx?sid=1.

157 *Ibid.*, 21.

158 *Ibid.*, 5.

159 Further discussed in Annie Murphy Paul, "Building the 21st Century Learner: A New Vision for Testing," *Scientific American (*August 2015): 55-61.

160 Stolen from the title of one of Don Murray's books, *Write to Learn*, 8th ed. (Boston, MA: Wadsworth Publishing, 2004).

161 Michael Maxwell, *Student's Friend* (website) www.studentsfriend.com. Ofer Bar-Yosef as discussed in Steven Mithen, *After the Ice: A Global Human History, 20,000 – 5000 BC* (Cambridge, MA: Harvard UP, 2003), 59.

162 While I enthusiastically recommend the Story of the World series for the elementary school student, I am much less comfortable with the approach suggested by Jessie Wise and Susan Wise Bauer in the *Well-Trained Mind* in later years. After their strong, globally focused introduction, their middle school and high school histories are much more narrowly focused on European and American history; the Great Books reading list does not take on a single work or period of history outside of the "Western Civilization" band. That is not enough in our global world. In addition, the Great Books approach to studying history is a good adjunct to studying the history, but it does not substitute for having an understanding of what happened, where and why. For example, a student who has read Scott Anderson's *Lawrence in Arabia*, Thomas Friedman's *From Beirut to Jerusalem*, and William Cleveland's *A History of the Modern Middle East* will have a far better understanding of the history and politics of the middle east than Wise and

Bauer's "classically educated" student whose only exposure to the entire region is a few stories in elementary school, an outline in middle school, and selections from the Bible and Quran in high school. Historical books are vital part of history, but they are not the sum total of history, not for white Europeans, and most certainly not for the nations and cultures unrepresented in a United States / European great books list. *Cf.* Susan Wise Bauer and Jessie Wise, *The Well-Trained Mind: A Guide to Classical Education at Home,* 2ⁿᵈ ed. (New York: W. W. Norton & Co., 2004).

163 Daniel T. Willingham, *Why Don't Students Like School? A Cognitive Scientist Answers Questions About How the Mind Works and What it Means for the Classroom* (San Francisco: Jossey-Bass/John Wiley & Sons, 2009), 41.

164 Sherri L. Fulp, *Status of Elementary School Science Teaching:2000 National Survey of Science and Mathematics Education* (Chapel Hill, NC: Horizon Research, Inc., December 2002), 2, 5 and 9, accessed March 9, 2016, 2000survey.horizonresearch.com/reports/elem_science /elem_science.pdf.

165 *Ibid.*

166 Jerome Bruner, *The Process of Education* (Cambridge: Harvard UP, 1960), 33.

167 Fulp, *Status of Elementary School Science Teaching,* 11.

168 Julie Thomas, Toni Ivey, and Jim Puckette, "Where Is Earth Science? Mining for Opportunities in Chemistry, Physics, and Biology,"*Journal of Geoscience Education* 61, no. 1 (February 2013): 113-119, accessed February 1, 2016, nagt-jge.org/doi/full/10.5408/12-319.1.

169 "Middle Grades Science Textbooks: A Benchmarks-Based Evaluation," (Evaluation reports of Life Sciences, Physical Sciences, and Earth Sciences.) *AAAS Project 2061* (website), American Association for the Advancement of Science (2002), accessed March 19, 2016, www.project2061.org/publications/textbook/mgsci/report/index.htm.

170 Donald P. Hayes, *A Spectrum of Natural Texts: Measurements of the Lexical Demand Levels,* Ms. (Ithica, NY: Cornell Dept. of Sociology, 2002), accessed January 30, 2015, www.soc.cornell.edu/hayes-lexical-analysis/schoolbooks/Papers/ASpectrumOfNaturalTexts.pdf and D. P. Hayes, "The Growing Inaccessibility of Science," *Nature* 356 (1992): 739-740, accessed January 30, 2015, /www.soc.cornell.edu/hayes-lexical-analysis/schoolbooks/Papers/HayesGrowingInaccessibility1992.pdf.

171 Blair Lee, "Why 'Neutral' Science isn't Neutral," *SEA Homeschoolers: Secular, Ecclectic, Academic Blog* (October 5, 2015), accessed March 13, 2016, seahomeschooler.com/why-neutral-science-isnt-neutral/.

172 Discussion of biology teachers not teaching evolution in Michael B. Berkman and Eric Plutzer, "Defeating Creationism in the Courtroom, But Not in the Classroom," *Science* 331, issue 6016 (January 28, 2011):404-405. Summarized in Nicholas Bakalar, "On Evolution, Biology Teacher Stray

From Lesson Plan," *New York Times* (7 Feb 2011), accessed January 26, 2015, www.nytimes.com/2011/02/08/science/08creationism.html. Discussion of elementary school teacher backgrounds in Sherri L. Fulp, *Status of Elementary School Science Teaching: 2000 National Survey of Science and Mathematics Education* (Chapel Hill, NC: Horizon Research, Inc., December 2002), 11, accessed March 9, 2016, 2000survey.horizon-research.com/reports/elem_science/elem_science.pdf.

173 Kate L. Turabian, *Student's Guide to Writing College Papers,* 4th Ed. Revised by Gregory G. Colomb, Joseph M. Williams, and the Univ. of Chicago Press Editorial Staff (Chicago: Univ. of Chicago Press, 2010), 114.

174 Robert Bruce Thompson. *Standard/Honors Home School Chemistry Laboratory Kit CK01A Instruction Manual.* Revision 1.0.7 (January 10, 2013), 15.

175 William H. Armstrong, *Study is Hard Work,* 2nd ed. (Boston: David R. Godine, Publisher, 1995), 97.

176 Gabriel Wyner, *Fluent Forever: How to Learn Any Language Fast and Never Forget It* (New York: Harmony Books (Random House LLC), 2014), Kindle location 1592.

177 *Ibid., passim.*

178 *Ibid.,* Kindle location 1542.

179 Defense Language Institute Foreign Language Center (website), accessed February 21, 2015, www.dliflc.edu/languagesatdli.html. The Foreign Service Institute has similar categories, discussed in Wyner, Kindle location 220.

180 Benny Lewis, *Fluent in 3 Months:How Anyone at Any Age Can Learn to Speak Any Language from Anywhere in the World* (New York: HarperOne. 2014), 87.

181 Doug Lemov, *Teach Like a Champion: 49 Techniques that Put Students on the Path to College* (San Francisco, CA: Jossey-Bass, 2010), Kindle location 391.

182 *Ibid.,* Kindle location 3571.

183 Steve Biddulph, *The Secrets of Happy Children: Why Children Behave the Way They Do -- and What You Can Do to Help Them to be Optimistic, Loving, Capable, and Happy* (Marlowe, 2002).

184 David A. Sousa. *How the Brain Learns: A Classroom Teacher's Guide* (Thousand Oaks, CA: Corwin Press, Inc., 2001), 88-91.

185 *Ibid.,* 95

186 Salman Khan, *The One World Schoolhouse: Education Reimagined* (New York: Twelve, 2012), 20.

187 Lemov, *Teach Like a Champion,* Kindle location 4978 and 5017.

188 *Ibid.,* Kindle location 2438.

189 David Sousa, "Impact of Circadian Rhythms on Schools and Classrooms," *How the Brain Learns: The Blog (Educational Neuroscience for Teachers)* (October 17, 2011), accessed May 22, 2016, howthebrainlearns.wordpress.com/2011/10/17/impact-of-circadian-rhythms-

on-schools-and-classrooms.

190 For example, "The Crucial Role of Recess in School," *American Academy of Pediatrics Policy Statement* 131, Issue 1 (January 2013), accessed April 4, 2016, pediatrics.aappublications.org/content/131/1/183.

191 John Taylor Gatto, "The Six-Lesson Schoolteacher," accessed April 4, 2016, www.cantrip.org/gatto.html.

192 Douglas Adams, *The Hitchhiker's Guide to the Galaxy,* (London: Pan Books, 2005), 79.

193 I first read about Bronson and Merryman's "The Lost Hour" in Marina Koestler Ruben, *How to Tutor Your Own Child: Boost Grades and Inspire a Lifelong Love of Learning – Without Paying for a Professional Tutor.* (Berkeley, California: Ten Speed Press (Random House), 2011).

194 Po Bronson and Ashley Merryman, *NurtureShock: New Thinking About Children*, 2nd ed. (New York: Twelve, 2011).

195 *Ibid.*, Kindle location 385.

196 *Ibid.*, Kindle location 401.

197 *Ibid.*, Kindle location 440.

198 Daniel Willingham, "Are Sleepy Students Learning?" *American Educator* (Winter 2012-2013): 35-39.

199 Bronson and Merryman, *NurtureShock*, Kindle location 428.

200 As cited in Ruben, *How to Tutor Your Own Child*, Kindle location 693.

201 Bronson and Merryman, *NurtureShock*, Kindle location 417.

202 Willingham, "Are Sleepy Students Learning?"

203 E.D. Hirsh, Jr., *Core Knowledge Sequence: Content and Skill Guidelines for Grades K–8* (Charlottesville, VA: The Core Knowledge Foundation, 2010), accessed January 17, 2013, www.coreknowledge.org/mimik/mimik_uploads/documents/480/CKFSequence_Rev.pdf

204 This section was originally published 25 March 2016 in my blog, *Homeschool Teacher Blog*, homeschoolteacherblog.wordpress.com /2016/03/20/school-in-a-box-out-of-the-box/.

About the Author

K ate Laird graduated from Harvard with a degree in history, a
good set of study skills, and a 100-ton captain's license.

Her first teaching job began seven days after graduation,
tutoring three children on a sailboat crossing the Pacific. That
"year off" turned into twenty-five, as she worked on boats around
the world, sometimes pausing to write about it.

In the middle, she taught for another two years at the
University of New Hampshire, while earning an MA in English,
but then didn't think much more about education until it came
time to teach her two daughters. The last twelve years have been
devoted to their educations, as the family worked and traveled on
the edges of civilization from Greenland to Antarctica, Tierra del
Fuego to New Zealand, through the South Pacific to Japan, and
now to Alaska.

You can find her online at www.katelairdbooks.com.

Made in the USA
San Bernardino, CA
09 November 2016